HOW TO DEFEND YOURSELF, YOUR FAMILY, AND YOUR HOME

A Complete Guide to Self-Protection

HOW TO DEFEND YOURSELF, YOUR FAMILY, AND YOUR HOME

A Complete Guide to Self-Protection

BY GEORGE HUNTER

DAVID McKAY COMPANY, INC.

New York

HOW TO DEFEND YOURSELF,
YOUR FAMILY, AND YOUR HOME

Library of Congress Catalog Card Number: 66-28811
MANUFACTURED IN THE UNITED STATES OF AMERICA

ACKNOWLEDGMENTS

The following organizations supplied information, documents, or illustrations to the author:

Federal Bureau of Investigation

The New York City Police Department

The National Rifle Association

U.S. Air Force

U.S. Army

The American Kennel Club

Literally hundreds of commercial companies also helped with drawings, photographs, and technical information. The author wishes to thank the people in these organizations who took the time to help him, and he hopes that this book will help to make their lives and the lives of their families happier and safer.

GEORGE HUNTER

Contents

CHAPTER I

Planning and Tactics

WHY is self-protection needed in a country with numerous, well-equipped police? A glance at your local newspaper almost any day in the week gives the answer. Robbery, theft, rape, murder, assault, and riot are commonplace in almost every city and many towns in the United States. Today, criminals find it profitable to invade the suburbs, and criminally inclined groups of adolescents have sprung up in some of the "best" neighborhoods. Even the finest police department often cannot reach the victim in time to prevent the crime. Horrible attacks are committed in the privacy of the homes of the victims. The recent murder of eight student nurses in their Chicago apartment is only one example.

According to statistics released by the Federal Bureau of Investigation, crime has increased five times as fast as the population over the last five years. If this soaring crime-increase rate continues, it is probable that most of us will be victims of some kind of serious crime at least once in our lives, or at the very least, will have a friend or relative who becomes a victim. If such things are possible, it seems entirely apparent that it is worth a little foresight, work, and expense to prevent them. This should be particularly apparent to parents. The emotional harm to an adolescent victim of a violent rape is enormous. A boy or girl assaulted by a sex pervert usually recovers from the physical damage, but the memory of the attack

1

There are several solutions to crime nowadays

and fear of a repetition will haunt him for years and may cause considerable psychological damage.

SELF-PROTECTION MEANS PLANNING

Fortunately, there is much that the individual can do. Self-protection should be carefully and systematically planned. If you go over your apartment or house and check it for all security weaknesses, and then correct them with good hardware and security procedures, you will be fairly safe. You should also check over your security situation in the street and when using public transportation and provide for avoidance and defense for yourself and members of your family. It is foolish to install good locks on all doors and windows if you sleep with one window wide open and fail to use the stoppers or snubs on the others. It is also obvious that even good hardware is useless if you leave your home vacant for long periods and advertise your absence by allowing newspapers and bottles of milk to accumulate on the doorstep. In planning self-protection, you must use all appropriate means and know *in advance* what you will do in the event someone breaks into your home or attacks you or a member of your family in the street.

A few people are amused by a person who devotes a fair amount of attention to locks, bars, and personal self-defense. Let me say this—if you have ever been a victim of a serious crime, you will not laugh at someone who attempts to provide a reasonable degree of security. And the whole point of planned self-protection is that it can reduce the chances of being the victim of a crime even in the most crime-infested neighborhoods.

Much of the burden of self-protection falls on women. Women spend a great deal of time in the home alone or with small children. They are also frequently victims of crimes committed in the street. Women should therefore understand the proper use of locks, alarms, and the tactics of self-defense as well as or better than men. Unfortunately, many women are comparatively uninformed about mechanical devices such as locks. All too often, entirely adequate hardware is installed in a home, and a woman or girl becomes a victim of a criminal because she failed, for instance, to lock a door securely.

2

The reader will find that most of the defense installations described in this book are well within the means and skills of the typical woman "do-it-yourselfer" or her husband. With a little information and a few basic tools, even a comparatively inexperienced person can install locks and other security devices which will keep out all but the most determined intruders.

EXTERNAL DEFENSES AND THE SECURITY ROOM

There is much to be said for setting up a security room to which women and children can go if an intruder does succeed in getting inside the house or apartment. Such security rooms should be equipped at the very least with a telephone, secure window locks or gratings, and good, quick-functioning locks on all doors leading to the rest of the home. Many people never think of installing locks on interior doors within their homes, but it's one of the most useful methods of providing comparative safety at little cost. For instance, a locked door at the head of the cellar stairs will probably frustrate an intruder who has successfully entered the cellar by jimmying or breaking one of five to eight windows with which most cellars are equipped. Behind the locked door of the security room, there will be time to call the police, or in the last resort, to get a defense weapon ready. Most criminals, however, will leave in a hurry if they realize that the intended victim is behind a locked door using a telephone.

Often, crime can be prevented through proper police surveillance. Unfortunately, many people "mind their own business" so well that they would never think of calling the police about a suspicious person in their neighborhood or apartment house. Keeping the police informed is the first line of defense. In some neighborhoods, however, the police are so swamped with crime that they are unable to cope with such reports from citizens. In these areas, all one can do is rely on self-protection. For instance, in one crime-ridden luxury suburb, the citizens have organized a protective patrol. There are approximately forty houses, and these forty families provide at least two participants for a twenty-four-hour patrol. Those who work on patrol do so in two-hour shifts. During daylight hours, two automobiles drive the community's roads. They're operated by women

3

who note the license numbers of all cars entering the area and take photographs of strangers they find there if at all possible. All neighborhood cars are equipped with fluorescent stickers bearing the insignia of the neighborhood civic association so that they can easily be distinguished from strange cars. At night, two men from the community patrol the streets in radio-equipped cars. They report all strangers immediately to the police by radio.

Formerly, burglaries were occurring about once a week in this neighborhood, and it was only a matter of time before someone would have surprised one of the criminals in the act with a murder as the probable result. Now crime has been reduced to zero. And none of the patrol members runs much risk. They never speak to suspicious persons—they simply take note of license-plate numbers and photograph strangers, and report suspicious persons and happenings as quickly as possible. But because these efforts have been publicized in the local newspaper, criminals know that this particular suburb is quite dangerous for them and they stay away. These patrols can be organized in your neighborhood or apartment house, too, if the situation calls for it. Forming a strong neighborhood civic association is the first step.

The border of your property can be protected with many kinds of fencing and walls, all of which deter criminals. Those who live in apartments obviously cannot erect fences and walls, but they can pay some attention to how the entrances are locked and how the locks are released. Sometimes tenants will press the release buttons in their apartments whenever anyone rings a bell at the entrance—a practice that will sooner or later admit a criminal. Those who live in apartments can also make it a point to be aware of the superintendent's or doorman's attitude toward security. If security is weak at the doors of the apartment house or in its halls, pressure should be brought on the owners or management to remedy the situation. This is often neglected until *after* a serious crime has been committed. You may be the victim of that first crime. Adequate security hardware can be installed in almost any apartment more easily than in the average suburban house simply because there are fewer entrances and windows.

A good watchdog is often enough to discourage a determined

intruder. But choosing and training the dog is not a simple matter. It's not enough to use friendly Fido (ten years old and a lover of all men with hamburger) to guard your home. It takes a capable and carefully trained dog to do the job. This book gives some hints on training.

If the doors or windows of an apartment or a house are nearly covered by evergreens and shrubs, a housebreaker has the cover he needs to work on the locks. The same is true of porches without locked exterior doors. It almost goes without saying, one would think, that windows and doors should be provided with good locks. But anyone who knows a little about locksmithing will tell you that the average American home is equipped largely with useless junk. Choosing the right lock for each door and window, and supervising its installation or installing locks oneself requires knowledge.

Noise and Time Are the Real Barriers

All locking devices provide two obstacles to the intruder—noise and time. In order to break in, the criminal must make a fair amount of noise. Similarly, it takes time to climb a wall, subdue a dog, and force one or two locks. If the average intruder encounters a series of obstacles, he will probably give up or make so much noise that he will arouse someone. Even the door of a city apartment can be equipped with hardware that will provide a series of barriers for the housebreaker.

Noise and the time factor provide the best chance for security. Self-protection should be designed to take advantage of this fact. Put yourself in the place of the intruder and take each route of entrance separately in order to estimate the security risks. Then provide as many noisy, time-consuming obstacles as possible. For instance, if an obvious route involves climbing a fence, breaking a window lock and the lock of the interior door of the security room, the inhabitants of the house are fairly safe. If you add a noisy alarm device, you are even more secure, and if you plan your defense actions in advance, you're still more secure. Each entry route deserves attention to make sure that as many barriers as possible are provided. Check to see that the number of barriers along each route are approximately the same. If one route is blocked by

5

three barriers, and another by only one, some effort is wasted. It is quite easy for the skilled housebreaker to select the easiest way to break in.

But the intruder may reach the locked door of the security room. Almost every criminal will give up when he encounters a series of barriers, but some dangerous criminals may not. These people will go to any lengths to get what they want and often are not aware of the risks they are running. This is particularly true of the drug addict and the sex criminal. Fortunately, most of these criminals are not skilled in housebreaking and they usually have inadequate tools, so they make a great deal of noise in overcoming a barrier.

Few people realize it, but the skilled housebreaker is really not very dangerous. He's something of a craftsman, and the last thing he wants to do is get into a dangerous situation involving physical violence, though sometimes he may make a mistake that leads to it. The average American family is not likely to attract a highly skilled, well-equipped burglar simply because the average American home does not contain enough of value to warrant his attention. Highly skilled criminals devote their attention to the rich or to commercial establishments.

But it is barely possible that you may find yourself with a criminal trying to break the last barrier—the locked door of the security room, usually a bedroom equipped with a telephone. Of course, the first recourse is a telephone call to the police. But it often takes quite a while for police to arrive even in an emergency.

Remember that a criminal who has violated multiple security barriers is usually of the most dangerous type. He would not have taken all the risks if he were not. As a last resort, in the absence of outside help, most people are willing to use a weapon of some kind, particularly to defend children. For those who have moral objections against using lethal weapons even in self-defense, there are several less-powerful devices. For instance, small tear-gas projectors are now available to the public in most states and cities. Tear-gas shells for ordinary firearms are also legally available in most places. These gas weapons do no permanent harm unless the gas is directed straight into the eyes. If properly used, these gas projectors incapacitate for fifteen or twenty minutes during which the intended

6

victim can flee. A club is usually not lethal, but when properly used, it can subdue even the most violent person. And these weapons can be used effectively by almost anyone if the criminal is in an awkward position such as halfway through a broken window or a shattered door. Even firearms can be used without doing permanent physical harm. A warning shot fired so that it will hit no one, or even the sound of a gun being cooked (prepared to fire) will send most criminals running. If you do decide to use weapons of any kind, you must act within the law of self-defense, and the law is discussed in some detail in Chapter IV of this book. The author does not advocate the purchase or use of firearms by persons who do not have adequate training in their safe use, but there are millions of veterans who have such training and anybody can take a course in gun safety. These courses are briefly described in Chapter VI.

TACTICS IN ROBBERIES AND ATTACKS

At home, most determined women and elderly men can use the various protective devices described in this book quite effectively. It takes little strength. In the street, on public transportation, in halls and passageways, and particularly in the self-service elevator (one of the most dangerous forms of transportation), the chances for successful defense are less. Some people are strong enough to put up a good unarmed defense against a criminal, but many others are incapable of effective physical resistance unless they have adequate training. The average man's physique gives him about twice as much strength as the average woman. In any case, however, the chief tactic of defense is avoidance, and this is true for men as well as women.

If you do a good job of avoiding danger, there's every likelihood that you'll never need physical defenses. Yet, if the average person is caught in a dangerous situation, he or she often needs an effective defense weapon, and I do not mean a rolled-up newspaper or an umbrella. At the very least, some practice at the most useful forms of hand-to-hand resistance is needed, particularly releases—methods of breaking chokes, bear hugs, and other common grips. If absolutely necessary, even a slight woman or girl can disable a powerful criminal with a sudden blow or kick, but she must take

7

him by surprise, and practice is needed. Fortunately, many hand-to-hand defenses are easily self-taught.

Don't Resist in a Robbery

The criminal bent on a robbery generally believes the victim will be unarmed and unable to put up a good hand-to-hand defense. Most women carry their valuables in their purses. To a criminal, this makes a woman a more attractive target than a man. Little physical contact or danger is involved in snatching a purse. Even if the woman does resist, one punch in the face or a knee kick in the stomach will probably be enough to stop it. A man is entirely different because he carries his money in a wallet inside a pocket. To rob a man, the criminal must stop him and demand that he turn over his money. This gives the intended victim time to resist. If the criminal has chosen the wrong man, he may get very determined opposition. Instead of stopping the intended victim and threatening him, therefore, the criminal or a group of them may simply knock him senseless first and then remove his wallet. Some muggers don't mind killing their victim as their first step.

The last thing a woman should do is put herself in the same category with younger men by resisting during robberies. The same thing could be said of older men. Hand over valuables if threatened and release your grip on purse or briefcase if the thief tries to pull it away. This is very cowardly, of course, but it's better to lose money than to wind up with a broken cheekbone or a fractured skull. This is the right thing to do unless you are prepared to risk your life.

Carry only a few dollars and use checks or the credit system to pay your bills. Ordinarily, there's no reason why you should carry large amounts with you. In an emergency, put a folded wad of bills inside your shoe where you can constantly feel it with your toes or put it in an envelope pinned inside your clothes. It's very poor practice to display large amounts of cash in public places. Some people forget this when they change large bills at stores. It's always better to pay by check immediately or to let the storekeeper bill you and pay through the mail. This is one very good reason for establishing your credit with the merchants you patronize.

If a robbery is attempted, however, don't resist or even call out for assistance unless you have every reason to believe that resistance will be effective and safe or that there are people close by who will come to your assistance. And don't depend too much on assistance from strangers. In large cities particularly, there are thousands of people who will watch while you are robbed or beaten. They apparently think they are watching a TV drama. They're very interested in a spectacle, but often they will not raise a finger, and sometimes they make no effort to call the police. Miss Catherine Genovese was slowly stabbed to death in a suburb of New York while dozens of neighbors watched. None of them called the police. Countless times, men have been severely beaten in crowded places by criminals and not one person tried to help them or summon police.

In an ordinary armed robbery, it may be difficult to remain calm and comply immediately with the criminal's orders. The sight of a knife or a pistol is often terrifying. It may help to think about the criminal's intentions. If a person points a gun or knife at you or threatens you with some other weapon, he probably will not use it unless you resist. For instance, if a gun is aimed at you, ask yourself: "Why hasn't he already shot me?" The answer is pretty obvious, but it's very reassuring and may help you to remain calm. The criminal does not wish to risk the death penalty or a long term in prison and is using the *threat* of bodily harm. If he intended to kill, he would already have done so. His intention is robbery, and he won't use the weapon if he can avoid it.

Jittery, unstable teenagers are usually the most dangerous. They are often so nervous and have so little control of themselves that they may pull the trigger or strike with a knife if you show the slightest sign of resistance or even reluctance. If confronted by one of these dangerous adolescents, it sometimes helps to say, "Yes, of course I will," in response to his directions, or "Here it is," when handing over your valuables, and to make any other soothing, obliging remarks that seem appropriate. Somehow, the sound of a sweetly reasonable voice is often very reassuring to this type of criminal. If you put on a convincing act, you will probably avoid physical harm.

9

In all robberies, try to look over the criminal carefully for identifying marks and distinctive physical characteristics. Don't be obvious about it, but look at his face and general physical makeup. Then select a person you know who resembles the criminal and remember your acquaintance's name so that later you can recall the criminal's general appearance. For instance, you may decide that the criminal looks just like the vice-president of your company but that he has larger ears and a receding chin. Then note specific things such as the color of his eyes and look for scars, tattoo marks, amputated fingers, etc. You should almost always report the crime to the police, and such individual characteristics may be helpful if you are asked to pick the criminal out of a group of similar men in a police lineup.

All this does not mean that you should turn over your money to a half-grown boy or a tottering drunk when you're sure that you can get away from him or that you can resist effectively or summon assistance. You must judge the situation intelligently and act accordingly.

Rape, Abduction, and Assault

With a rapist or a person intent on physical harm, the situation is entirely different. You should resist, but you want your resistance to be effective. Another crime—abduction—almost always calls for resistance. Abduction or kidnapping is a very serious crime in this country. A person who risks the punishments usually inflicted for kidnapping is almost always a very dangerous criminal.

Don't resist a determined criminal armed with a knife by poking a hatpin at him or using a nailfile as a knife, as one publication on defense advises. Don't try to ward off a determined abductor by pushing a lighted cigarette or cigar in his face (another common and equally stupid piece of advice). Unless you can use hand-to-hand defenses effectively, you need a powerful weapon or, at the very least, an effective repellent gas or spray.

Newspapers and popular literature of other kinds often advise readers to defend themselves with ineffective weapons. For instance, one book tells readers to carry a corkscrew, presumably because it's legal to do so in some cities. The intent is to stab or slash at

10

the criminal with this "weapon." Even if he's wearing ordinary lightweight clothing, stabbing or slashing a criminal with a corkscrew, a nailfile, or a screwdriver is ineffective. These weapons will not penetrate clothing. If the criminal is wearing an overcoat, using such a weapon is like trying to pierce a suit of armor with a knitting needle (another recommended and ridiculous weapon). With these ineffective pointed instruments, the target can only be the pear-shaped hollow under the adam's apple or the side of the throat. Some people are calm enough and determined enough so that they can strike these small targets with these weapons effectively, but it is difficult. Even these ineffective weapons, however, may cause considerable legal trouble if they are not used within the law of self-defense, and in many cities carrying them is forbidden.

What if the criminal is hurt with one of these ineffective weapons? He may have been intent on assault or rape, but now he has been stabbed or slashed, probably in the face, with a weapon that usually will only wound. His reaction? He'll probably commit murder.

The same reasoning applies to many easily learned physical defenses. For instance, some "authorities" advise that the intended victim should break a finger. The advice usually goes as follows: If the criminal grasps you by the wrist, use all the fingers of your other hand to pry up a finger. Hold the finger in the palm of your hand and bend it sharply and forcefully backward.

Of course, the criminal's finger will be dislocated or broken because the full strength of one hand is used against only one of his fingers—usually the pinky. This does not disable the criminal, and the pain of the minor injury may anger him so much that your life will be in danger. Sometimes—when dealing with a drunk or a half-serious but overly enthusiastic acquaintance—it pays to use a fairly painful release, but you must be prepared to follow up. If a painful release causes anger and a dangerous attack, the renewed attack must be stopped before it can do any real harm by using a disabling blow or kick, or by using some sort of defense device such as gas or liquid repellent, acting within the limits set by the law of self-defense. To believe that you are safe because you have learned a few simple releases is actually to be falsely confident, and this false confidence may cost your life or a serious injury.

It's almost impossible to lay down hard-and-fast rules for defense situations involving real physical danger. Your own best judgment is always needed. Even the basic idea that a woman should always resist rape may sometimes be wrong. During the recent wave of rapes in Boston, one woman escaped death by submitting to the rapist. She did so because she felt that resistance was hopeless. She knew that the criminal who was committing the series of rapes almost always strangled his victims afterward. During the rape, she carefully avoided looking at the rapist's face and told him over and over that she was not looking at him and did not want to be able to identify him. She was dealing with a disordered mind, and it worked. Of course, the woman would have been better off if she could have kept the rapist out of her home in the first place, and good security hardware would have accomplished that. And she would not have been obliged to go through this horrible experience if she had had adequate defense devices in her apartment and had known how to use them safely and effectively.

Some Nonlethal Defense Devices

The increased number of attacks on women and elderly men have created a demand for repellent sprays in small, easily handled cans with a button release. These sprays are usually made of concentrated pepper derivatives. When sprayed into the face of an attacker, they cause temporary blindness and convulsive sneezing. They're fairly effective, but not as much so as the tear-gas projectors discussed elsewhere in this book. Rebuff and Bodi-gard, selling for about $2.00, and several other sprays, however, may ward off an attack that would otherwise become very dangerous if no resistance were offered. Some of these sprays dispense a chemical dye along with the pepper derivative which colors the attacker a bright green or purple so that the police can easily pick him up. A bright-green would-be rapist or mugger really stands out in a crowd.

These sprays will not completely disable an attacker. If you use one, try to get away from the criminal just as rapidly as you can. Sometimes, however, a really determined person can hang on to the intended victim despite the spray's effects. Usually, however, the criminal cannot see. At such times, knowing the more common wrestling releases is most useful.

In some areas, various law-enforcement agencies are trying to prevent the sale of these sprays. Just why remains something of a mystery. New York's former Markets Commissioner said, "We have enough of a jungle in this city without adding this stuff to it. . . . Can you imagine what this would do in a crowded subway car?" Yes, of course, one can imagine it, and the subway is one of the places where a woman or an elderly or comparatively defenseless man would find such a spray most useful. As yet, however, these sprays are available in most cities and are not generally considered to be dangerous weapons, though at any time carrying one of these sprays may be prohibited in your city. Just because a spray is on sale in your town doesn't mean that you may carry one with you— it may still come under the provisions of a law prohibiting concealed weapons. It pays to check local regulations, though I must say that sometimes even the police give remarkably vague answers. Use of one of these sprays except in legal self-defense may also make it possible for someone to sue you if it should happen that the spray does inflict permanent harm or in the event the criminal success- fully pretends that it did.

FIREARMS

Many persons have the mistaken idea that firearms in the home are illegal. Because of this, they deprive themselves of the most effective means of repelling a dangerous attack. Although this book does not advocate use of firearms by people who do not know how to use them safely, there's no denying that they are the most potent defense weapon.

In fact, there is no city or state which entirely forbids firearms in the home. In some cities and some entire states, carrying concealed weapons away from home is illegal unless a license has been ob- tained, but only New York State forbids mere *possession* of a fire- arm capable of being concealed under clothing, whether or not that weapon is taken out of the home. Even in New York, however, a license for possession of a concealable firearm in the home can be obtained, and sometimes it is possible to obtain a license to carry

13

concealed weapons in New York. Some of the states with weapons laws are liberal about issuing concealed-weapons permits; other states and cities will not issue these permits except to bank guards, private security personnel, and shopkeepers. This makes it very convenient for the criminal because he is almost always sure that his victim will be unarmed if encountered outside the home. The best way to find out about these laws is to apply for a permit. In many Southern and Western states, however, no license is required to carry concealed firearms, and in the majority of states, a pistol can be kept in the home.

Everywhere in this country, however, a citizen has the right to possess a rifle or a shotgun not capable of being concealed under clothing. These weapons may be purchased and kept in the home without a license or permit. Only one city—Philadelphia—currently requires the citizen to register rifles and shotguns with the police. Other cities and some states may enact laws requiring the registration of shoulder firearms, but certainly no law entirely prohibiting possession of firearms can be enacted because the Constitution of the United States guarantees every citizen the right to keep and bear arms. A law prohibiting firearms of any kind would only disarm the law-abiding person while criminals would continue to use firearms illegally. The average citizen will not break the law even if the law is mistaken or badly conceived, but a dangerous criminal does not worry about being caught with firearms or other dangerous concealed weapons since they're often a necessary part of his equipment. Chapter IV discusses weapons laws in more detail.

If you have scruples against killing or disabling a dangerous criminal, you should be aware that these attitudes may cause increased danger to others in your family. For instance, if you're unwilling to use force of any kind, you may find yourself faced with a situation in which you'll be obliged to watch helplessly while a criminal attacks one of your children or some other helpless member of your family. If you are completely unwilling to use weapons, you have a heavy obligation to make sure that your attitudes do not place innocent people in danger of death or severe bodily harm. In the United States today, small children are not safe from the attacks of sex degenerates, and eighty-year-old women have been

14

raped, mutilated, and murdered. With or without weapons, your obligation to provide security for yourself and your family is very great and will probably become greater as time passes. Fortunately, however, there is much that you can do to protect yourself and your family short of using a gun.

CHAPTER II

Avoidance

AVOIDANCE is the best possible defense. Avoid the criminal and you won't be obliged to risk your life to defend yourself. One of the chief hazards in avoiding trouble is your own attitude. Many people are superstitious—don't think about danger and it won't happen, but it does happen and there's no reason why you should be immune. It's easy enough to form the habit of being alert to danger. In order to do so, you don't have to be in a constant state of fright. All you need do is look around you each time you enter a new situation, estimate the risks, and get out of there if the situation seems dangerous. Checking each new situation for danger doesn't take much effort. It soon becomes a habit which can provide you with a large degree of safety.

Another common cause of unnecessary danger is fear of embarrassment. Loud and determined calls for assistance are a good defense in many situations. A willingness to avoid danger by rapid retreat is also important. But many people are so concerned about avoiding embarrassment that they will not call for assistance until the very last minute—sometimes until it is much too late. Others will not, for instance, step out of a self-service elevator if a drunken hulk is about to enter it.

16

If you're a stranger, it will take you some time before you know any city well enough to identify its hazardous areas. Some neighborhoods become dangerous as soon as the sun goes down. In the daytime, they consist of workaday streets with everyone going about his business in an orderly, quiet way. After dark, the drunks, violent groups of adolescents, and less-obvious criminal types appear. Since you'll be going home after dark on many nights, it pays to investigate both by day and by night any neighborhood where you might live. This is particularly true for the head of a family who plans to install his wife and children in a new apartment.

It also pays to know which neighborhoods are on the edge of criminal areas. For instance, some decent areas in large cities are "targets" for criminals and degenerates who live only a short distance away in an urban slum. The housebreaker, the rapist, and the degenerate usually does not favor his own neighborhood. There are too few worthwhile targets for the thief and burglar and there are too few attractive women and children. Instead, they raid the nearby decent neighborhood.

If you're to select an apartment or house in a fairly safe place, you need time to read the newspapers, particularly the crime news, and to familiarize yourself with the geography of the town and its transportation routes. If you come to the city from another place, try to stay with relatives or trustworthy friends. Women often stay at a residence home for women only. Stay in a temporary residence for two or three months until you really know what sort of living quarters are available and where they are located, and then decide what would be best for a person of your means. If you are married, stay in a hotel with your family until you familiarize yourself with the city.

When hunting for permanent quarters, don't be too anxious to sign a lease. Once you've signed it, you'll usually be obliged to pay the full amount of the rent for the term of the lease even if you don't stay. Don't accept the verbal assurances of the agent or owner that they will "let you terminate any time you wish to go." Some apartment managers and home-rental agents know perfectly well

17

that they have undesirable property to rent and this deliberate lie is their method of trapping a tenant.

If you sign a lease for an apartment and there's no provision for easy termination, you may find yourself trapped in the same building with a group of drug addicts or other dangerous people. You'll probably find that you can't do anything about your unsavory neighbors and that you'll have to live with them for the term of the lease unless you can pay it off.

Take a little time to investigate the neighborhood and the building before you sign anything. Ask questions—ask if the superintendent lives on the property and don't rent in a building where he's a part-timer and away at night. Speak to the superintendent and find out how long he's worked at the address. If he's been there for several years, he's usually fairly dependable. See if you can get the opinions of other tenants. No one is safe in an apartment building where the superintendent is careless, perhaps because he drinks to excess. Drunken building superintendents are a plague in many cities. If you can, rent an apartment where a responsible, careful owner lives on the premises. Owner-operated housing units are usually the best. The owner who lives on the premises is usually concerned about cleanliness and safety and has the authority to do something about bad conditions.

Even if the agent or landlord tells you that there's a big demand for the apartment or house and that it will be snapped up immediately if you don't take it, make sure that it's a safe proposition before you sign anything. Sometimes, you can put a deposit on an apartment—usually one month's rent—and it will be held for you for a specified time. If you decide not to take it, you lose only a limited amount. Housing is not as scarce as it once was. You'll probably find what you want and what you can afford in safe circumstances if you keep looking long enough.

If you live in a safe place but work in a dangerous area or commute through one, you're risking trouble. Check a prospective place of employment as thoroughly as you check the place where you plan to live. Try riding to and from it by the shortest transportation route both at night and in the daytime. Take several walks around the employer's neighborhood during the noon hour and eat

18

in the restaurants. Remember that you may work after normal closing hours and that you'll be obliged to go home late at night. If a young woman is asked to work overtime, and there have been attacks on women in the neighborhood, she has every right to ask her employer for a male escort to the nearest safe transportation station or to her own door. If such an escort is not forthcoming, she has reasonable grounds for refusing to work overtime. Several large employers have been providing *armed* escorts for overtime workers. No reasonable employer will force you to work overtime in dangerous circumstances.

TAKING OVER NEW PREMISES

After you have found an apartment or house that you like, it's worth investing a few dollars to make sure that it's safe. It is usual for the management or the real-estate agent to turn over a set of keys to a new tenant or owner. Where do these keys come from? They're often the set used by the previous owner or tenant. You do not know much about him. He may have copies of the keys and he may intend to use them after the new tenant or owner—you—moves in. He may have passed his copies on to criminal friends. Change the lock tumblers when you move in. The superintendent or owner of an apartment building may object to this. Some management people insist on having a key to each tenant's apartment so that they can enter it in the event of a fire or a break in a water pipe. If this objection is made, place a set of your new keys inside a sealed envelope before you hand them over. If the envelope is opened, you'll know someone used that set of keys. Under these circumstances, few superintendents will use the keys unless there is a legitimate reason. Since envelopes can be steamed open, it's a good idea to seal the flap and the ends with old-fashioned sealing wax—even candle wax will do if you apply it carefully and use a seal ring or some other distinctive metal object to place a mark on each blob of wax sealing the flap and both ends. If the superintendent remarks that you're very suspicious, tell him that he's quite correct.

So much caution about keys may seem a bit extreme, but it's very useful to know if others are entering your premises from time to time. Many cities are plagued by the inside burglary. A dishonest superintendent or some other building employee keeps a constant check on the contents of apartments, using the house keys to do so. When he finds one with enough of value to make a burglary worthwhile, he goes ahead or calls in another person. The door is opened when the dishonest employee knows that it's safe to remove the apartment's contents through the halls. After everything has been removed, and the stolen articles are safely off the premises, the criminal breaks a window leading to a fire escape to make it appear that the apartment was burglarized from the outside. The door is then locked again. If there are several burglaries in your building and it's difficult to understand how the thieves could have gotten away with bulky furnishings each time without attracting attention, it may pay to interest yourself in the activities of the building-service employees.

Incidentally, it's very unwise to leave a spare key in some hiding place outside the door—under a milkbox, under the welcome mat, or in the azalea bush. A capable housebreaker almost always checks these "hiding places" in order to save wear and tear on his tools. Don't mark your keys with your name and address.

Most leases provide that the owner of the premises or the super-intendent is to have "ready access" to the apartment. This does *not* in itself require you to turn over a complete set of keys. All you must do is allow authorized people to enter if requested to do so, and under most leases, you can choose the time—after working hours if necessary. If a lease provides that you must turn over a set of keys, it's sometimes possible to have that clause altered. If not, rely on the sealed-envelope device or avoid taking that particular apartment.

Your keys are perhaps your most valuable possession. Losing them may lead to a burglary or worse. If you lose the keys; it's easy for the person who finds them to enter your home.

Why most women carry their keys in their purses is a great mystery. There's usually plenty of identification in a purse so that a purse snatcher can easily determine where the owner lives. Even an ordinary purse snatcher may be tempted to enter a home because he finds a set of keys. In some places, it's customary for one criminal to sell sets of keys with identification to another criminal. If you do lose a set of keys and there is identification with them, it's only sensible to change the tumbler units. But it's much cheaper to carry your door keys in a pocket or on a chain. Usually there are only one or two keys that you really must take with you. Restrict yourself to carrying only one or two keys so that they may be easily concealed. By the way, it's much safer to live in an apartment building where the main entrance is kept locked, though such buildings are increasingly difficult to find. At any rate, a small pocket with a zipper or a snap-closing sewn on the inside of a belt or clothing is the safest place for keys.

Thieves sometimes return handbags or wallets after they have removed the money. They stuff such things into a mailbox, and if there's identification, the post office will send them back to the owners. Don't jump to the conclusion that the thief is being chivalrous. Stuffing a purse or wallet into a mailbox is often a good way of getting rid of incriminating evidence. Sometimes it will be returned with keys still inside. The usual reaction is to breathe a sigh of relief because the lock tumblers will not need changing. Don't ever fall for this particular trap. It only takes a few seconds to make an impression of a set of keys in a soft bar of soap or wax. Then a skilled man can make keys that will fit your door. A record of the address is kept and the keys are returned to prevent suspicion. The criminal may be very pleased to trap you alone in your home. Change the tumblers if you run into this series of events— do it whenever keys are returned to you after an unexplained absence. If you find particles of wax or soap on your keys at any time, you can be sure you're on somebody's list.

Be aware of who's on duty as doorman, superintendent, or elevator operator in your apartment building. Most of these people have access to the management's set of keys. If an employee leaves, change the tumblers on your locks. If old Walter, a superintendent you have learned to trust, is suddenly taken off the job and replaced by a shiftless lout, change the tumblers. You really don't have to worry about house passkeys if you change tumblers when you move in. Passkeys are made to fit a general pattern of lock tumblers and the chances are small that a house passkey will fit new lock tumblers selected at random. Sometimes, you can test this by asking an employee to open your door for you. Tell him you've misplaced your keys. If the passkey does not work—as it shouldn't—suddenly "discover" your own keys. Most employees in larger housing units won't disturb themselves because the passkey doesn't fit one apartment's lock.

If you're moving into an apartment, you'll be obliged to put a name plate or card downstairs beside your mailbox in the lobby or in some other prominent place. Women should avoid identifying themselves by using only the initial of their given names without the usual "Miss" or "Mrs." No one would know for sure that J. Jones is a woman. The resident of the apartment might possibly be a 300-pound wrestler or a champion pistol shot.

IDENTIFICATION OF STOLEN PROPERTY

To prevent permanent loss of your valuable property, go over every costly item for serial numbers and keep a list of them along with the manufacturer's name and the model number or style designation. If there's no serial number, write down the manufacturer's name and the model or style designation. Often it's possible to paste gummed labels bearing your name inside valuables where they cannot be seen. For instance, you can glue one inside most electric clocks and radios after unscrewing the back panels. You can even do this with watches if the label is small enough.

AFTER A BURGLARY

If you come home and find that your door has been jimmied or look up and see that one of your windows has been broken, don't go in. Instead, go to the nearest telephone and call the police. If you go inside, you may find that the criminal is still there and you may be hurt. If you live in a private home, and have any reason to believe someone may have entered it during your absence, take a few minutes to walk slowly around your house. Look at each window and door. If a door has been forced or if any of the windows are broken, don't enter—call the police. Many people have

22

been hurt or even killed because they unexpectedly interrupted a housebreaker.

EXTENDED ABSENCE

When you leave your home for a vacation or other extended absence, make sure that at least one light is on and the radio is playing so that the place seems occupied. Your electrical equipment must be in good condition so that you can do this safely without danger of a fire. You don't have to play the radio so loudly that it annoys neighbors. Criminals usually check carefully before breaking in, and the sound of a radio playing softly is often enough to keep them out. Don't draw all the blinds or pull down all the shades—it's a dead giveaway.

Of course, you should close and lock all the doors and windows. This is some indication that the occupants are absent, of course, but usually the radio and the lights will dispel that impression. If you have a home air conditioner that protrudes out of the wall or a window, closing all windows in the summer is not an indication that you are away. Many people seal their homes entirely and rely on the air conditioner for all ventilation.

Cut off milk and newspaper deliveries and arrange to have the post office hold your mail or have a friend remove the delivered mail from your box. A stuffed mailbox and an array of milk bottles or packages informs everyone that you are absent.

There's a photo-electric device which turns lights off and on morning and evening. The Nite-Guard and similar devices are quite expensive (around $12.00) because they are equipped with a light-sensitive cell. When natural light falls below a certain level, the device turns on the current. As soon as there's enough natural light, the device turns the current off again just as you would do yourself. Similar devices turn the current on at a set time every day by means of a timing apparatus that is set like an alarm clock. Both devices can be used to start a radio playing.

If you leave home for two weeks or more, let someone you trust know where you are so that you can be called if there's trouble. Even if you don't interrupt your vacation, police are sometimes more anxious to recover stolen property if the owner telephones

23

and asks them about the burglary. Also, you may be able to give them useful information such as the location of the list of serial numbers of your valuables.

In the suburbs, try to hire a trustworthy neighborhood boy to cut your grass and water the lawn. If a heavy growth of grass or brown, drying shrubbery shows, it's a sure indicator of extended absence.

Make it a point *not* to announce your trip to the local newspaper before you leave. Some people like to see a newspaper announcement that they will visit Bermuda via the *Ocean Monarch,* sailing September 15th, complete with the address of the vacationing family. Housebreakers like to see such announcements too. Announce your trip to the society editor when you return. You'll be able to give her more information and perhaps a photograph of yourself in some interesting vacation activity.

If the police in your neighborhood are diligent, it is worth informing them that you will be away. They'll pay special attention to your house during patrols. In urban areas, however, it's usually not worthwhile. The police simply cannot check every vacant apartment.

THE SELF-SERVICE ELEVATOR

.Self-service elevators can be very dangerous. You should always consider using the stairs instead of the elevator if you suspect danger. On the stairs or in hallways, you have room to run and it's much more likely that someone will hear you if you cry out. If you are living in a dangerous situation, it may be necessary for you to make a self-imposed rule never to use the elevator unless you are with someone you know. Many criminals hesitate to tackle two people at once.

When you enter the elevator at the ground floor, place your foot so that it will prevent the door from closing. Then push the button for your floor. If the indicator light tells you that the elevator is, instead, bound for the basement, get out at once. Someone may be down there using the elevator to bring you to him.

If you are already in the elevator alone and a dangerous-looking person tries to enter, get out again. If he's an innocent person, he'll think that you intended to get off at that floor. But if he tries to prevent you from getting off, start shouting for help immediately and try to keep a foot where it will prevent the door from closing.

If you are waiting for the elevator on a landing and it arrives with a suspicious person already in it, don't get in. Most innocent people will believe that you were waiting for the elevator to take you in the opposite direction and will think nothing of your failure to enter. If the person attempts to get off the elevator, he may have a legitimate reason for doing so, but he may be intent on robbery or rape. In these cases, make for the stairs immediately or ring the bell of an occupied apartment and keep on ringing it. At least, you're not inside the elevator with the criminal and you have some chance of escaping or fending him off. Don't try to reenter your own apartment if there is no one inside who can help you. You'll probably unlock the door and the criminal will then push you inside the empty apartment and follow.

If you are trapped inside an elevator with a criminal, it's often best to use the alarm button and to call out at the top of your lungs. Elevator alarms are intended to call the attention of the superintendent to a jammed elevator. Often, the individual in the car cannot hear the alarm sounding because the buzzer or bell is located in the lobby or a maintenance room. Don't stop pressing the alarm merely because you can't hear it sounding. Know exactly where the alarm button is in the elevator and make a habit of standing near it. If you live in the suburbs and seldom use self-service elevators, it still pays to be alert when you do use them. It only takes a second to check the location of the alarm button. Do this as you select the button for your floor. If you do live in an apartment building, test the buzzer or alarm bell in the elevator at least every six months. When the superintendent appears, tell him you pressed the alarm by mistake. If no one appears, find out why and make sure that the alarm is repaired or that the management is told about the superintendent's failure to respond. Be pleasant about it, but register a complaint. You pay rent, and you're entitled to reasonable security. If necessary, tell the superintendent exactly what you are doing.

ROOMMATES

If you're unmarried, it pays to be careful about those with whom you share your quarters. If the person with whom you live is careless about locking doors and windows or about entering the apartment with strangers, you might as well camp out on a subway platform. Try to rent the apartment or house with the lease in your name and only afterward look for a person with whom to share the costs. If the person turns out to be less than you expected, force him or her to leave. To do this, your lease must be written so that it allows another person to live with you but does not require that person to be a party to the document. Some leases are written so that only the people who sign it may occupy the premises. In most two-party leases, the other person has as much right to occupy the premises as you do.

KEEP A RECORD OF APPOINTMENTS

For women, the comparative stranger is usually much more dangerous than anyone she knows well. It's something of a safeguard to make sure that some trusted friend knows the name and address of anyone with whom a woman plans to associate alone. If a person constantly avoids telling you where he works and will not introduce you to friends or relatives, he's usually not trustworthy.

TELEPHONE TACTICS

You need a telephone. It's almost always the quickest way to summon the police. Locate your telephone beside your bed so that you can reach it quickly if aroused during the night.

Write the telephone number of the police on a piece of paper and glue it down where it can easily be seen. Sometimes you can be so flustered that you'll be unable to remember the number even if you think you have it memorized. The number of your local precinct is best, though some cities have a special city-wide emergency number. If you must call in the dark and cannot remember the number or cannot dial in the dark, dial "O" for operator—the last hole in the telephone dial. When she comes on the line, tell her,

"This is an emergency. I need police." Even this brief statement may be enough. If the line is kept open at your end, the telephone operator can almost always trace the phone and its location. If you do have time, however, give her your name, the address, and your apartment number, in that order. Only after these essentials have been given should you take the time to state the nature of the emergency.

Your telephone can also be a source of danger and annoyance. Most burglaries in large cities are committed during daylight when people are away at work. If a criminal intends to break into an apartment or house, he often uses the telephone to check the tenant's working hours. It's very simple to look at the names on the mailbox and to look up a given name in the telephone book. Then it's a matter of a few regular calls to determine when the apartment or house is usually unoccupied. If the criminal does get an answer when he expects the apartment to be empty, it's easy enough to say, "Sorry, wrong number," and hang up. Therefore, don't ever advertise your telephone number, and it may be best to keep it unlisted.

If for some reason, you must list your telephone number in the directory, and you are a woman living alone, it's best to make sure that only the initial of your first name appears, just as any sensible woman would do with her listing in the lobby of her building. Some criminals and crank callers scan telephone books for female names in their neighborhoods and try to "get acquainted" over the phone. Don't let them know that you're a woman.

If you have an unlisted number, you have an advantage, but you can throw it away very easily. For instance, if the telephone rings and the caller asks, "What number is this?" don't ever give it to him. One kind of crank calls numbers at random, and if he finds your voice attractive and you give the number, you'll form an acquaintance that you'll regret, particularly when the crank calls over and over again at two and three in the morning. If you get this kind of question, simply ask what number the caller wants. If he doesn't give the right number, tell him so and hang up. If he does give the right number, ask him what his business is and with whom he wishes to speak. If he doesn't give logical reasons for calling and the correct name, hang up. Don't regard the telephone as an imperious voice which you must always answer. You wouldn't think of giving your telephone number to a stranger in the street, so why should you do so over the telephone? And don't be more liberal with information when it's a female caller. Women are often used to extract information that's later used by male housebreakers.

If you do have a listed number, you should be very cautious. A criminal may learn your name and your address. The next recourse is to the telephone book to find out your telephone number. When he calls, he'll try to identify your voice and fish for information. When the telephone rings, say "Hello." Let the caller take it from there and hang up immediately if you find he has no legitimate reason for calling. You can be just as polite over the telephone as you wish, but don't talk much and never volunteer information about yourself. Above all, never let yourself fall for any statement which would take you outside your home. All kinds of things are offered. You can win free dance lessons or a new car if you'll report at such and such an address to participate in a contest or quiz show. You may win a free steamship ticket to Europe if you can pass a test being given at such and such address. The caller may attack you in the hall of your apartment building or you may find your home stripped when you return from the wild-goose chase.

Criminals often use the false telephone survey to gather information. The telephone rings and a polite voice asks you to participate in a survey being conducted by a research organization. First of all, you're asked to give your name, your address, and perhaps your age. Then, if the criminal is skilled enough, he'll ask quite a few innocent questions among which will be a query on the worth of your personal property and another on when you plan to take your vacation. That sounds almost unbelievable, doesn't it? But this criminal technique has worked well for years. If you think that the survey is worthwhile and you decide you want to participate, tell the caller that you will give him the information if he'll send you a letter asking for it. If your telephone number is not listed, don't volunteer your name and address, however. After all, most of the legitimate survey organizations obtain names of participants from published lists, and the caller should already know your name and address. If a letter asking for such information is sent to you without the name and address of a responsible organization that can be checked in dependable directories, don't answer it.

On rare occasions, it's possible for a person to trap a telephone caller who annoys with obscene language. If you get a series of such calls, make an arrangement with the police and the telephone company so that they can locate the caller's phone. If all goes well, you may be asked to participate as a witness against the individual or to meet him out in the street under the watchful eye of a detective. Do this only if your city has a stiff system of penalties for such offenses. If not, it's better simply to hang up as soon as you hear the first dirty word. In some areas, obscene telephone calls are regarded as simple mischief and the caller will be out of jail (if he ever sees the inside of one) in a few days. Then you may be in for a renewed series of calls or even worse. Sometimes you can stop a series of these calls simply by picking up the phone and saying quietly—but loudly enough so that you can be heard over the wire —"Here's that man again, officer," or some similar ominous sentence. The caller will usually hang up. Most of these telephone callers have the mentality of small children, and it's often easy to deceive them. Remember, however, that some of these people can be extremely dangerous.

For a fee, the telephone company in many cities will install a special plug so that you can disconnect your telephone entirely at night. This stops annoying calls, but you are cutting yourself off entirely from legitimate outside calls. In an emergency such as a fire on the lower floors of your building, you cannot be reached. It's often better to turn the volume of the telephone bell or buzzer down just low enough so that you will hear it if the phone rings continuously. Most telephones now have a volume adjustment. If not, your telephone company may be able to install one. Taking your phone off the hook is also useful on some occasions if you can safely do so. It annoys the telephone company and cuts you off from emergency calls, but sometimes it's necessary. In many cities you'll find that the telephone company will send a very loud, high-pitched signal over the open phone if you leave it off the hook for a very long period. If you're having telephone trouble and wish to

29

keep the phone on the hook, it sometimes helps to arrange a telephone code. Tell your friends and relatives, for instance, to call and let the phone ring three times and then to hang up. This will inform you that someone you know wants to reach you. If the caller then calls again immediately, you can be sure that you are receiving a legitimate call. Otherwise, don't answer the phone.

Of course, you should change the telephone number when you first move into your apartment. It's unwise to inherit a telephone number as the author once did. The former occupant of the apartment turned out to be a bookmaker and his clients called every hour of the night and were very irate when they found I could not supply his new number.

IN THE STREET

Women are usually fairly cautious about where they go, particularly after dark. Most men never give a thought to the matter unless they have already been victims of robberies or worse crimes. Some neighborhoods are so dangerous, however, that it pays to stay out of them under any circumstances. Avoidance is always less troublesome than physical resistance.

If you suspect that you may run into trouble, walk near the curb. Stay away from building fronts and the entrances to hallways and alleys. If, however, you are attacked, it helps to have some solid object at your back—a wall, a post, or a mailbox will do.

It helps to know the location of the nearest fire-alarm or police call box. Keep an eye out for them, particularly if you think you are being followed. Police call boxes may be used by civilians in emergencies. Never hesitate to open them and use the phone if you need help. Of course, you should never pull a fire alarm unless you are sure you are dealing with a criminal, but if you do find yourself in a dangerous situation, pull the alarm. Sometimes, if the potential attacker is merely following you at a distance, you can frighten him off by standing with your hand on the fire-alarm lever. Few criminals will act if they know that a fire company will arrive on the scene in a few minutes. You must not expect to avoid being arrested for the trouble you'll be causing the fire department. If you were really in desperate need, however, it's unlikely that you would be convicted.

When walking alone, some people are reluctant to face trouble because, somehow, they feel it will go away if they ignore it. For instance, some women will let a man follow them for blocks. Only at the last moment will they turn to face him or make some effort to get help. It often happens that they wait too long. If an attacker gets his hands on you, you'll be obliged to fight him off. It's easier to act early even though you may sometimes be mistaken. If someone follows you, test him by crossing the street, walking a block or two and then recrossing the street or by making some other rather odd maneuver. If he follows each of your movements, you can be sure that he is actually following you.

When you are sure, go into the nearest store or public place. Go into a telephone booth or use the storekeeper's phone to call the police. Of course, the person who followed you will probably no longer be there when the police arrive, but he may see the police car and then he'll realize that you are not such easy game. Again— it does no harm to avail yourself of the police in such circumstances, and a responsible police department encourages you to do so.

If you are followed in a street lined with private residences, try to remain calm and march up to a house where the lights are on. Ring the bell just as though you were expected. When the door opens, clearly and calmly explain what is happening and ask the householder to let you in. Plead for help. If you're a respectable person, most people will try to help you. Surprisingly, it depends mostly on how you're dressed. Dirty blue jeans do not get the same sympathy as a suit. Even if you happen on an unsympathetic or fearful householder, all is not lost. The mere fact that you are talking with someone may frighten the criminal away. Even if you are not allowed inside the house, appeal to the occupant to call the police. Though there may be exceptions, it's usually best to stay on the doorstep if you're denied entrance. The criminal does not know what is happening. He may conclude that you are waiting for another person before entering. If you wait long enough, a group of people may appear and you will be able to appeal to them for assistance.

Never try to elude a follower by entering the doorway of a darkened building or the lobby of a multiple dwelling. Many attacks occur in such places, and the criminal will be only too happy to follow you in. This applies to the entrance of your own home. It's better to stay out in the open if you are being followed. At least in the street, there's a better chance to attract attention. If you try to race the attacker to your door, you may lose the race by a step or two and find yourself trapped. Don't waste time when you come home late. Have your keys out before you reach the entrance. Open doors quickly and lock them quickly behind you.

It's unwise to lead a follower to your home. He may be pleased to know exactly where you live. He may intend to come back later when you are not aware of him. If you know you're being followed, go elsewhere until you can shake him. One woman I know was faced with this problem and walked seven blocks through a dangerous neighborhood with a dangerous-looking lout following her. He disappeared when she entered the local police precinct house.

You may want to purchase a portable alarm. For instance, there's the Invento Alarm at about $10.00 which makes a violent whistling noise that can be heard for blocks. Basically, there are two types of alarms—one type rings or sounds only when a lever is depressed and held there. The other type goes on making noise until exhausted if the release is pressed only once. The first type is best. You may come across a situation in which the criminal threatens to kill you unless you turn off the alarm and under these circumstances it's best to do so. You can also buy a police whistle for a dollar or two. If attacked, blow many short, loud blasts. These alarms and all defense hardware are useless if you bury them at the bottom of your purse or pocket. Make an effort to keep them on top of the other things you carry. If you have the slightest suspicion that trouble is brewing, get out your defensive device and hold it in your hand ready for use.

Of course, one of the best ways for a criminal to look you over is to do so in a public place such as a restaurant, a bowling alley, or even a church or synagogue. It's important to avoid being followed when you leave a public place. One way to check on this is to leave the building by one door and, if you think someone is

32

following, return by another. If there's only one entrance, go back in again and stay for a while. If the same person shows up inside, it's probably best to seek assistance.

PUBLIC TRANSPORTATION

Many robberies, attacks, and even rapes occur on public transportation—particularly on subway platforms and in subway cars.

On the subway late at night, always try to sit in the car with the motorman or the conductor. Since many subways no longer have conductors, you're usually safest in the first car where the motorman's cab is located. On buses, it's best to sit near the driver. Select a seat that is not in the corner of the car or in a corner formed by the backs of the seats. It's usually safest to sit near a door so that you can dodge out of it if a group of unruly people enter. You can often do so behind their backs. Try to time your move so that you get out just as the door closes so that they are prevented from following. But be careful not to do this if you must leave the train for a deserted, dangerous platform.

If most people leave the subway car in which you are sitting, get up and make your way forward until you find more people. Always go forward in the train toward the motorman. You may be in a situation where the entire train is almost empty. If you go toward the rear, you may run into trouble. If you are near the motorman's cab, you can at least bang on his door with your heels while your back is pressed on the door and try to fend off the attacker. Some subways have communications systems which enable the motorman to call ahead for assistance. At the very least, the motorman can shout out of the cab's window when he reaches the next stop. Never hesitate to pull the emergency cord or to use a glass-fronted alarm pull after breaking the glass. Use a little judgment, however, since these alarms usually cause the motorman to stop the train. After stopping, he will often look for the trouble, but one man may not be enough assistance. In this situation, it may be best to try to hold out until you reach the next stop.

Uniformed servicemen, firemen, postal employees, and in fact, any man in a government uniform is usually the best source of assistance. In a recent case in Philadelphia, a young girl was being

33

dragged into a deserted subway tunnel by a large group of danger-ous teenagers. The obvious intention was rape. There were thirty or forty people standing on the platform, but only one man tried to help. He was a Navy enlisted man, and he certainly deserves some sort of medal. He was severely beaten, but he delayed the gang and the police arrived in time.

In dangerous areas, stand in a lighted place when waiting for a train, preferably near the change booth. Try to avoid subway stops where there is no attended change booth. If you must use them, have your change or token ready and try to wait in the street until you hear the subway train rumbling into the station. Then go down the stairs and get on the train as quickly as you can. It's better to wait under a light out in the open than it is to wait on a deserted subway platform. When waiting at an attended change booth, don't go through the turnstile until the train is almost at a stop. If attacked in such a situation, you may find that the attendant in the booth may be unwilling to risk injury by coming to your assistance. After all, he is not a policeman. But he usually has a telephone and can call for assistance. Despite a man's greater strength, this advice is not inappropriate for men where violent muggings frequently occur.

If you travel with another person, you have a better chance of avoiding trouble. When leaving home or a gathering late at night, try to find someone else who is going the same way and travel together.

Travel and Your Car

If you travel, don't drop your security guard. People often for-get about self-protection on vacations and sometimes they regret it. If you have special defense devices such as an alarm and a repel-lent dispenser, by all means take them with you when you go, but be sure they are legal where you visit.

In strange sleeping quarters such as hotels, don't rely too much on ordinary door locks. Hotels and motels commonly have many passkeys, and it's not always possible to prevent someone from making copies. Also, locks on doors in such places are often flimsy or simple to pick. If your room door is equipped with a chain or manually-operated bolt, use it and you're fairly safe. Many hotels place signs in their rooms requesting guests to do so for their own protection. If your room does not have a chain or bolt, try to lock the door in some other way. The Eaton Yale and Towne Co. makes the Travelock, available at most hardware stores. This device is a portable key lock that can be used to lock almost any door from the inside. It has a hooklike arrangement which you place against the jamb. The hook catches the frame of the door on the outside. Then the door is closed on it and the body of the lock is shoved up against the closed door. The key is turned and the door is securely locked. There's another device that consists simply of an expanding wedge on which you close the door. There's no key, but when you flip a lever, the wedge expands and the door is jammed shut. If you do use a key device, place the key on a stand beside your bed. You may want to get out of the room in a hurry, and you'll want to lay your hand on that key as quickly as you can. You can also lock a door by propping a chair back under the doorknob.

Windows are another problem. It's usually quite difficult to secure them unless they are completely closed, and sometimes this is difficult if you need ventilation. Some hotels and motels do equip their room windows with snub devices so that the windows can be fixed in place when open enough to admit air but not an unwanted visitor. Look for these devices when you're shown a room. If the windows are not equipped with them, go elsewhere if possible. After all, you customarily inspect a motel room to assure yourself that it's clean and comfortable. Why not devote a few seconds to your security? If you absolutely must stay in a place with insecure window devices, put several ashtrays or other objects where they will fall on the floor with a crash if the window is moved or if someone tries to enter.

Travel by car can also be extremely dangerous. This was recently demonstrated in a case that occurred in Newark, New Jersey. A nurse was sitting in her parked automobile. A group of adolescent criminals opened the car's door, pulled out the nurse, and took her to a deserted building where she was raped over and over again by the various members of the gang. As an amusement, her skin was burned with cigarettes and her hair was set on fire. She survived and the criminals were arrested. In this case, the New Jersey judi-

35

cial system acted with speed and the average sentence for the gang members was fifty years in prison. This is no real compensation to the victim, however, who would have been quite safe if she had kept her car doors locked.

Don't park in front of a bar or even a soda fountain where teenagers congregate. They may damage your car, and there's more likelihood that you'll run into a dangerous person or group in such places. If you can't find a safe place, try to park in an attended parking lot or garage. Never leave valuables or any object that would attract thieves in any place visible from the outside of the car. Remember that so much as a fifty-cent piece may induce teenage criminals to break a car's window.

Of course, you should always remove your keys from the ignition after you have parked and take them with you. Car keys are just as important as house keys. Don't "conceal" a spare key under the hood or taped to the inside of the bumper. Experienced thieves know where to look for them.

When you approach your parked car, have your keys ready in your hand. The more time you spend fumbling with the door and the ignition, the more opportunity there is for someone to attempt a robbery or an attack. You're comparatively safe when your car is moving, so get it going as quickly as possible. When you first unlock the door of your car, glance over the back of the seat to make sure that you do not have an unwanted passenger.

After you are sure there's no one in the car, lock all the doors and keep them locked all the while you are in motion. Keep as many windows as possible completely closed, and if you simply must have one open for ventilation, open it only partway—never enough to admit a hand and arm. Rely for most of your air on the hood ventilator.

Many people have been attacked in stopped cars. Therefore, try to keep your automobile in motion. Leave an interval ahead of you, if traffic is moving slowly, so that you have some chance to speed up if only for a few feet. If someone tries to enter your car, your safest method of defense is to accelerate rapidly.

If you can legally make use of some defense device such as a tear-gas projector, keep it within easy reach of your hand while

36

driving, particularly if you are passing through a slum. Even a heavy automobile wrench on the seat beside you can be very useful if a dangerous criminal puts his arm or head through a window. Use such a device only in accordance with the law of self-defense as discussed in Chapter IV.

Your safest bet is to drive a hardtop rather than a convertible. It's easy to slash a convertible top with a knife. Even with a hardtop, keep the doors locked. Groups of teenagers have smashed the windows of a car in an effort to get at the person inside for no better reason than the motorist's efforts to drive through a street where a neighborhood ballgame was going on.

If your car breaks down on the road, you may run into serious trouble, particularly if this happens at night. In this situation, your chief objective should be to get help from police or an authorized towing service. Don't be too quick to accept help from a truck driver or some other unofficial source. You may feel that you are being too suspicious and rude if you refuse help from another motorist. There's a polite way to do so, however. If another driver stops and offers help, ask him to call at the next service station or police barracks to report your situation. Most decent people will be glad to do this, and you run no risk. Don't get out of your car to speak with someone who stops unless you are quite sure you can handle the situation if he proves to be dangerous. Normally, you should keep the doors locked, stay inside, and roll down a window to speak with him. Roll it down only partway and keep your hand on the handle, ready to roll it up again.

At night, you can signal for help by blinking your lights. In the daytime, or at night, blow your horn—blow it three times, pause and then blow another set of three blasts. If you can do so safely, it also helps to get out of the car long enough to raise your hood or to tie a white rag or handkerchief to the radio aerial. Almost anyone will realize that your car is stopped because of a breakdown. On well-traveled highways and parkways, police usually maintain regular patrols, so don't wander off—they'll be along sooner or later. On country roads, you may be obliged to wait a long time, but help will eventually arrive. Your worst situation is to break down in a city slum late at night. If necessary, wait it out until the sun comes up and you see people in groups on their way to work. You're comparatively safe in your locked car, particularly if you have a defense device. You're not safe at all when walking long distances if you're unfamiliar with the neighborhood.

Signal for help with lights or horn only when there's a possibility of being seen. Don't keep it up if there are no cars or people in sight. If you wear your battery down, you'll be unable to signal when someone does come along. A flashlight is a very useful thing to have along if your battery does become exhausted.

Is it really necessary to add that you should never pick up hitchhikers? Police have been saying it for years, but every year a few people are killed by hitchhikers.

IF IT DOES HAPPEN

In a serious attempt at assault or rape, use any available means to repulse the criminal. You are completely justified in using dangerous kicks and blows. It's important to remember, however, that hand-to-hand defenses are regulated by the law of self-defense. A blow or a kick can be just as deadly as any weapon. Be sure you are acting legally.

If possible, use surprise tactics. You can fake a fainting spell or try to appear so confused that you seem incapable of resistance. This condition is only too easy to imitate if the criminal has struck you. In a rape attempt, for instance, the criminal will turn his attention to removing the victim's clothing after he's sure the person is helpless. This is the moment that should be used to disable the attacker. Kick, or use any weapon to inflict a swift, disabling blow.

The clothing worn by women is important in defense. Sixty years ago, women wore complicated things such as bustles and voluminous skirts and petticoats. Sometimes this decorative apparel was useful in deterring a sexual criminal since he had a hard time managing all that cloth and whalebone. Modern clothing can be used for this purpose. If a woman is wearing a strong, snug girdle or other foundation garment with a closed crotch, a rapist will be obliged to use both hands to remove it. To do so, he will have to put aside any weapon he may have. As he does this or takes his hands away from the throat or arms and begins to struggle with the clothing, there's a very good opportunity to disable him. A weapon is useful in this situation, but almost any woman can do quite well with blows and kicks if she knows how.

Few people realize it, but many rapes are caused because a woman refuses a man in a sneering, contemptuous manner. Saying "No" in a polite, seemingly considerate way even if the approach has been coarse is an excellent avoidance tactic. Evident disgust is always dangerous since it may trigger violence.

Even determined resistance may not always be successful. In the ordinary course of events, the victim of a rape will be taken to an emergency hospital by the police. In some areas, large public hospitals offer very poor care because of overcrowding and low budgets. After a rape, the victim needs a delicate internal examination to determine if there is any damage and she also may require immediate surgery. The physician usually administers a very thorough douche in order to prevent disease. This douche may also prevent pregnancy. It should be administered just as quickly as possible. In crowded public hospitals, delay is common. If the victim is in a fertile phase of her monthly cycle, the douche may come too late and then she will be forced to bear the criminal's child. In some states, women may legally obtain an abortion if a physician certifies that one is needed for reasons of health. In some places, this certification may be obtained after a rape if the doctor is willing to swear that the pregnancy is endangering the victim's mental health. To obtain such certification, however, the crime must have been reported to the police when it occurred or the legal agency may not regard the occurrence as a rape. Abortions after rape are easily obtained in Europe, particularly in Sweden and Poland.

If possible, male victims of assault should also try to receive care from their own doctors. In large public hospitals, a certain attitude commonly prevails about persons who arrive in the emergency room with broken noses, cuts, broken teeth, or stab wounds. Since the hospital sees many cases of this kind and most of them result from fights between drunks or near-criminals, it's often assumed that most of those who come in with such injuries got pretty nearly what they deserved. No one, therefore, makes much of an effort to treat these injuries quickly or considerately in many public institutions. Even if you are obliged to suffer some additional pain to do so, it's often best to go to your own doctor if you are ever so unfortunate as to be hurt in an assault. Of course, if the injury is very serious, seek help wherever it can be obtained.

CHAPTER III

Security Hardware and Barriers

A^N independent testing organization examines new security
devices such as safes and locks, and rates their efficiency.
The standard used is the amount of time it would take a criminal
to breach the security barrier with the best available tools if the
criminal were sure he could work without interruption. You would
be amazed at the shortness of the time rating given to large and
very expensive security devices. A bank vault costing hundreds of
thousands of dollars and weighing many tons sometimes gets a
security rating of only half an hour. A very expensive time-com-
bination lock may have a rating of ten minutes.

What can you do to protect yourself against the highly skilled,
well-equipped housebreaker with only the rather simple locks available at the hardware store? The answer is quite plain—you can do
almost nothing. Even a good pin-tumbler lock of the type commonly used in home protection can be picked in a few seconds
without making much noise. This is demonstrated at the conven-
tions of the American Locksmiths Association. At this convention,
there's usually a lockpicking contest in which expert locksmiths
participate. Those who manage the contest often choose a new lock
on sale to the public, often one advertised as completely pickproof.
Each locksmith in the contest picks the lock, racing against the
stopwatch. In one contest, an extremely skilled locksmith picked a

new pin-tumbler lock in exactly one second. Unless you are using the old-fashioned and completely worthless warded lock, the doors of your apartment or house are equipped with pin-tumbler locks.

For the private citizen as well as the bank manager, the message is plain. No amount of money spent on security hardware will keep criminals out unless these devices are backed up by alertness and good security procedures planned in advance. The bank manager, of course, relies on complex electronic alarms and armed guards to deny the criminal the uninterrupted time he needs to breach the security hardware. The private person can install an alarm system in his home too, but it's usually so elementary that a skilled criminal can detect it and silence it in a few seconds. Don't put your entire trust in locks and other security hardware. You must plan in advance what you will do if your security hardware is breached while you are at home, and you must stay alert so that you can avoid interrupting a dangerous criminal if he enters your home when you are away.

Fortunately, the really skilled housebreaker or burglar seldom shows up at the average American home because he is not interested in the small gains he would acquire from breaking into such a place. If you install security hardware, your opponent is usually a half-grown adolescent with no better tools than a crowbar or jimmy, one hand-operated drill, and a hacksaw blade. This type of person commits 80 or 90 percent of all the forced entries that occur in the United States.

The ill-equipped teen-age housebreaker can be extremely dangerous, however, because he is often very nervous and may become violent when a calm, first-class housebreaker would retreat as quickly as possible. The sexually-disturbed person, the maniac, and the criminal under the influence of alcohol or drugs can be very dangerous too. Fortunately, the violent housebreaker is rather uncommon, and he's almost always entirely unskilled and poorly equipped. The rapist's idea of a successful housebreaking is smashing a window or breaking down a door with a great amount of noise that will arouse anyone in the house.

The nightmare of many law-enforcement people is a rapist, maniac, or murderous adolescent who is a highly skilled locksmith.

Such a person could enter almost any American home in a very short time without making the slightest noise. As far as I know, there has never been such a person. Apparently, the man who is willing to study the locksmith's trade in school or through books is so constructed that he will not commit a violent crime if he can avoid it. On the other hand, the man who is interested in rape or violence for its own sake will not devote many hours of hard study to learning how to pick a lock noiselessly or even to learning how to use drills and saws skillfully and noiselessly.

In some cities, however, skilled men devote all their time to the locksmithing aspect of crime and sell ready-made keys to others who commit burglary. For instance, one of these men may be called in as a "consultant" who will make a key for a particular lock by inserting a sensitive key blank, and hand filing it according to the markings obtained. Strangely enough, these criminals are very careful about their customers. They'd attract inconvenient attention if they made a practice of selling their services to strong-arm men, rapists, and other violent persons. One has to be a bona fide member of the housebreaking fraternity with a demonstrated nonviolent record to deal with a good criminal locksmith.

Well, do you feel secure? You have a right to relax only if you have gone over every window and door in your home carefully to check it for security weaknesses and have installed all the hardware needed to keep a rather unskilled criminal out. Not many people have done that.

Should you install all the security hardware detailed in this chapter? In most cases, you don't need locks, gratings, and alarms on every opening, and probably some of the items are not necessary in the average situation, though they may be very useful if you find yourself living in a very dangerous situation. If you tried to install all the hardware mentioned in this chapter, it would cost a fortune, and much of the work would be wasted effort. Select the hardware in terms of your real needs.

DOORS

Before installing locks or other security hardware, examine the door, the doorframe, and the hinges carefully to determine if they are strong enough. The favorite tool of the average housebreaker or burglar is a jimmy—a small crowbar which is forced between the doorframe and the edge of the door and used as a lever. On the lock side of the door, the jimmy is inserted in the crack, and the housebreaker attempts to wrench the lock or bend it so that the tongue of the lock disengages from the receiver. That is, the tongue is forced out of the slot in which it normally rests when the door is locked. If the lock and the receiver are strong, however, and the jimmy does not work, the criminal often tries to use his jimmy on the hinge side. Sometimes, the doorframe is so old and dried out that one wrench with a good jimmy or bar pulls the screws of the hinges right out of the holes. Then the door can be opened even if the lock does not disengage. Sometimes, the wood of the door itself is rotten and the screws on the hinge side of the door will pull out. The original installation may have been faulty. For instance, some carpenters use screws that are too short to hold against a determined effort, or the screws may be made of poor steel that rusts away in a damp climate if the wood is porous and soaks up moisture. Unfortunately, there is no rule of thumb. In good hardwood, a ¾-inch wood screw will hold well, but in soft, porous pine, a 3-inch screw may be too short.

To guard against entry on the hinge side, you should remove the screws entirely and examine them for strength and to make sure that they are long enough. Examine the wood of the frame and the door to make sure that it is not powder dry, cracked, or rotten. In older houses, I've sometimes been amazed to find that the hinge screws were so loose that they could be removed after only two or three turns with a screwdriver.

If the screws are loose but the wood is sound, replace the old screws with longer ones that hold properly. Sometimes it pays to use long, sheet-metal screws of the self-tapping type that are threaded all the way to the head. If longer, thicker screws are needed, they may not pass through the holes in the hinge plates. If necessary, take the hinges to a machine shop or automobile repair shop, and have the holes reamed out to the required size and countersunk to accommodate the larger screws. If you take the new screws as well as the hinges to the shop, the mechanic will have

44

no difficulty. If the wood in the frame or door is not sound where the old screws were located, but is strong enough close by, have new holes drilled through the hinge plates a half inch or more from the old ones. Fill the old screw holes in door and frame with hardwood pegs cut off flush with the surface. This serves to reinforce the wood, particularly if the pegs are first soaked in a good wood glue. You can do all this work yourself if you have a $\frac{1}{4}$-inch electric drill with the necessary bits or even an old-fashioned carpenter's drill.

If a wooden doorframe is in very poor condition, the only remedy is replacement with new, solid wood. Remove the rotten or dried-out pieces with a hammer and chisel and install new wood, making sure that it is solidly anchored to the rest of the structure, preferably with screws. Countersink all screw holes and cover the screwheads with wooden plugs or a good grade of wood putty or composition. Use white oak if it is available or a good grade of longleaf pine. The ordinary soft pine available in most lumberyards is simply not strong enough to be used in doorframes. If the door itself is in poor condition, it should be replaced.

The most satisfactory type of door for a house or apartment is solid hardwood, $1\frac{1}{2}$ or 2 inches thick. It should fit the doorframe properly with a crack no more than $\frac{1}{64}$-inch wide between the frame and the door. Never buy an old-fashioned door consisting of several thin wooden panels and a thicker frame for use in an outside entrance. Even worse are very lightweight doors with only one large panel or the so-called "Swedish door," which has a wooden frame covered with a very thin sheet of plywood or veneer on the outside and the inside, leaving a hollow space between. These doors should be used only between rooms inside the dwelling where a strong barrier is not required. The thin panels of wood in such doors can be broken with one solid blow of a fist wrapped tightly in a towel. It's surprising how quickly and noiselessly this can be done. Once the panel is broken, the lock can usually be opened easily by reaching through the hole.

The lock in a paneled door can also be opened quietly and fairly quickly by drilling a small hole through one of the thin panels near the lock and then sawing out a larger hole with a compass saw or other thin-bladed saw. This is a common technique with rather un-skilled operators.

A solid hardwood door can be cut through with carpenter's tools, but it takes considerable time and the housebreaker will make a great deal of noise in the process. I prefer the solid hardwood door to doors made with one or more thin metal panels. These metal doors are common in apartment houses in large cities where fire regulations require metal doors. These doors usually have a hollow-metal frame which is constructed of rather strong, quite thick metal. But the panel is only sheet metal and it is only about $\frac{1}{64}$-inch thick. Soft metal is often used. There are many ways to break through the thin, sheet-metal door. For instance, a drill will go through the panel in a second or two, and then a larger hole can be sawed out with a hacksaw blade held in the hand. A thick glove or even a cloth wrapping protects the housebreaker's hand against the saw teeth. Some housebreakers use a simpler method. A hunting knife is sharpened to a needle point. The criminal drives this knife through the panel near the lock with one strong blow. By putting all his weight on the knife, the criminal makes one vertical cut by pulling the knife straight down. This cut is about 8 inches long. Then he makes another vertical cut about 4 inches away. The strip of metal between the two cuts is forced inward by strong pressure or even a blow from a gloved fist. This provides enough room to reach inside and open the lock.

A thick hardwood door provides much more protection than a paneled, sheet-metal door unless the metal of the panel is excep-tionally thick. In an apartment house, it pays to replace a thin sheet-metal door with good wood, provided you can get permission to do so and the wooden door does not violate fire laws, which require metal doors in multiple dwellings in many cities. If the metal door must remain, it may be wise to hire a metalworker to cover the entire outside surface with a hard metal plate at least $\frac{1}{8}$-inch thick fastened to the door with nonretractable screws. In every large city there are companies that specialize in this form of protective hardware, and they're usually listed among the lock-smiths in the classified telephone directory. You can do this kind

46

of work yourself provided you have a good drill and buy the metal plate cut to size.

If you cannot obtain permission to replace a weak door, you can still strengthen the door on the inside. In many apartment houses, the lease or the landlord forbids permanent alterations without specific written permission, but since security has become a matter of life or death in many cities, reinforcing a paneled door at the risk of breaking the lease seems like a worthwhile project even if you're caught at it by the landlord. If you do a neat job, the alteration is not often noticed because it's on the inside, and since the alteration actually improves the property, I wouldn't worry about the consequences unless the alterations violate fire laws.

Figure 3-1 shows my own method of strengthening a door with one or more large panels, wood or metal. In this case, the door is wooden with the usual four panels, but the same method can be used with any paneled metal door. If possible, remove the door from the hinges and lay it flat on the floor, as level as possible. If doorknobs and other hardware prevent laying the door flat on the floor, place it on several pieces of lumber. Fill the panels with a good grade of ready-mixed concrete, available at any hardware store, to which has been added very fine gravel or pebbles no larger than $\frac{1}{4}$-inch thick. Don't worry too much about how much gravel you add or how many pebbles, as long as there are lots of them. The concrete will be entirely sealed up in a tight compartment and it really doesn't matter too much if the concrete cracks, though the pebbles or gravel should be firmly bedded. With the door level, make sure that the concrete mixture does not hump up higher than the face of the doorframe. Allow the mixture to dry thoroughly and then cut a piece of $\frac{1}{4}$-inch plywood large enough to cover all the panels and overlap onto the door's frame about one inch. Fasten the plywood to the door with wood screws, countersunk and plugged, and surround the plywood with $\frac{1}{4}$-inch, quarter-round molding. This makes a very neat job if properly painted or stained, and the limited size of the panel eliminates interference with the doorknob and lock. If necessary, however, the plywood panel can be cut to fit around the doorknob and lock, though some-

47

FIGURE 3-1: Reinforcing a Thinly Paneled Door.

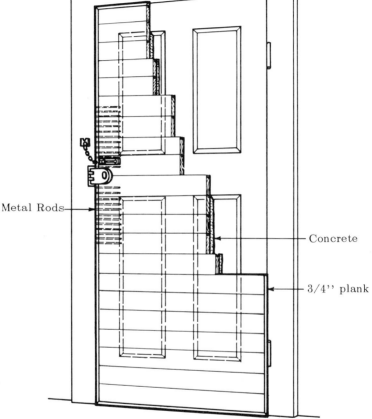

Metal Rods

Concrete

3/4'' plank

Remove door from hinges and lay flat on floor. Fill hollows
in front of panels with concrete mixed with small pebbles or
gravel. Cover entire surface with 3/4-inch-thick plank
screwed to door around edges. If door must remain on
hinges, work from bottom with plank filling hollows with
concrete as you reach them. Metal $\frac{1}{4}$-inch rods above and
below lock prevent drilling or sawing from the outside.

48

times it's better to remove them and put them back on top of the plywood—it's usually thin enough.

If for some reason the door cannot be removed from the hinges, you can put the concrete mixture in the panel cavities while the door is standing. Simply use tongue-and-groove planking, cut to the proper width and about 2 inches wide. Hardwood tongue-and-groove flooring is ideal. Starting at the bottom of the door, screw several planks to the door, starting an inch or two below the panels. Then fill in concrete and gravel to the height of the planks. Continue the process to the top of the door, taking several evenings if necessary. As long as the cavities are thoroughly filled, the concrete does not have to bind together at each joint. When finished, surround the planking with quarter-round molding.

Sometimes the wooden panels in a door are thin at the edges but rise in the center to an increased thickness which would make the coating of concrete and gravel extremely thin. Careful work with a wood chisel and a plane will thin down the center of the panel in order to accommodate a thicker coating of concrete.

This type of strengthened door makes it practically impossible for a thief to cut through a panel. Thieves usually use a drill first and a saw later to get through thin metal or wood panels. I once did this installation for a friend. About a year later, a housebreaker attacked that door. A jimmy did not work because I had installed good locks and hinges, though he tried manfully. Next, he used a drill to start a small hole so that he could unlock from the inside. The mixture of gravel and concrete ground the face right off his $\frac{1}{2}$-inch carpenter's drill, as I discovered because he threw it down in disgust when he stalked off. Even if he had cut the small hole, the concrete mixture would have ground the teeth off his saw. Personally, I felt that I had won a great victory against a criminal, and perhaps I saved my friend's life. If she had come home when that criminal was inside the apartment, she might have been killed. Security hardware is like that. You don't quite appreciate it until it frustrates a criminal.

If you block access through the panels, isn't it possible for the housebreaker to cut through the frame of the door near the lock? It's possible, of course, but the frame of a wooden door is usually quite thick, and cutting through it takes a bit of time. The metal frame of a door is usually constructed of thick sheet metal and is a more serious obstacle than the sheet metal of the thin panel. To make doubly sure, however, use metal pins in the frame of a wooden door. Figure 3-1 shows where they should be driven. I favor short lengths of $\frac{1}{4}$-inch drill rod, obtainable at any good hardware store, for this purpose. Drill $\frac{1}{4}$-inch holes in the edge of the door $\frac{3}{8}$-inch apart, 6 or 7 inches above and below the lock, almost the full depth of the wooden frame. The location of these holes is shown in the illustration. Cut the drill rods with a file about half an inch shorter than the depth of the holes and drive the rods into the holes. Cap them with wood putty or hardwood pegs. If a housebreaker tries to cut through the frame around the lock, he'll soon find that it's a tough job.

Installing all this concrete and metal in a door increases its weight considerably. In order to do it, you must have hinges solidly anchored in good wood. If, however, the door does sag, mount a rubber-wheeled furniture caster on the inside of the door so that the wheel supports the increased weight. Doors should always open easily when unlocked to provide a quick exit in case of fire.

In some older buildings, each apartment's door has an overhead transom that admits air. When these transoms were very popular in the 1890's, most cities had their quota of "transom burglars," who made a specialty of squirming through the narrow openings after forcing the transom open. If you are unfortunate enough to live in an apartment with one of these transoms, it's best to install a grating over the opening.

Use a little imagination when improving your hardware, and always try to view your finished work from the point of view of a criminal. I once advised a friend about strengthening the door to his apartment and gave him all the advice I have given here. He carried it out in exemplary fashion by concreting his paneled door and improving the locks. But when I inspected his work, I found that his hinges were defective. He lived in an old Victorian town house that had been cut up into apartments. His apartment consisted of several rooms which had formerly been part of the master suite. The door opened outward onto an improvised hall, and the

50

hinge pins were on the *outside*. In spite of all his time-consuming efforts, it would have taken a thief only a few seconds to knock out the hinge pins and pry open the door. When I pointed this out to him, he told me I should have warned him. My reply was that I had never seen an outside door with the hinge pins exposed to someone in the hall. This is the kind of thing that you should guard against, and the only way to do it is to imagine that you are trying to break in.

Door Locks and Viewers

The only lock that cannot be picked (manipulated without force) is a sliding bolt, chain, or similar device that has no keyhole on the outside. Even a number-combination lock with a dial instead of a keyhole can be opened from the outside by a skilled man who does not know the combination.

The most common dead barriers without either keyholes or combination dials are the sliding bolt and the door chain. Both can be installed so that they cannot be circumvented or forced from the outside. All that's needed is a strong door and jamb with a very narrow crack between them so that a hacksaw blade or piece of wire cannot be inserted. Most outside doors are fitted into frames that receive the door's edge in a corner formed by molding so that nothing can be inserted between door and jamb because of the right angle formed by the molding. Check your outside doors to make sure that this is true. If not, use heavy hardwood molding to form a right angle. Inspecting any properly installed door will cue you in.

Sliding bolts and chains cannot be used to lock up when you leave your home since they cannot be locked from the outside, but each outside door in your home should have a dead bolt to back up the regular, keyed door lock. I prefer the chain rather than the sliding bolt because it permits one to open the door partway to receive letters, mail and small packages without losing security. A door chain should never be installed so that it permits the door to be opened more than two inches when the chain is on, and one inch is preferable.

The most common fault in door-chain installations is that quite

51

short screws are used. It's astonishing, but the screws supplied with door chains are often only $\frac{3}{4}$ of an inch long. If these screws are used in ordinary pine door frames, a powerful man can jerk them right out merely by throwing his weight against the door. Almost all house and apartment doors open inward. Use screws that are at least two inches long, and make sure they go into solid wood. Normally, the permanently-fastened, anchor end of the chain should be screwed to the frame, and the receiver (slotted part to take the free end of the chain) should be fastened to the door. The harder the door is pushed, the more firmly the sliding fitting at the end of the chain is held in the receiver. This arrangement is more difficult for an intruder since he's obliged to reach right around the edge of the door in order to touch the slide in which the free end of the chain is anchored, and this is impossible if the opening is fairly narrow.

A door chain is very reassuring when an unknown person knocks on your door or rings the bell. You can keep the chain on while you unlock the door to interview the caller through the narrow crack. If you are suspicious of the caller, do not put your hand too near the crack, and under no circumstances put your hand through it. If the caller is a criminal, he may be able to grasp your hand and twist your fingers painfully enough to force you to take off the chain. Keeping the opening narrow makes it more difficult to do this.

If a criminal tries to put his hand through the crack to manipulate the chain, your response should depend on your other security hardware and how serious the danger is. If the criminal is not armed with a gun, it's probably best to slam the door on his hand or fingers. Slam it good and hard by putting your shoulder against the door and using all your weight. Don't attempt to hold the fingers or hand in the door jamb. Your objective is to make the criminal remove his hand so that you can lock the door again with the regular door lock. After one solid smash, jerk the door open as far as the chain will permit, and then slam it again, and again if that is necessary. Even a dangerous criminal will soon get the idea that it's best to remove his mangled hand. When he does so, quickly close the door and put on the ordinary lock. Call the police imme-

52

diately and tell them to look for someone with broken fingers. It's difficult for a criminal to explain such an injury because his mangled hand demonstrates that he tried to enter your home forcefully. You should be very careful not to injure an innocent person in this way, but just why an innocent person would put his hand into the narrow opening between door and jamb is difficult to imagine. You must use your own judgment, remembering that excessive force is forbidden under the law of self-defense.

Sometimes, however, the criminal is strong and heavy enough to force the door to the limit that the chain will permit and hold it there in spite of your attempts to slam the door. This is not really dangerous. If you have installed the chain properly so that there is a minimum of slack in the chain, the would-be intruder's own weight will keep the end of the chain in the receiver, and he will be unable to remove it unless he lessens his pressure on the door to create a little slack in the chain. Most often, this movement will make the crack so narrow that he will be unable to insert his hand. If he succeeds in doing so, however, that's the time to slam the door on his fingers. All the while this is going on, you should be yelling your head off for help.

Door chains, of course, are of no use unless you put them on when you are at home. In a dangerous neighborhood, it's a very good idea to keep the chain on all the time. Let's suppose that a criminal intruder picks or forces the regular lock while you are inside the apartment or house. Most often, the noise will arouse you, but sometimes it will not. After the ordinary lock or locks are picked or forced, the criminal will come up against the door chain when he tries to open the door. If all appears to be quiet, he may try to cut the chain. Normally, this is difficult to do with a hacksaw or a file unless the criminal can hold the chain with a pair of pliers or a tension wrench and use the cutting tool with his other hand. Some housebreakers use very large, commercial bolt cutters for this purpose. These tools have handles two or three feet long and tool-steel cutting jaws. They're much too large and clumsy to be carried conveniently, so they're rarely employed except by criminals who have taken the trouble to disguise themselves as tradesmen. These commercial bolt cutters sheer through a door chain in less than a

53

second. If you see the blades of a large cutter on your chain, you have very little time to get away.

In any situation where a criminal proves too powerful for you in a contest involving a door chain, or manages to get bolt cutters on the chain, you should use the better part of valor and retire to the security room. Once you're there, you have a bit of time to call the police and get a weapon ready—though it's not much time if the criminal has effective tools. You should also retire to the security room promptly if you have reason to believe that the criminal is armed with a gun. Normally, a knife or the other less effective weapons cannot be used through the narrow crack, though tear gas or a repellent spray would be effective.

There's only one way to test a door-chain installation. After all the work is done, try to break it yourself. If you don't have much weight and strength, ask some powerful friend to do it. Put the chain on with the other lock or locks off, and ask him to throw his full weight against the door, but in such a way that he will not injure himself. Sometimes the heads of weak or defective screws will break right off, and the screws may pull out. If self-tapping metal screws have been driven into a metal frame or a metal door, the metal holding them in place may prove to be weak. Testing in this way also will reveal a weak chain. Always buy door chains with welded links rather than links that are merely bent into shape. A welded chain can break, however, if one of the welds sealing the ends of a link together is defective. Some apartment-house owners install trashy hardware to save money, and welded chains are not popular with these people because they are more expensive. When you move into a new apartment, test all existing security hardware, including the door chain. I wouldn't attempt to test the hardness of a door chain with a large bolt cutter because the result is a foregone conclusion—no chain of this type can withstand a good cutter. Chains come in many lengths, designs, and quality grades. Spend some money and get a strong chain. Make a careful installation, leaving only the narrowest opening possible. Your life may depend on it.

The outside door or doors of an apartment or house should be equipped with a viewer—an improved peephole. Several good ones are on the market. The best type is a simple metal tube that can be installed in a single hole drilled right through the door. Usually, the hole is only ¼-inch in diameter. Viewers with very short barrels are available for use with doors that have thin panels. A viewer is usually made in two parts. One part is inserted in the hole from the outside, and the inner part screws into the exterior part, forming a tight seal that's almost impossible to unscrew from the outside. Good viewers have glass lenses inside the tube. These lenses permit a wide-angle view so that a person inside can see a great deal by looking through it. If the tube were not equipped with the wide-angle lens, the view would be very restricted, and there's a possibility that you might not see enough of the person outside to form a judgment of him. With a wide-angle viewer, you can also see if there is more than one person. The lens or lenses have another purpose. They're usually made of thick glass, and since they're small in diameter, they're difficult to poke out with an ice pick or a metal rod. Sometimes, a thief will do this in order to insert a wire so that he can make an attempt to open your locks from the inside. If you install the viewer high enough, it will be quite a distance from your locks, and it's almost impossible to open a door in this way if the locks are properly installed. Some viewers have a pane of one-way glass or a lens made of the same material. With this type, it's possible to see the caller without being seen yourself.

The lock on the outside door is probably your most important security barrier, and yet few people examine this lock closely to see that it is well made and in good condition.

Figure 3-2 shows an ordinary, old-fashioned key for a warded lock, the key for a modern pin-tumbler lock, and a cutaway view of a key in a pin-tumbler unit. These pin-tumbler units can be easily removed and replaced if a change of key is needed. It's wise to do this whenever you move into a new home. The screws that hold the tumbler unit in place are usually found on the edge of the door where the lock fits into the frame. Remove these screws, and the tumbler unit either screws out or drops out of the lock body. Remove the tumbler units on all doors when you first move into a new apartment or house and take them to a reliable hardware store or a licensed locksmith and ask for replacements with differ-

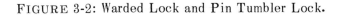
FIGURE 3-2: Warded Lock and Pin Tumbler Lock.

Old-fashioned warded-lock key, top, operates an ineffective lock that can be opened easily with a hairpin or a cheap set of skeleton keys. Center drawing shows pin-tumbler key and bottom drawing shows the key in a pin-tumbler cylinder or core. These cores can be easily removed from lock if change of key is needed.

56

ent key patterns. Since the tradesman has your samples, he will know exactly what you need. Take no chances—don't give him your name and address. By replacing tumblers, you can make a former occupant's keys useless at a cost of about $2.00 per lock.

Don't use an old-fashioned warded lock in any situation requiring good security hardware. The warded-lock key operates the lock by passing though a series of metal bars called wards. These wards are in fixed positions inside the lock and fit into the cuts or "bites" in the old-fashioned key. Almost every hardware or variety store sells a great assortment of skeleton keys that will fit almost any warded lock. To breach the security provided by a warded lock, all the criminal needs is five or six of these skeleton keys. He uses one after another until he finds the right one, and the lock will open very quietly. Dangerous criminals are capable of buying a large selection of skeleton keys in order to gain admittance to a home. At best, the warded lock should be regarded as a "privacy device," used only when security against dangerous persons is not required.

The outside door of your home should be equipped with a good pin-tumbler lock, properly and strongly installed. Test the installation by having a heavyweight friend throw his weight against the door in the same manner used in testing a door chain.

If the criminal cannot simply break the lock off its mountings through sheer weight, and he does not have skill enough to pick the tumbler, he will probably try to circumvent the lock with a jimmy or by depressing the lock's tongue. A crowbar or jimmy is inserted in the crack between door and jamb and leverage is used in order to force the tongue of the lock out of the receiver. Sometimes, the lever will bend or distort the lock or the receiver so that the tongue will disengage. For this reason, you should never use a lock on an outside door if that lock is equipped with a wedge-shaped tongue. These tongues close automatically when you push the door closed behind you. This type of lock is often called a "night-latch," though why remains a mystery because they're unsafe at night as well as in the daytime. The lock with a wedge-shaped tongue is very convenient because you do not have to use the lock's knob or a key to lock up behind you when you enter or leave, but these locks are very dangerous because they can easily be opened with a jimmy or even a strong screwdriver. The metal tool is shoved into the crack in front of the tongue and then driven against the slant of the wedge or worked back and forth until the tongue is depressed and the door can be opened. Because of the wedge or triangular shape, the tongue is easily depressed and with a minimum of noise. If the crack between door and jamb is fairly wide and there is no right-angle recess to prevent direct access to the tongue, even simpler tools can be used. There's the "loid" burglar who uses a celluloid playing card or other flat, stiff piece of plastic. The card is inserted in the crack above the lock and is then worked downward against the wedge-shaped tongue. With a little manipulation, the card pushes the tongue quietly back toward the lock and the door is opened. Though many of these night latches are equipped with modern pin tumblers, the shape of the tongue makes them unsuitable for any important door.

At the very least, a pin-tumbler lock should have a large, rather long tongue of a rectangular shape that fits into a deep, strong receiver on the door frame. It's much more difficult to manipulate or jimmy a long rectangular tongue than it is to deal with a triangular tongue. If I were buying this type of lock, I would insist on a large, heavy lock of the type customarily used in warehouses and other commercial establishments. They're big, ugly, and roughly finished, but they work.

Another type of lock, however, is much smaller, more nicely finished and a much better security barrier than even the square-tongued industrial lock. Personally, I favor it above all the other pin-tumbler locks. This is the ring-and-bar lock produced by the New England Lock and Hardware Company under the trade name *Segalock*. A very fine lock of the same type is produced by Eaton, Yale and Towne. Figure 3-3 shows this type of lock. It does not have the usual slotted receiver for the tongue. Instead, the receiver consists of a metal plate with two sturdy rings. This receiver is mounted on the right angle formed by the edge of the doorframe and is held in place with as many as seven heavy screws. The locking bar of the lock itself moves vertically through both these rings when the key is turned. Because the locking bar fits through the

58

FIGURE 3-3: Ring-and-bar Pin Tumbler Lock.

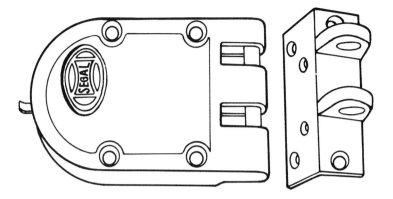

This type of lock, manufactured by several companies, is impossible to jimmy. It is much superior to any lock with a wedge-shaped or square tongue.

rings and the end of the bar fits into a round hole in the frame of the lock, a jimmy is ineffective. If the criminal cannot pick this lock, he is forced to cut away the entire door around the lock in order to get at it from the inside so that he can turn the knob. The criminal can also chew away enough of the wood to insert a hacksaw blade so that he can saw through the rings and bar, but this is a lot of work and makes much noise. I saw the results of one crude housebreaker's efforts along these lines. The door was thick hardwood and the thief could not cut right through it after he found out that he could not jimmy the lock, though he chewed away a lot of wood with his jimmy and could actually see the rings and bar from the outside. Because he could not get through on the lock side, he tried to jimmy the hinges, but failed in that attempt too and finally gave up in disgust. With this type of lock, the entire frame and door edge can be removed or beaten out of shape and the lock will hold as long as the thief cannot reach the knob. The lock in the illustration is Model 666 of the Segalock line (New

59

England Lock and Hardware), and heavier versions are available from the same company.

In some cases, however, this lock may not be enough. This is particularly true when the door itself is weak and cannot be strengthened. For instance, in some apartments, doors consisting of many small panes of glass framed by narrow wood strips are used to separate a small entrance hall from the main hall of the apartment. These glass doors are not to be trusted because one pane can be knocked out and the lock opened from the inside. In some cases, the landlord will not allow the tenant to replace a weak, thin door with a heavier one. In these cases, the Model 688 Segalock is very useful. This lock, and similar types manufactured by other companies, has the same locking bar-ring construction, but it has no opening knob on the inside. Instead, the lock has one keyhole on the outside and another keyhole on the inside. The door must be locked with a key both when you enter and when you leave. This is somewhat inconvenient when you are merely returning home, but remember that you used the key to open the door. If you already have the key in your hand, you can easily lock the door after you have entered. Even if a criminal cuts a hole through a weak door, he still cannot open this lock by turning a knob. Of course, a housebreaker may try to cut a hole large enough to admit his whole body right through the door, but this is only done with very weak doors in circumstances where the criminal can make a great deal of noise.

Any lock with a keyhole on both sides instead of a lever or knob on the inside can be dangerous if fire breaks out. Let us say that you leave your home in the morning to go to work and that you lock the door behind you leaving your wife and children inside. If your wife cannot find the key, she cannot unlock the door. If there's a fire, disaster can be the result. With these locks, it's a good idea to hang an extra key on a nail or peg high up out of the reach of children so that it is always available. Don't hang the key near the door or a housebreaker may be able to reach it after cutting a hole through the door.

The Fox Police Lock Company, 46 W. 21st Street, New York, N. Y., makes a lock that has no tongue. The Fox brace lock is shown in Figure 3-4 with one of the internal parts. The lock depends on a long steel bar that fits into a lock body mounted on the door. The bottom end of the bar fits into a hollow in a metal plate which is recessed into the floor and screwed in place. The lock is equipped with a modern pin-tumbler unit. When you use the key from the outside, the bar is pushed over into a blind socket in the lock body and it braces the door closed. In essence, this lock operates in much the same way as a chair shoved under a doorknob.

The only way to open a Fox Police Lock without picking it or using a key is to cut a hole right through the door and move the bar into the unlocked position from the inside. When the lock is open, the bar slides up through a ring in the lock body as the door is pushed inward. The opening is wide enough to admit a person carrying a large package. If the door must be opened completely, the bar is lifted out of the socket in the floor and is then easily removed from the retaining ring on the back of the lock. When the door is locked, however, the bar does stick out into the room some distance and causes some inconvenience, and the installation is not the most attractive in the world. And yet, thousands of these locks are sold every year in crime-infested areas because of their obvious strength. When an unskilled housebreaker finds that a lock has no tongue whatsoever, he's inclined to give up and move on to easier pickings.

The Fox brace lock does have one disadvantage, however. When operating in the manner described above, it can be opened if a hole is cut through the door, and the hole doesn't have to be large. All that's needed is an aperture large enough to admit a stiff wire with which the bar can be pushed to one side. Normally, this lock is secured after one enters merely by pushing the bar into the locked position. If you wish to guard against someone cutting a hole through the door, however, you can set the lock so that it functions as a deadlock. That is, you can adjust the lock, or have a locksmith do the work, so that the bar cannot be moved from side to side. Once the door is locked with a key from the outside, the bar will not move though pushed firmly, if this adjustment is made. To do this, one uses the cam pin shown in Figure 3-4. Remove the back plate of the lock with a screwdriver. It's held by only two screws.

61

FIGURE 3-4: Fox Brace Lock.

Locked

Bar slides into slot
to open when key is
turned from outside.

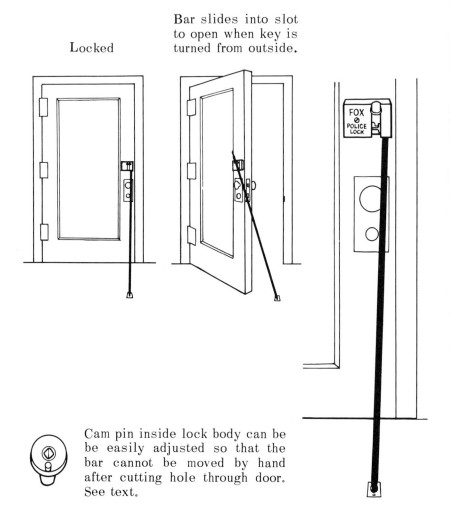

Cam pin inside lock body can be
be easily adjusted so that the
bar cannot be moved by hand
after cutting hole through door.
See text.

The Fox brace lock has no tongue. Instead, the door is held
closed by a long steel rod which fits into a metal socket let into
the floor. The lock is equipped with a modern pin-tumbler core
operated with a key from the outside.

You'll soon locate this circular cam pin, which is merely set on a pivot inside the lock. It can be removed with the fingers without unscrewing anything. If the pin on the circular cam is in the topmost position shown in the illustration, the lock functions as a latch. It can be opened by moving the bar from the inside. If you remove the cam from its pivot and move the pin a quarter turn to the right and replace the cam on the pivot, the lock cannot be opened by moving the bar. It's a very simple adjustment that can be made in a few seconds.

Using a Fox brace lock as a deadlock causes no inconvenience if you are living alone, but if there is another person, he or she will be securely locked inside once the key is turned from the outside. If the lock is used in this way, you must also install a bar or chain so that you can lock the door when you are inside.

One of the advantages of the Fox brace lock is that it is easily installed. The company furnishes complete directions for determining the location of the socket in the floor. Once that's installed, the lock itself is simply screwed to the inside of the door—a matter of ten minutes' work with a drill and screwdriver. This requires no careful inletting of metalwork into wood, common with more conventional locks. The lock is particularly easy to install on metal doors if sturdy self-tapping metal screws are used.

An inexperienced person, however, sometimes makes a dangerous mistake when installing the Fox brace lock. Commonly, it's used on an old-fashioned wooden door that has a large keyhole right through it for a warded lock. It's very easy for a thief to put a stiff wire through the old warded-lock keyhole and push the brace lock into the unlocked position if the lock is not functioning as a deadlock. If you cannot replace the door, fill the cavity of the old warded lock with concrete containing many small pieces of gravel or small pebbles as described previously for strengthening paneled doors. As long as you block the keyhole securely, the installation is secure. Sometimes, it's best to remove the inside fittings of the old warded lock entirely, including the inside doorknob, and cover the hole with a metal plate $\frac{1}{4}$-inch thick, held in place with strong, nonretractable screws. By the way, you'll have to secure the outside doorknob to the door with a long wood screw if you remove the

FIGURE 3-5: Pin-tumbler Core.

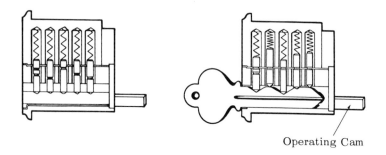

Operating Cam

When locked, separations in two-part, spring-loaded pins are at random lengths. With the correct key, pattern of the key places separations in a straight line so that the key can be turned, which activates the cam that moves the lock's tongue.

inside knob since you'll need something with which to pull the door open.

If you install a good door and a good pin-tumbler lock, you're safe against almost every crude housebreaker. What about the man who can pick locks? To pick a lock, the criminal inserts a small wrench in the keyhole and turns the tumbler slug with it just as though he were using a key. The wrench has an opening in its head through which the criminal inserts the lock pick. This pick is usually a piece of thin, very stiff wire bent into a right angle at the end. With this pick, the thief solves the puzzle of the tumblers. There are five pin-tumblers in most modern locks, as shown in Figure 3-5. Each pin is driven by a spring and each pin is in two pieces. When you insert your key, the lower ends of the pins fit into the notches in the key and align themselves so that the separation between the two-piece pins forms a straight line. The second drawing shows the pins in this unlocking position. The separation between the upper and lower portions of the pins permits the tumbler plug to rotate inside the larger tumbler unit, and when this rotation occurs, a cam or bar projecting from the back of the plug uses the force of the rotation to retract the tongue out of the receiver. Take apart any pin-tumbler lock and you'll see how this basically-simple mechanism works.

The thief has no key, so he solves the puzzle of the varying lengths of the pins with his pick by dealing with each of the five pins one at a time. When the criminal applies pressure with his keyhole wrench, one of the five pins will bind before the other four. This is because manufacturing tolerances are not perfect, and even in a finely machined lock, one pin will react to the mechanical pressure before the others. By touching each of the pins in turn with his pick, the thief locates the pin that binds first. Then he releases the pressure of his wrench slightly and pushes that pin upward. Renewed pressure with the wrench holds the pin in its partly unlocked position. The thief repeats the process with the next pin that binds, and pushes it up, and so on until he has moved all five pins slightly. Then the thief finds himself dealing with the first pin again, but the process goes on until all five pins are moved to the unlocked position, and the plug rotates, opening the lock. I'm quite unskilled with a pick myself, but I can unlock most pin-tumblers in fifteen minutes without a key. Some very skilled people can do it in a second or two.

To guard against this type of manipulation, most manufacturers of good locks install pin-tumblers with mushroom heads. These pins catch on the corner of their holes when pushed with a pick instead of a key, but a skilled man can overcome even this obstacle. The only real insurance against this kind of manipulation is to increase the number of pins so that the time needed to pick the lock is greatly increased. The Sargent Hardware Company, New Haven, Connecticut, makes a new pin-tumbler unit which has three sets of pin-tumblers arranged radially around the keyhole. The key is of the unconventional shape shown in Figure 3-6. Because the criminal must manipulate three sets of pins, he'll take a great deal more time to pick the lock, and because the operation is much more complicated, the new tumbler unit makes the operation completely out of the question for almost all criminals. Just seeing the unconventional shape of the keyhole is often enough to send even a fairly skilled man in search of an easier job. Your local hardware-store

FIGURE 3-6: Sargent Radial-lock Key.

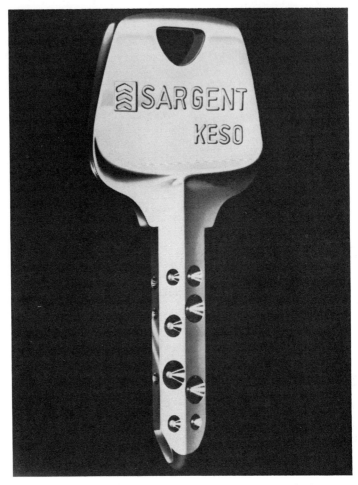

A new lock core by Sargent has three rows of pin tumblers, arranged radially. This provides triple sets of barriers for the lock pick. Though a very skilled burglar might pick this lock, it would take a very long time. The key is of an entirely new design. The new cores can be screwed into many existing locks with little trouble. Photo enlarged to show design.

dealer can order one of these new pin-tumbler units for your existing pin-tumbler lock. I suggest, however, that you remove the old tumbler and take it to the hardware store with you so that the clerk can order one of the new units that will fit the original installation. There are two basic types of tumbler units. One is held in place by a screw thread cut into the barrel of the tumbler unit. The other type is secured with two long machine bolts. The screw-in type and the one held with two bolts are standard in size and shape no matter who manufactures them, but the correct type must be ordered.

The dial-combination lock is sometimes preferred because it has no keyhole and therefore cannot be picked. Yet, the dial-combination lock (padlock or receiver lock) can be manipulated. The dial is simply rotated left and right until the criminal feels the lock make the first adjustment for opening. The criminal must repeat the process to find the second number, and usually a third. In cheap combination locks, the manufacturing process is so crude that even a fairly unskilled person can find the combination by a process of experimentation if he has time enough. A few dial-combination locks are manufactured for doors that operate a tongue in a receiver in the same manner as an ordinary pin-tumbler lock. Some of them are crudely made and are therefore easy to open. Others are finely manufactured and are extremely difficult to manipulate, but they are quite expensive.

If you use a combination lock of any kind, don't write the combination down in a "secret" place on the wall near the lock. If you can't remember the numbers, write them on a piece of paper and carry it with you. (If your memory for numbers is that poor, you might as well be carrying a key.) As soon as many thieves see a combination lock, they look around for the combination written nearby on the house wall or on a windowsill. If the money to be gained is enough, the criminal sometimes uses a 30X rifleman's spotting scope. With a good telescope mounted on a tripod in a room across the street, it's quite easy to read the combination over the occupant's shoulder as he dials. A disguised criminal sometimes pretends to be a deliveryman and arrives just as the homeowner is entering his home and reads the combination while waiting patiently as the combination is dialed.

67

Padlocks are useful in securing cellar doors, garage doors, and doors on sheds. Don't buy a trashy padlock or trashy padlock hardware. Even some good padlocks are easy enough to open with a jimmy or bar by shoving the tool through the curved bail and jerking the lock open, but a cheap one opens with a minimum of effort and they are easy to pick. If you must use a padlock, get a large, heavy one intended for commercial use. Most of them are quite hard to jimmy. Padlocks should be used only where high security is not required. As with other security hardware, the screws fastening the hasp to the shed or garage should be long and inserted into sound wood. If you buy a padlock, look it over carefully for numbers and symbols on the outside other than the manufacturer's regular trademark. Many padlocks are coded. That is, a number or a symbol or both tell a locksmith the shape of the key needed to open the lock. That is a great convenience for locksmiths who constantly get calls to open locks from persons who have lost their keys, but information on these key codes has leaked to criminals, and coded padlocks are going out of fashion for that reason. Nevertheless, many of them are still around and a few are still being sold. If you have one or buy one, file the symbols or numbers off, and touch up the raw metal with a weatherproof paint to prevent rust or corrosion.

The shape and arrangement of a door frame or a door sometimes makes it necessary to expose the heads of screws used to fasten security hardware. Normally, all screw heads should be on the inside, and almost all hasps, hinges, locks, bolts, and chains are made this way. If you are forced to drive a screw from the outside, perhaps to permanently close an opening, it's sometimes best to countersink the screw hole a half inch or so. Drive the screws well below the surface of the wood or metal and fill the openings with wood filler that will dry hard, or drip molten lead or solder into the hole on top of the screw, making sure that the slot in the screw fills up. Be careful about fire if you use lead or solder. If you use several screws and fill all the slots, it becomes a major project to remove the screws. Non-retractable screws are also available in most hardware stores. The heads of these screws have specially manufactured slots that take an ordinary screwdriver, but the upper-left and lower-right quarters of the screw head are machined away at a slant so that the screw can be driven into the wood but cannot be removed. The screwdriver simply doesn't grip the screw-head when it is turned counterclockwise. Non-retractable screws are excellent if you're putting up an expensive outdoor fixture such as a sundial or a spotlight, but remember that you'll have a difficult job removing the fitting yourself if you ever decide to move. The only way in which it can be done is to file off the screwheads level with the holes and then use an electric drill to drill away the remaining head of the screw. You'll never get the threaded part of the screw out of the wood.

You can save quite a bit of money if you install your own locks. The tools needed to install a modern pin-tumbler lock are:

- A carpenter's drill (brace)
- A $1\frac{1}{4}$-inch diameter carpenter's bit (drill)
- A set of screwdrivers
- Hammer and wood chisels if metalwork must be recessed into wood

In the installation of a pin-tumbler lock, first roughly locate the lock and the receiver on door and frame. Put the lock and the receiver together and then simply hold them on the door with the separation between the two parts over the crack. This will pinpoint the location of the pin-tumbler unit. Then use your $1\frac{1}{4}$-inch bit to drill a hole right through the door to accommodate the pin-tumbler unit. Install the pin-tumbler unit in the hole and then attach the lock itself to the cam or activating rod coming out of the tumbler unit. Last, install the receiver on the door jamb.

The $1\frac{1}{4}$-inch drill bit is used to drill a hole right through the door to accommodate the pin-tumbler unit. Almost all of these units will fit neatly, but not too snugly, in a hole with a $1\frac{1}{4}$-inch diameter because these units are all slightly smaller. If you can locate the hole in the right position and drill it at right angles to the surface of the door, most of your work is done. Good locks are almost always packed with directions showing how they should be installed.

If not, make it a point to disassemble an installation similar to the one you plan. Disassembling a pin-tumbler lock into its major components can be done with a screwdriver from the inside in a few minutes and it's worthwhile practice if you've never installed such a lock before. If your carpentry is a little shaky, practice installing the lock before you actually work on the project. Get two pieces of plank as thick as your door. One piece represents the door and the other the frame. If you can locate the hole for the tumbler unit and screw holes on these two pieces of wood and install the lock correctly across the crack, you'll have no trouble with the real work.

Most outside doors installed in apartment houses and housing-development homes are put in with a lock already in place. Commonly, these locks are of the lightweight variety, and many of them are component parts of doorknobs. Alternatively, the builder usually puts in a cheap night latch with a wedge-shaped tongue or some other inadequate lock. I would not depend on any of these devices. For instance, the usual lock that forms a part of the doorknob can be broken right off its mounting with one sharp blow of a heavy hammer. The entire knob comes away. Then it's just a matter of using a pair of pliers to get hold of the mechanism that activates the lock's tongue.

Two locks are better than one. If you have a situation in which a fairly great degree of security is required (and most people do), equip every outside door with two heavy pin-tumbler locks. This is another way of increasing the number of pins that a lock picker must manipulate, and two locks doubles the work of a man who uses a jimmy or saw. Remove or deactivate the old lock so that you won't be obliged to use it. Locking and unlocking two locks is enough.

To sum up door hardware, each outside door should be equipped with:

- Two sturdy pin-tumbler locks
- A good chain
- A wide-angle viewer

Expensive? Yes, it is, but this equipment may save your life.

70

Put yourself in the position of an unskilled or poorly equipped housebreaker who cannot pick door locks quietly or who does not have the necessary tools to cut through a door or jimmy it open quietly. This type of thief almost invariably attempts to break in through a window. He's standing on the fire escape outside an apartment or in the flower bed outside the window of a suburban house. Naturally, he has made a telephone call to make sure that no one is at home or has found this out in some other way. Yet, he still does not wish to make much noise or spend a great deal of time breaking in because a neighbor may hear or see him. Windows do not have locks with external keyholes, so it is never possible to pick a window lock. He must force the window in some way to get inside, and therefore, an ordinary glass window is a better barrier than most people believe. It's seldom possible simply to heave a rock through the glass and then reach inside to undo the window catch or lock from the inside because that would arouse someone. A large picture window with thick plate glass that is permanently closed and sealed into its frame is probably a better barrier than any door because breaking the large piece of glass could arouse someone at least a block away.

One of the more simple methods of getting through ordinary glass is to cover the glass with wide strips of adhesive tape. Then the thief breaks the glass under the tape with a hammer or some other heavy object. Often, a large stone can be found on the premises. This stone is pressed up against the tape, not thrown through the glass. Pressure is slowly increased until the glass under the tape breaks. The tape deadens most of the noise and prevents large pieces from falling. Once the glass is shattered, the thief puts down his hammer or stone and clears away tape and glass. Then he reaches inside and undoes the window catch. Key locks on windows are rare.

Sometimes, a glass cutter or a diamond is used. The glass is scored deeply with the cutter to form a square near the window catch large enough to admit the hand and forearm. The cutter does not go right through the glass, but the square can easily be broken

71

out. After scoring the glass, the housebreaker covers the square with wide adhesive tape, overlapping onto the rest of the glass by several inches. Then any heavy object can be used to force out the square.

In some metal-framed casement windows, the glass is held in place with putty on the outside. Usually, these metal-framed windows have six small panes. A pane near the window catch is selected, and the thief uses the point of a knife to remove the putty. This can be done without making the slightest noise if the point of the knife is carefully ground so that it conforms to the triangular shape in which the putty rests. A pair of needle-nose pliers is used to remove the small wire clips that the glazier inserted to hold the glass in place before putting in the putty. After all putty and the clips have been removed, the window pane often drops right out into the thief's hands. If not, the thief moistens a rubber suction cup (a toilet plunger is often used), and presses it against the window until the cup gets a good seal and then pulls the pane out of the frame.

Several other methods are used, but all of them involve fairly quiet removal of the glass so that the thief can reach inside to get at the window catch or lock. There's really no way you can prevent a criminal from getting through ordinary window glass if he has enough time and can work undisturbed. Therefore, one of the simplest precautions is to clear away shrubs that prevent passersby and neighbors from seeing your windows. Installing lights at the corners of your house so that they will illuminate the windows on the outside at night is a good idea too, though few people will leave these lights on all night unless they have reason to expect illegal entry.

If the glass can be easily breached, it's apparent that the window catch and/or lock is important. If, however, the window is of the old-fashioned type consisting of two overlapping, quite large panes inside wooden framing, it's almost always possible for the criminal to break out one entire pane and climb through the large opening even though he cannot undo the window catch. This operation on a conventional "double-hung" wooden-framed window, however, involves a lot of time and noise since a large amount of glass must be removed.

If the window is metal framed, there are usually six or possibly nine small panes of glass held by metal strips that are welded together into one unit. This type of window (usually called a casement window) is most often hinged at one side and opens when a small crank is turned. It's easy to make a metal-framed casement window fairly secure. Let's say that the thief removes a pane of glass near the window catch but finds that it is equipped with a key lock or that some other locking device keeps the metal frame in place. The criminal still cannot get into the house or apartment because the metal strips keep him out. The metal framing holding the small panes of glass actually forms a network of bars. If the thief finds that he cannot open the window, he can, however, get in by using a hacksaw to cut through the metal strips to make a large enough opening to climb through. In this operation, the thief must first remove at least four of the small panes of glass. Then he must saw through the metal strips in at least four places to make a large opening. In most cases, the metal strips used to frame the small panes are made of very soft steel, and only a few strokes of a hacksaw are needed to cut them. And yet, removing four panes of glass and cutting the metal in four places takes considerable time, though it can be done fairly quietly. Quite a few thieves will give up the minute they find out that they cannot undo a window catch or lock. If the criminal persists, it's also possible that he will use a jimmy or a saw on the window catch or other locking device.

Very few window catches with key locks as component parts are available for metal-framed casement windows. There are a few small keyhole locks that can be used on these casement windows. These locks do not have a finely machined pin-tumbler unit. Instead, a very simple disk-tumbler lock is used, and it must be of a lightweight variety because there is seldom room enough to install a heavy lock. The small receiver is usually secured to the window frame with two small metal screws, and this means drilling and tapping the frame to receive the screws. The metal strip in the window itself must be drilled and tapped so that the body of the lock

FIGURE 3-7: Key-operated Window Lock.

Top socket is used when window is left open
for ventilation. This type of lock can be used
only in double-hung, wooden framed windows.

can be screwed to it. But since the metal of the frame and the
window itself is often soft, and it's always thin, there is never metal
enough or room enough to make a really strong installation for a
lock using a key. I've seen many such installations, and not one of

them was strong enough to withstand a blow from a heavy hammer or a good jimmy. In addition, the screws holding the lock and the receiver to the metal can be unscrewed and the entire lock removed quite easily. If you install one of these window locks on a metal or a wooden window, fill up the heads of any exposed screws with wood filler or solder or use non-retractable screws.

The situation is somewhat better with the old-fashioned double-hung wooden window frame. Figure 3-7 shows a lock screwed into place on a wooden window. Many similar devices are sold. As the figure shows, they are usually screwed to the top of the lower half of the window and a bar (tongue) projects into a hole bored into the top part of the sliding window. Since the wood of the frame is rather bulky, there's room enough to use sturdy, rather long screws, but it must be admitted that the lock itself is rather small and lightly built. The tongue goes into a metal cup which is sunk in the wood and two cups are usually used. One is located in a position that will keep the window locked when it is completely closed. The other is a few inches above the completely closed position and is used when the window must be left partly open for ventilation.

An amateur installation involving a simple pin in a hole is often more effective than one of these window locks. Figure 3-8 shows how to use a metal pin in an ordinary casement window catch for a metal-framed window. A ¼-inch hole was drilled right through the window catch and a $\frac{1}{4}$-inch diameter metal pin is inserted in the hole to lock the catch. The tongue of the catch cannot be moved because the pin holds it solidly in the frame of the catch. The pin is cut off flush with the side of the window catch, and the flat end of the pin is painted or otherwise finished to resemble the surface of the catch. The blind end of the pin often comes up against the wall surrounding the recessed window. When a housebreaker encounters such an installation, he usually has more trouble with it than he has with a keyed lock. The cut-off pin finished to resemble the surface of the catch is hardly noticeable, particularly in the dark. All the thief knows is that the window catch will not open, but quite often he cannot tell why. Of course, the criminal can use his jimmy to pry off the whole window catch, but that takes time and makes a bit of noise.

75

FIGURE 3-8: Locking Pin in Window Catch for Metal-framed Window.

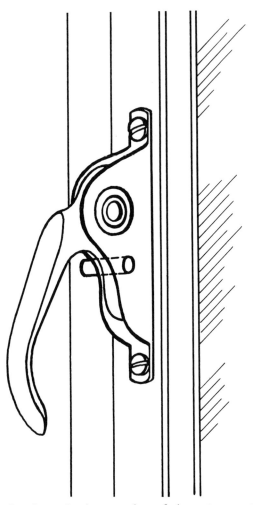

Drill a hole through the catch and insert a metal pin to lock the catch. Make sure the pin can be easily removed with a magnet or a knife blade to avoid being trapped in a fire (see text). Improvised pin locks of this type are effective because a criminal does not know precisely how they work.

The home owner simply puts these pins into their holes when leaving his house or apartment or retiring for the night. It's quite easy to shove the pins into the holes, but it's difficult to remove them. If the pin goes right through the catch and the other end comes up against a wall, a knife can be inserted behind the pin to push it out again.

A simple metal pin through a window catch or through the wooden or metal frame of the window can be used in many different ways. For instance, with wooden-framed windows, the holes can be drilled through the wooden window frame into the sash. Then a pin is cut to the right length to come flush with the top of the hole. I like to use a pin that is a bit smaller in diameter than the hole in which it is used. A magnet can then be used to remove the pin from the hole. Of course, a criminal can use a magnet too, but thieves don't carry magnets with them, and if they do not know the location of the pin because you place it in an inconvenient and inconspicuous position, opening the window becomes extremely difficult. If you put two or three pins in each window, it becomes almost impossible. These pins are really puzzle locks of the simplest kind, but they can be ingeniously used to puzzle a thief so badly that he will give up. They can be used in both metal and wooden-framed windows. You can also use pins to secure screens and screen doors in the summer, and to close a hiding place where you conceal valuables or a weapon.

If a pin is inserted in a tight hole that grips it firmly, a magnet cannot be used to remove it when you wish to open the window. In such installations, it's best to countersink the hole just a bit so that the head of the pin can be gripped with needle-nose pliers. Of course, the thief will be able to locate these exposed pins more easily than ones that are cut off even with the surface, but if the pins are cleverly placed, he usually doesn't find them because most often he doesn't know what to look or feel for.

These locking pins are particularly useful if you must leave a window partly open for ventilation. With the window open enough to admit air but not a thief, drill a hole for your pin through the wooden frame and into the sash. To locate the position where the hole in the frame and the hole in the sash match when you are

77

inserting the pin requires a little jiggling sometimes unless you make an inconspicuous pencil line showing the exact position of the sliding window when the holes match. With metal-framed windows that open when a crank is turned, a locking-pin hole can often be drilled through the crank mechanism when the crank has been turned to the partly open position.

To make locking pins, I prefer to use drill rod from which electric-drill bits are made. Broken drill bits can also be used. Drill rod is available in most good hardware stores. It's usually so hard and stiff that it must be cut with a good file while held in a vise. I like to use $\frac{1}{4}$-inch rod, but pins as small as $\frac{1}{8}$ inch in diameter are effective precisely because they are harder for a criminal to locate. If you use very thin rod, put in a few more pins to give added strength.

With all locks and pins, all members of the household should be able to open the locks or remove the pins quickly. The danger is fire. If a fire breaks out in the home, it may be necessary to leave by a window. If windows are difficult to open or the key cannot be found, someone may be burned to death. With key-locked windows or locked gratings, keep a key in each room in a location known to all members of the household. With pins, a pair of pliers or a magnet should be kept in each room where the pins are used.

If you live in rented quarters, remember that your lease may forbid the installation of permanent hardware unless the permission of the landlord is obtained, and be careful not to violate fire regulations by installing a permanent barrier that would endanger anyone's life.

Sometimes a homeowner in a difficult situation decides to use what could be called aggressive hardware. Instead of merely installing protective security hardware, he decides to go all out by using snares, spring guns, metal-jawed animal traps, deadfalls, or even trap doors located beneath windows or inside doors. Don't do it! In most places, the law forbids the use of these extremely dangerous devices for a very good reason. If, for instance, you put a powerful animal trap under a window where a criminal has previously entered, it may endanger an innocent person, perhaps a child. Another possible victim of such an arrangement is a fireman

78

who enters your home in order to put out a fire. If you install such a device, you'll lay yourself open to a criminal charge in most states, and in all of them you may be sued for any injury inflicted on innocent people.

Home air conditioners can also be a source of danger. These units are usually installed in a window that is opened partway to receive the box-like apparatus. Since home air-conditioning units are quite valuable, thieves very often remove them from their mountings from the outside and cart them off to the nearest receiver of stolen goods. Removing the air-conditioner also makes a convenient opening through which a thief can enter the home. If you are making such an installation, guard against theft by using large, heavy angle irons. Bolt one leg of the angle to the machine's sheet metal housing with a heavy bolt or two with the nuts inside the housing, and fasten the other leg of the angle to the wall with large wood screws or toggle bolts that will hold firmly in the plaster wall. The more angle irons you use, the more secure the installation. You must guard against removal of the machine, but you must also guard against having it shoved back into the room by a criminal so that he can enter. Most firms which specialize in installing these machines know about security arrangements; see to it that the firm makes a strong installation. Don't, however, entirely block the exit permanently because of the fire hazard unless there is another exit close by in the same room. If one half of the window can still be used as an exit in an emergency, the installation is safe as long as the opening is large enough to permit the occupants to crawl through it.

WINDOW GRATINGS AND BARS

There's no doubt that a fairly clever man with good tools can breach window locks or even pins if he has enough time and can work undisturbed. In a really dangerous situation, therefore, you may wish to install window gratings.

Permanently installed bars across any window are very hazardous. These bars are usually inserted in holes drilled in masonry or they are permanently fastened with non-retractable screws. This type of installation makes a home look like a prison, and if a fire

79

breaks out, it's impossible to leave by way of a window. For this reason, some cities have completely outlawed the use of permanent window bars, and in a few localities, even folding window gratings may be held illegal. Check local regulations before installing anything of this type. The danger of permanent bars and gratings has been demonstrated several times in the United States during factory and mental-institution fires when those inside the buildings died horrible deaths because they could not escape through the windows.

To avoid this fire hazard, folding window gratings are used. These gratings consist of strips of steel in a criss-cross pattern held together by rivets at each intersection of the strips or bars. Similar gratings are used to cover the plate glass windows of many stores. One side of the grating is permanently fastened to the wall inside the home. When the grating is folded back, it forms a compact, vertical mass which is easily covered by window draperies. Unfolding the grating over the window takes only a second or two, and on the other side, the grating is locked into place with one or two padlocks through U-bolts or bails installed in the wall or with an integral key lock, the tongue of which fits into a receiver fastened to the wall.

A competent home mechanic can easily install these folding window gratings himself provided he buys the right hardware from a reliable supplier. The installation only amounts to fastening one side of the grating permanently to the wall and installing the lock receiver or padlock hardware on the other side. If you're not equipped to do the work yourself, any locksmith will do it or give you the name of a competent tradesman who can.

It's important to buy these gratings large enough so that the lockwork and hinges will be out of reach of a person outside the window who is using a crowbar or a jimmy. Make sure that the grating overlaps beyond the window opening by at least one foot. If two, three, or more windows are close together, buy a large grating that will cover all of them in one installation. Large gratings are available because storekeepers commonly require them for display windows. Some of these commercial gratings roll down over the windows instead of folding back to one side.

Test the quality of the steel in folding gratings. Some steels are so soft that a few strokes with a hacksaw will cut quite a thick bar or strip made from them. Unfortunately, some security-hardware dealers are not very scrupulous about the quality of the steel they use in gratings. I remember one dealer who was highly indignant because a customer complained when thieves cut through a window grating in a few minutes and took everything of value in his home. The dealer said, "Well, if they're going to saw out the grating, there isn't much you can do to stop them." Actually, if hard steel is used and the metal strips are fairly close together, the housebreaker will be obliged to take a long time to enter. For instance, if the criminal must make ten saw cuts, and each cut takes twenty minutes due to the hardness of the metal, the work will take over three hours, and that's beyond the safety limit of almost any housebreaker.

Take a hacksaw with you when you are ordering your equipment and test it when it is delivered. Without showing the hacksaw, ask the dealer how long it would take a man to saw through one of the strips in the grating. If he's trying to pass off soft steel on you, he'll probably give some satisfactory but vague answer. Then ask him if you can test the grating by trying to saw through one of the strips. If you get a blank refusal, take your trade elsewhere. If the strips are made of satisfactory hard steel, you will do little or no damage with an ordinary hacksaw. There's no reason for the dealer to prevent you from making the test unless he's trying to cheat you. The metal rivets that hold a folding grating together should also be of hard steel. Rivets can be tested with a $\frac{1}{4}$-inch electric drill. If the drill eats away a rivet head in a few seconds, reject the whole grating. Don't be timid about making these tests—your life may depend on the quality of the steel.

Gratings or "window gates," as they're often called, range in price from $18 to about $50 per normal-sized window. The smaller the amount spent, the softer the steel and the lower the quality of the lockwork and hinges. Some window gates are worked up into beautiful designs resembling old Spanish and French ironwork, and these gates may cost as much as $300 per window. Instead of folding back, some of these decorative gratings are hinged at one side and open like a door. Again, be careful that the hinges and the lock mechanism are far enough from the window itself so that they cannot be reached with a pry bar or saw. With decorative window gratings, be especially careful to test the metal in items that resemble curved wrought iron in graceful whorls. Some of these gratings actually *are* wrought iron. A strip or bar made of this material can be cut with a hacksaw or file in a very short time. Wrought iron used in security hardware is about as easy to cut as wood.

Gratings on your windows may not be necessary in a quiet, safe neighborhood with good police protection, but this kind of hardware is becoming increasingly common in large cities. In some places, an apartment that is not equipped with this type of metalwork on every window will be burglarized within a week. In the suburban home, it's seldom necessary to install folding gratings on every window. Usually, window locks or pins are enough on the windows that are seen by every passerby. If you have one or two windows that are in concealed locations, however, window gratings might be an excellent way to secure them. I'd also put window gates on the window or windows of a security room in order to make quite sure that a criminal cannot enter the security room from the outside.

The anchor side of the grating or the hinges and the lock receiver must be securely fastened to the wall with large, heavy-duty screws similar to those used in fastening door hinges. Make sure that these screws go into the centers of wooden studs behind a plaster wall and that these studs are in good condition. If the gratings are going into a masonry wall, it's best to cut out large holes and mortar the holding bolts or toggles into place. Locating a stud behind a plaster surface is usually a matter of tapping lightly with a hammer handle until you find the stud by the dullness of the sound. The sound made when you tap hollow plaster is entirely different. After the stud is located, put a $\frac{1}{64}$-inch drill bit in your drill and make a series of holes across the stud in a horizontal line. By the resistance offered to the drill, you will find both edges of the stud and the screws for your hardware can be centered. The holes in the plaster can be filled with wood filler or plaster and painted over later. It's extremely dangerous to drive the screws not knowing exactly where the center of the upright 2 by 4-inch stud is located since the screws may only go into the edge of the wood and may pull out very easily as a result. Sometimes, when the wood is hard to locate or one discovers that the studs are rotten because the drill penetrates too easily, the plaster must be broken away and new wood installed. This is also necessary when the space is not right and a stud cannot be found in the correct position to take the hardware.

With all such installations, make sure that the key for gratings is located in a place known to each member of the household in case a fire breaks out. As a safety measure, it's a good idea to have a key for the gratings in every room where they are installed.

Security Room Hardware

A properly-equipped security room should have the following:

- A thick hardwood door in the doorway leading to the rest of the house secured to the frame with good hinges and heavy screws in sound wood;

- A quick-functioning pin-tumbler lock on the inside of the door, backed up with a door chain;

- Window gates on all windows;

- A telephone with a long extension cord so that it can be taken out of the line of fire from the entrance;

- If possible, a light switch controlling a light in the next room;

- A weapon concealed in a secure hiding place.

A viewer is not needed on a security-room door, and a good lock backed with a chain instead of another pin-tumbler lock is enough to provide you with the time needed to call the police and to get a weapon ready. The light switch is used to distract the attention of an intruder as mentioned elsewhere in this book.

Every parent is aware of the havoc that can be caused by a child who locks himself into the bathroom. The hazard is even greater with a security room because the hardware and the door are much stronger. Therefore, install the lock and chain high up on the door, well out of the reach of a small child, and make it a point to keep a key for the lock hidden somewhere outside the security room. The door and window hardware should open quickly and easily from the inside in case of fire.

FENCES, WALLS, AND HEDGES

There's a tendency to laugh at the old New England adage that good fences make good neighbors, but in these days of crime and vandalism, the adage is a statement of fact. A good fence, wall, hedge or combination of them is useful for several reasons. If you do not have a borderline barrier, most people feel perfectly free to enter your property. If you do have a barrier near the property line, vandals and criminals will think twice about entering, since trespassing is a minor crime in most states. Climbing a fence or other barrier is strong evidence of trespassing under many local laws. Merely crossing a property line may not be considered serious enough to constitute trespassing. Maintaining a borderline barrier of some kind, therefore, often prevents a criminal or vandal from scouting your property for a crime later on. The person with a criminal record dislikes being caught halfway over a fence.

Of course, any person may enter an unlocked gate in order to reach the door of the house. For this reason, it's wise to fence the walk leading to the door. In other words, regard the walk to the door as public property, but fence it off on both sides to prevent the criminal or vandal from wandering off it onto the rest of your property, perhaps in order to look for an easy entrance into the house. Even if you do fence off the walk, a gate at the sidewalk end is still a good idea since it can be wired so that a bell or buzzer goes off in the house whenever the gate is opened. Rigging the gates in your fence with simple alarms is an excellent idea since it gives you the earliest possible warning of an intruder's approach, and this is particularly useful at night. Most people who rig up alarms on their gates turn them off in the daytime since the normal traffic in and out of the house would keep the alarm going on and off throughout the day. Most vandals and criminals never suspect an alarm on an unlocked fence gate and will enter freely, tripping the alarm.

Before building any kind of fence or wall or planting a hedge, you should check local regulations. The rules governing the installation of fences, walls, and hedges are often stated in the community's building code, but they may be included in other ordinances. It's important to know what you may and may not do in the way of exterior barriers. For instance, some towns have very strict rules about the height of fences. These communities often limit the height of a fence to three or four feet because higher fences are thought to be unattractive. In some places, the exterior barrier must be set back a specified number of feet from the property line or the sidewalk in order to provide a more airy, spacious atmosphere. Some towns entirely prohibit the use of barbed wire in fences because it has been found that it is dangerous for children. If you fail to check on local regulations, you may spend hundreds of dollars on a fence or hedge only to be served with a notice of violation and an order to remove the barrier.

In erecting any of these barriers, it's wise to remember that you are responsible for injuries that they may cause, such as wounds inflicted on children by barbed wire or broken glass on top of a wall. Some property owners resent this very much, claiming that they have the right to do as they please on their own property, but in most towns and cities, the law does not take this view.

The "attractive-nuisance" doctrine followed by most state courts should also be borne in mind. The doctrine does not apply to adults who are simply labeled trespassers or worse if they illegally enter onto private land. Children under an age set by law are quite another problem. This makes it difficult for the homeowner because adolescents are committing increasingly serious crimes. Under the attractive-nuisance doctrine, the property owner can be sued if a child trespasser is injured on his property and it can be demonstrated that the property owner maintained an attractive nuisance, that is, any structure or object that would attract a child and cause an injury. For instance, if you have several fruit trees in your garden, children may climb a fence in order to take the fruit. This is a common failing among many children, and most people ignore it or issue a mild warning. But if the child is injured while on your property, perhaps by falling out of the apple tree or into an excavation or perhaps the old well at the foot of the garden, you can be sued for damages, and some courts will levy a large amount.

The way to guard against this is to maintain a good borderline barrier—not because most fences will keep children out (they can climb almost anything), but because the fence is excellent evidence in court that you made an effort to keep children off your property. Actually, however, you should back up the fence with a home-owner's multi-purpose insurance policy with a clause that covers attractive-nuisance suits. You should read any existing policy very carefully to see that you are covered in this respect.

The fence itself may be a hazard to children. If, for instance, you erect a high wall and cover the top with broken glass or metal spikes, as the custom was fifty years ago, a child may try to climb that wall in order to get into your garden or simply to see what's on the other side of the wall. If the youngster is severely injured by glass, spikes, or a fall, a suit may be brought. In many places, a jury will refuse to grant damages, but this is not always true, particularly if the fence or wall is obviously very dangerous. If I had one of these old-fashioned "man-killing" fences or walls, I'd remove the iron spikes or broken glass as soon as possible.

The problem then, is to construct a borderline barrier that will keep most children and trespassers out without causing unnecessary injury. Unfortunately, the law pertaining to injuries and regulations governing setback and height make it almost impossible to construct a secure borderline barrier in most areas. This can be remedied to some extent by installing alarms on the gates; nevertheless, it's true that most legal fences are not effective barriers. This is in sharp contrast to the customs in such countries as Mexico and Spain where practically every piece of property owned by anyone with even a little money is surrounded by a very high wall with barred gates. If conditions in the United States continue to breed criminals at the present rate, perhaps we will have to revise our building codes to allow the construction of more effective borderline barriers. One notices that municipalities and state governments don't obey their own rules on fences very often. The law in a given area may require a setback of four feet and a maximum height of three feet, but when the state or city erects a fence around an official building, it's often six feet high, right on the border of the property, and may be topped by barbed wire or spikes.

The brick or stone wall is disappearing in the United States. Few are built nowadays, and the old ones are gradually crumbling away. Apparently, most Americans move so often that they are not interested in making the major investment required for a brick or stone wall. High, solid walls have one major security disadvantage. If a wall or fence is solid and high enough, it cuts off the view of the house, and that's one of the worst things you can do with a border-line barrier. If passersby and people in cars can see your house, you're much less likely to be burglarized than a neighbor who cuts off the view of his home with a high barrier.

For this reason, most people settle on a woven-wire fence or a wooden picket fence with fairly large spaces between the upright pickets. The wooden picket fence of a moderate height is not an effective barrier because it can be climbed, but it does serve notice on everyone that it encloses private property. There's no doubt that a wooden picket fence is the safest possible choice from the liability point of view, provided the tops of the pickets are *not* sharpened. It's difficult for a child to injure himself climbing this kind of fence, and if he or she manages to do so, most juries will not award large damages.

A good wooden fence deserves good maintenance, and that usually means painting every year unless the fence is constructed of cedar, which does not require this care. The fence should be constructed in 6-foot or 8-foot horizontal sections and nailed to posts sunk in the ground. These posts should be heavily creosoted to protect them from termites and other borers, or they should be 4 x 4-inch cedar, which is practically impervious to rot or borers. Probably creosote is the best solution because cedar fence posts are becoming increasingly expensive. The posts should be sunk at least three feet into the ground or they should be anchored in concrete.

A woven-wire fence is a bit more dangerous for children because their feet slip on the wire more easily than on wood, but these fences are becoming very common, and in some areas, a suit arising from the use of such a fence is unlikely, provided the woven wire is not dangerous on the top or bottom edges. In making woven-wire fencing, the manufacturer has two choices with the top and bottom edges of the wire. In some cases, the ends of the wire are merely cut off top and bottom so that short, spike-like ends protrude. This type of fencing is a good barrier because the spike-like ends catch on the clothing and make it difficult to climb the fence or squirm under it. These protruding ends, however, can be quite dangerous since a child may slip when climbing over, and one of the spikes may enter the eye or even the throat or groin. In some areas, it is extremely dangerous to erect this type of fence. A safer variety of woven-wire fencing has the ends of the stiff wires paired and looped around each other. This forms a smooth edge which will usually not injure anyone. Posts for woven-wire fences are usually $\frac{3}{4}$-inch galvanized steel and they should be securely anchored in concrete-filled post holes. The type of woven-wire fencing you choose should be carefully considered and local regulations should be consulted to determine if the unlooped wire fence is permitted.

Hedges are fairly good barriers, but the ordinary privet hedge so popular in the United States is more of a boundary marker than a barrier, as any small boy knows who has broken through one in order to recover a baseball. You can crawl under most privet hedges because the individual plants are usually fairly far apart close to the ground, and you can break your way through them because there are no thorns. Thick hedges can be dangerous if they are too high because they cut off the view of the house in the same way as a board fence or a wall.

Low thorn hedges of barberry, American holly, or multiflora rose (*rosa multiflora*) are fairly effective barriers as well as good border markers. If the thorn hedge is kept low enough, it is not much of a hazard to the active child because the thorns will be below eye level and few children are foolish enough to force their way through a thorn hedge headfirst. I know of no regulation barring thorn hedges, but in these days of protective laws, it is possible that some towns may have them. Multiflora rose is particularly effective. The individual plants interweave themselves so much that it's hard to break through even if you are wearing a heavy leather jacket and thick pants. The thorns catch in the clothing and hold one back. To a person in ordinary clothing, the thorns are intolerable. It is possible to cut through such a hedge with clippers, but it takes time and few criminals would care to be caught at it.

For a really effective barrier, combine a woven-wire fence with smooth looped ends and a rather wide planting of multiflora rose. Put the wire fence on the outside and the thorned plants on the inside. If the fence is four feet high, an intruder may climb it, but then he's faced with a drop into the tangled plants. Few people care to tackle such a barrier, but there's no denying that clipping and caring for the hedge is work. Many modern gardeners, however, favor the "wild look" and even a rather loose, unclipped multiflora rose hedge is a formidable barrier. Even a loosely-planted hedge should be cut on top, however, if it threatens to grow so high that it cuts off the view of the house. Clipping on top also forces the plants to grow thickly.

A bundle of 10 large multiflora rose bushes costs about $2.50 or $3.00. A bundle of smaller bushes costs about the same. The bushes should be planted about one foot apart for the smaller bushes and $1\frac{1}{2}$ feet apart for the larger ones. Two or three rows make a wide planting which is very effective behind a fence. The bushes should not be planted too close together. If crowded, they do not grow properly and they may not flower as much. The small roses that these plants bear are beautiful. Multiflora rose should be planted no earlier than mid-April in most northern states, and can be planted throughout the summer if there is enough water. The usual method is to spade the ground thoroughly as wide as required and plant the individual bushes after spading in peat moss and bone meal. When the first new growth appears, use commercial rose food and plenty of water. Deep watering is the key to fast growth. If roses grow well in your area, multiflora rose will probably prosper. If you are in doubt, consult a local nurseryman about a thorn hedge that will grow in your locality. He can also advise you on planting and care.

Even a safe woven-wire fence and a thorn hedge may lead to a suit if a child is foolish enough to climb the fence and then dive headfirst into the thorns, but few children are so foolish, and few juries are so liberal as to grant damages under these circumstances.

Commercial burglar alarms often make use of photo-electric cells. A "perimeter defense" is set up in which an invisible beam is focused on a light-sensitive cell. If the beam of light is broken, the alarm goes off or a signal is relayed to a central office which notifies the police or dispatches private security agents. By focusing the light beams across windows and doors, a complete system of barriers can be set up to protect the entire dwelling. Of course, if a criminal is aware of the system and looks for the projectors and receivers, it's often possible for him to squirm under them or step over them. Installing a photo-electric alarm system in a private home, however, is very effective because the criminal seldom expects to find such a system in an ordinary apartment or house. These systems are supplied by many organizations, and some companies also offer private police service tied in with the alarm system.

The Pinkerton Electro-Security Corp., 275 Main Street, Webster, Mass., has applied radar to the security problem. It manufactures a small radar unit which is capable of detecting an intruder anywhere in a certain space rather than when he crosses a line or enters an opening.

Photo-electric and radar alarms are quite expensive, and would not interest the average homeowner or renter. As the advertising material from many firms making this type of equipment demonstrates, the chief appeal is to storekeepers and owners of commercial establishments.

It's quite easy, however, for a fairly skilled do-it-yourselfer to rig up a good burglar-alarm system. The essential component of such a system is the automatic nipple switch. Millions of servicemen are familiar with this device. This switch has terminals for the wires and a prong or nipple which can be pressed in or allowed to pop up. The switch can be wired so that the connection is closed and current supplied to the alarm when the nipple is depressed or when it pops up. In the Navy, for instance, practically every cabin door is equipped with one of these switches. When the door or hatch is opened, the nipple pops up and the switch cuts off the current to all the cabin's lights so that the ship never shows a

FIGURE 3-9: Nipple Switch for Home-built Burglar Alarm.

Nipple

Terminals

The switch has three terminals. One, the "common," is always used. With the other two terminals, the switch can be wired to supply current when the nipple pops up or when it is depressed. In most burglar-alarm systems, the switch is wired so that the alarm goes off when the switch pops up.

light to enemy gunners or bombardiers because a door or hatch was carelessly opened.

Figure 3-9 shows one type of nipple switch manufactured by Micro Switch, Freeport, Illinois. This company makes a wide variety of these switches and sells large numbers of them to the Armed Forces. Almost any military-surplus store has them in stock and you can select the various types that will best suit your own installations. If necessary, write to the company for descriptive literature. Some nipple switches are capable of taking ordinary alternating house current, and these heavy-duty switches can be used to power electrical equipment such as a radio or the home's regular lighting system. By using a heavy-duty switch and house-current wiring, you can set up a burglar-alarm system that will turn on all the lights in the house and the radio as well.

Most of the switches, however, are small and capable of handling only the direct current ordinarily used to operate a door bell or buzzer. With these low-voltage, direct-current nipple switches, you must use regular bell wire, not the heavier wire employed with household appliances and lighting. An alarm circuit using these switches must include a transformer to convert house current to low-voltage direct current. The other components of the circuit are one or more switches for door and windows wired into the main line of the circuit, a main switch to turn the entire system on or off, and an alarm bell that will operate on low-voltage direct current. Any loud door bell will do as long as its sound cannot be confused with your ordinary door bell or buzzer. Figure 3-10 is a schematic drawing of such a system.

Most homes are equipped with a transformer that supplies current for the door buzzer or bell. If you're installing a direct-current alarm with bell wire, you can attach the alarm wires to the terminals of this transformer in addition to the wires for your door bell. The additional set of wires does not interfere with the functioning of the door bell. If your home does not have one of these transformers, you can install one or use four dry-cell batteries as your power source. If you use dry cells, you must test the alarm system from time to time to see that the batteries are not going dead.

Don't install electrical equipment of any type unless you know what you are doing when working with electricity, and don't do it even then if the law in your area prohibits electrical work by anyone except a licensed electrician. The danger of fire is too great, and you may void your fire insurance if you do the work yourself. An electrician will do all the work described here for a few dollars.

As the illustration shows, the Micro Switch has three terminals

92

FIGURE 3-10: Wiring Diagram For Burglar-alarm System.

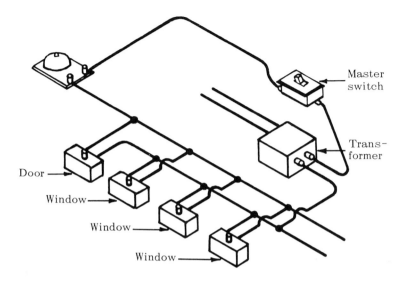

In this simplified system suitable for an apartment, the bell will go off whenever a door or window is opened and the nipple of its switch pops up.

instead of the usual two. One terminal is labeled "common" and the two others are labeled "closed" and "open." The common terminal must always be used. If the nipple of the switch must be depressed to close the circuit and activate the alarm bell, use the terminal labeled "open" and ignore the one labeled "closed." If the nipple must pop up to trip the alarm, use the closed terminal. In most burglar-alarm systems, the pop-up feature is used. Some of these switches have screw-post terminals similar to those used in lamp switches, while others have terminals to which the wires must be soldered or clipped.

Some nipple switches are bulky and hard to conceal, but the smaller varieties can be recessed into woodwork or even metal if properly insulated. If you can conceal the switch, the criminal who

FIGURE 3-11: Door-Alarm.

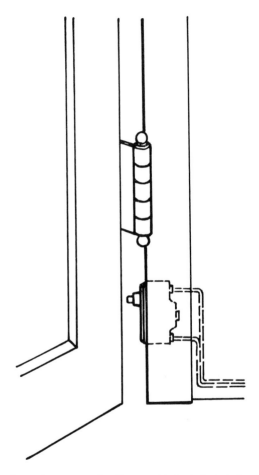

When the door is opened, the switch inlet into the jamb pops up and the alarm goes off. With a switch carefully inletted into the woodwork, the intruder may never notice it.

sets off the alarm will most often be unable to find the switch and tear it out to stop the ringing bell. Figure 3-11 shows a Micro Switch installed in a door jamb close to the bottom hinge. Only the button or nipple shows. When the door is opened, the nipple pops up, the circuit is closed, and the alarm bell sounds. Of course, the criminal can press the nipple back in with his fingers to shut off the alarm provided he notices the tiny switch recessed into the door frame, but that's unlikely. All the criminal knows is that an alarm bell is going off somewhere in the house and that it may be connected with a central office that will send police. Of course, that isn't true with this type of amateur installation, but the criminal doesn't know that, and the most common reaction is to get out of the situation as fast as possible.

You can rig up one of these Micro Switches for every door and window in your home and you can install a switch on every gate in your fence. It takes some skill to recess or conceal the switches, but it's really only a matter of simple carpentry. If you're a good carpenter but a poor electrician, recess the switches and then call in an electrician to do the wiring. If your carpentry or metalwork isn't too good, you may be content to simply fasten the switches to door and window frames without recessing them, but remember that the criminal may see them quickly and deactivate the system by ripping out a switch. Figure 3-12 shows two of these more clumsy installations, one on a garden gate and the other on a garage door. Some varieties of Micro Switch are equipped with long prongs instead of nipples so that the "reach" of the switch is greater, but these switches are bulky and can be easily spotted by a criminal. You can also use blocks of wood and metal strips to extend the reach of the switch as shown in Figure 3-12. Where possible, I prefer to recess the switch into the woodwork and conceal the wiring under molding and baseboards, or bury it in the wall. For instance, one of the most common installations is in the sill of a wooden, double-hung window. The switch is recessed into the woodwork and the pop-up feature is used. When the window is opened, the nipple springs up and the alarm sounds.

The master switch for the entire system should also be concealed so that the criminal cannot readily find it. Alternatively, you can

95

FIGURE 3-12: Alarms for Garden Gate and Garage Door.

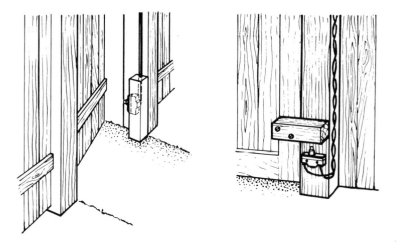

When the gate is opened or the garage door raised, the alarm goes off.

use a master switch that works when a key is turned in a lock. Key-lock master switches for low-voltage systems are available in many hardware stores. When leaving home, put the alarm system on by closing the master switch. When you open the door to leave, the alarm bell will sound for an instant before you close the door, but if you close the door quickly, the bell will not disturb anyone. Incidentally, if you have wired every door and window, the system acts as a reminder when you leave or retire for the night. The bell will sound if any of the windows or doors are open.

If possible, conceal the alarm bell too. One way to do this is to break open a hole in a plaster wall, install the bell by screwing it to a stud, and cover the opening with a picture or some other wall hanging. In that way, the criminal cannot usually locate the alarm bell quickly in order to suppress it. Of course, you must not smother the sound of the bell by hiding it too effectively.

A bell alarm is useful because it may frighten away a criminal

96

when you are not in, but it will also arouse you if someone tries to enter when you are at home.

Burglar lights are usually installed on a post some distance from the house. They are trained to shine on portions of the house wall that are ordinarily in darkness at night. With most suburban homes, one or two walls may be fairly well illuminated by street lights, but the back side of the house remains dark. If you mount a wide-angle spotlight some distance from the house, it will illuminate all these windows. Another method is to mount two spotlights high up on a corner of the house itself so that one spot shines on each wall. These lights should be wired so that they can be turned on with a switch located inside the security room. The power cable should be buried underground in metal conduits if the light is located at a distance on a post, and the post should be hollow to take the wires or cable. This will prevent a criminal from cutting the cable before he attempts to force his way into the house. With this arrangement, the light or lights can be turned on whenever you hear a suspicious noise outside, and often that's enough to frighten away the criminal. By using heavy-duty wiring in your burglar-alarm system, you can tie in exterior burglar lights so that they will go on even when you are not at home if someone raises a window or opens a door. Wiring the lights to work this way does not interfere with normal manual operation from the switch in the security room.

THE LAST WORD ON SECURITY HARDWARE

Almost any locksmith will tell you that the customer who spends the most on security hardware is the one who has just been the victim of a crime. After everything has been stolen or a personal attack has taken place, the victim runs to the nearest locksmith or hardware store and buys locks, gratings, alarms, chains, bolts, and everything and anything that might prevent another crime. After a criminal has successfully invaded your home, you know that a thief has been watching you, studying your habits, and planning to violate a place you have regarded as safe and that an unknown person has actually searched through your possessions. It's as though a prop had been pulled out from under the victim.

Panicky buying under these circumstances often leads to unnecessary expense, and you may also buy defective equipment. Some hardware dealers can be merciless in passing off inferior goods on the victim of a recent crime. If you need a locksmith, make sure that you deal with a licensed man. In most cities, the police will recommend a licensed locksmith located near your home.

Survey your home now for security weaknesses and start installing the hardware. Don't wait until after a crime has occurred because that crime may be murder or rape. If you can't afford all the equipment at once, buy one or two of the most necessary items and make a start. You owe it to yourself and your family.

CHAPTER IV

The Law of Self-Defense and Weapons

IF you have firmly decided that you will never use weapons, repellent sprays, tear gas, unarmed physical defenses, or weapons of any kind because they may injure or kill a criminal, it is not necessary for you to read this chapter since it deals with the laws governing self-defense. Even if you only plan to rely on unarmed personal defense, however, you should read the chapter very carefully because a kick, a blow, or one of the more sophisticated "nerve holds" used in unarmed personal combat can be just as damaging or deadly as any weapon—something that is often ignored by those who take karate and wrestling courses. Even a repellent spray of the mildest type is actually a weapon of a sort, and it's barely possible that it may injure the eyesight or that a person against whom such a spray is used may make the claim that the spray did cause some permanent injury in order to bring a profitable lawsuit.

If force of any kind is to be used, you should understand the law of self-defense. It's very important to know when force may be used and when it is forbidden. If you do not know, you may find yourself convicted of a crime or you may find yourself on the losing end of a very, very expensive civil lawsuit.

There is no easy way to study the law of self-defense. Reading a legal treatise may help,[1] but the legal language may be confusing and the legal practice of citing seemingly conflicting decisions for the benefit of other lawyers doesn't make for clarity. These legal works attempt to generalize about how the law of self-defense is enforced in fifty different states. Since the law does vary from state to state, there is always a possibility that the reader will be unable to discover the principles that apply in his own state. Even within one state, however, the law is not a simple, unchanging thing, always enforced in the same way in all similar cases. A given decision may vary from a previous decision in a similar case for reasons that would never occur to a layman. Local political pressures and racial tensions also affect the decisions of some courts and the way in which the police enforce the law no matter how high-principled some judges and officials may be. A perfectly legal action in one place may be considered illegal in another. A legal act may be considered illegal for a time even though an appeal to a higher court later justifies or excuses it.

A Conservative Guide to the Law

The average citizen therefore needs a guide to the law of self-defense, so conservative that following it will satisfy requirements for a claim of self-defense in as many cases as possible, no matter where the citizen acts.

The author has attempted to provide such a guide here, but he can make no guarantee that it will fully protect you in all cases should you ever be forced to claim self-defense. Yet, it does provide the safest possible guide to the use of force in self-defense precisely because it is based on the most conservative interpretation possible. It is based on what it is *practical* to do rather than on what is legally possible or permissible. If you wish to plan de-

[1] The best that I have been able to discover is Chapter 7 of "A Treatise on the Law of Crimes" (Clark and Marshall), 6th edition, revised by M. F. Wingersky, Chicago, Callaghan and Co., 1958. This work is frequently quoted in this chapter. A more theoretical treatment appears in "Criminal Law" by R. M. Perkins, pp. 880-919, The Foundation Press, Brooklyn, N. Y., 1957.

fense actions beyond the limits stated here, you should consult a lawyer practicing the criminal law in your own community.

The reader will find that this discussion includes some information on the tactics of self-defense. Tactics must be included here because it is impossible to separate legal considerations from what you will do in a dangerous situation. This is the difficulty that a person untrained in the law encounters when he attempts to study a legal treatise on self-defense. The legal writer discusses the law completely in the abstract with few concrete illustrations of what can and cannot be done, and as though the reader were some legal abstraction who could never be called up in court. Though tactics are introduced in this chapter to some degree, they are discussed more completely, and from a different point of view, elsewhere in this book.

Fortunately, the conservative interpretation of the law of self-defense is very easily and clearly summed up: *Take human life or use force only if an innocent person is in danger of severe bodily harm or death, and there is no other way to ward off the attack or safely retreat from it.* If you follow that single rule, the danger that you will be involved in a court action is reduced to a minimum. In our troubled times, there are people who are anxious to use the law of self-defense as an excuse for harming or killing other people. They therefore try to stretch the law of self-defense to include cases in which they themselves are actually the aggressors. Sometimes it is possible to do this, but very often an alert prosecutor and an intelligent jury see through the lie. If there is malice aforethought, the user of weapons or deadly force of any kind resulting in death will probably be convicted of murder even though he or she claims self-defense.

Many cases of self-defense involve killing or injuring a criminal whose identity is not known to the defender. For instance, if an armed, dangerous criminal attempts to force his way into your home, and you use force in legal self-defense, you will almost certainly be absolved of all blame even if the criminal is killed. Nevertheless, the relatives and friends of the criminal may not forgive you, and you may be forced to face them later on. It has happened

101

many times, particularly when the criminal has been involved with a tightly-organized group such as the Mafia or has belonged to a family of habitual criminals. Therefore, it's best not to use force if you can possibly avoid it even if you believe you are legally entitled to act. If someone is trying to stab you, however, or is injuring, raping, murdering, or kidnapping you or one of your children, you really do not have much choice. Strangely enough, the relatives and friends of the criminal may not seek revenge under these circumstances. Even criminals have some sense, and if they know that force was used only as a last resort, no action may be taken. Of course, no one can accurately predict what an insane or psychologically disturbed person will do.

Legal complications also are pretty frightening when you examine them closely. In some states, a claim of self-defense is taken pretty much on face value provided the person who makes the claim is a respected member of the community. In a small town, for instance, a good citizen who shoots a burglar found breaking forcefully into his home at night runs little risk. After all, he knows the sheriff, the prosecutor, and everyone who could be called as a witness or juror. In some jurisdictions, the only consequences of such an act are one visit by the sheriff and a very brief hearing in which the citizen makes some sort of declaration that he acted in legitimate self-defense. The author is not saying that this is the right way to handle such cases, but that's the way they actually are handled in many small towns, and that's why criminals usually avoid small towns. There are too many armed citizens who know their rights and who know that they will not be unjustly prosecuted if they act on them.

In a large city, the circumstances are entirely different. The prosecuting attorney, the police, and the jurors do not know the person who pleads self-defense. Though his background is investigated and character witnesses may be called, the defender remains a stranger and is treated as one. For instance, some law-enforcement authorities are justifiably cautious about accepting a claim of self-defense at face value. They want to assure themselves that the claim is correct so that they cannot be accused of laxity in enforcing the law. If the injured or dead person turns out to have a criminal record and the circumstances of the case point plainly to legitimate self-defense, there's usually little question about the innocence of the defender. On the other hand, if the injured or dead criminal had no criminal record and the circumstances are not so clear, the defender may find himself or herself involved in lengthy hearings and expensive court actions, despite the fact that he really did act with the best intentions in an entirely legal manner. It can't be otherwise because that would make it all too easy for criminals to claim self-defense to justify murder.

The whole matter of claiming self-defense places the person who makes the claim in a strange position. Under American law, the defendant is innocent until he is proved guilty. Under the laws of many European countries, the defendant is guilty until he succeeds in proving that he is innocent. In pleading self-defense after a killing or a severe bodily injury, the person who makes the claim admits that he has inflicted bodily harm or that he has killed someone. It is then up to him to demonstrate to the court's satisfaction that his action was justifiable or excusable. If he fails to do so, he may be convicted of an assault with intent to kill, manslaughter, or even murder. No matter what the legal reasoning behind these hearings is, they are often conducted under the European system—the defendant is guilty until he demonstrates that he is innocent. If the defender's motives were acceptable, and he acted legally, there is usually no difficulty about proving the point, but if the case is not clear, and the defender's motives were doubtful, he'll probably be convicted.

Policemen, prosecutors, jurors, and judges are only human beings, no matter how highly trained or what their moral principles may be. Though usually every effort is made to rule out prejudice and to preclude mistakes in a hearing or trial, mistaken judgments do occur. The fact that mistakes are made is demonstrated by the large number of cases in which a superior court reverses the decision of a lower court. In cases of self-defense, it sometimes happens that a lower court denies the claim and convicts the defendant unjustly of some form of assault, manslaughter, or murder. If the defender's actions were morally justified and legal, a superior court will usually reverse the conviction. Sometimes these cases are carried to the supreme court of the state before a just decision is handed down. Ultimately, of course, the defendant may be absolved of all blame, but the process is nerve-racking and very very expensive. If the defendant cannot raise bail, he will be imprisoned pending the appeals.

Court actions usually depend on the testimony of witnesses, and if any witness is a criminal, he may perjure himself. In many cases, the court action is a result of an occurrence in which the defender and the supposed criminal are the only witnesses. For instance, if a criminal breaks into an apartment or house, he is often alone with a single occupant. The same thing can happen in a street attack. The defender sometimes uses force, severely injures the criminal, and pleads self-defense. Put yourself in this situation for a moment. You have severely injured another human being you know to be a criminal. Let us say that this criminal attacked you with a weapon and that you were successful in warding off the attack and injured him in the process. When the matter comes up before the authorities, the only witness testifying before them other than yourself will be the injured criminal. Do you think for one minute that the criminal will testify honestly? The answer is almost always no. If he admitted that he attacked you, he would be asking for a long prison sentence. He will therefore try to lie his way out of the situation, and some of the lies that criminals can tell under such circumstances are really astonishing. The criminal may pretend to have had a legitimate reason for entering your home, and he may also claim that you attacked him. Since there is no other witness, he may just possibly be believed. If he has a criminal record and a weapon can be traced to him, and if there is physical evidence of criminal intent, such as burglar tools, his testimony will probably not be believed. In some cases, however, such clear evidence is not available, and then the defender may find himself in some difficulty.

Establishing a claim of self-defense can be very difficult if the criminal was *not* alone and there are several others who cooperate to rig up a believable tale, and if the defender has no friendly witnesses whom he can call. This type of attack frequently occurs in public places such as bars and restaurants and on the street when a person is attacked by a group of criminals. They will all tell the

104

same plausible lie, and the claim of self-defense may possibly be denied. They may all swear that *you* were the aggressor and that they (including the injured or dead criminal) acted in self-defense.

In addition to the possible difficulties with law-enforcement authorities, the person who claims self-defense sometimes runs into the civil law under which any person may be sued if he inflicts an injury or death on another. This commonly happens when the injured criminal senses the opportunity to collect large amounts of money from the defender's insurance company. In these cases, the criminal has two incentives for highly-embroidered, convincing perjury—money and avoiding a criminal conviction. Of course, if the defender establishes that he acted in legal self-defense, it's almost impossible for the criminal or his relatives to win a civil suit.

The Good Samaritan

All good citizens should come to the aid of anyone attacked by criminals. Do you agree with that statement? I certainly do, and most people do. In fact, the law in most jurisdictions makes it legal for any person to use a *necessary* degree of force to prevent a serious violent crime even though the intended victim of that crime is completely unknown to the person who acts to defend the innocent. By the way, there is no law or regulation requiring anyone to assist in the prevention of violent crimes, and as yet there are no laws requiring people even to call the police in such cases, though current agitation for such laws may result in their passage at any time.

There are certain disadvantages to springing to the defense of a complete stranger, however, and you should be aware of them. One of the most important is that the person you defend may not be willing to testify in the hearings in which you attempt to establish what happened. If in helping another person, you are forced to inflict some severe bodily harm or even to kill, your only legal course will be to claim self-defense. In effect, you say that you acted to protect another person against violent felonious attack and that your action was justifiable. Sometimes, when the criminal turns on the protector, the claim can be made that the protector was also acting in his own self-defense against an attack that resulted from his attempts to defend another. If the person who was originally attacked declines to testify, probably because of fear of retaliation by the criminal, the whole claim of self-defense is weakened. That people would leave someone who tried to protect them in legal jeopardy is horrifying, but it does happen. In such cases, the defender is faced with all the lies of the criminal without the principal witness who could testify for him. This particular legal hazard has sometimes been used by criminals to fleece courageous, law-abiding people. The bait is an attractive young lady or possibly a very old woman. She is attacked by one or two toughs who seem to beat her, take her purse, or even seem to attempt rape. The decent citizen springs to her defense and strikes one of the criminals, and a rough-and-tumble fight develops. Eventually, the police arrive and all participants are hauled off to the station house. Later, the woman says that she was merely arguing and not in any danger. The two toughs are actually her brothers or perhaps her son and husband. Of course, one of the men claims to be severely injured and sues. There may even be several planted witnesses who will swear to all this. The victim soon finds that he can settle the case out of court, but it's very expensive. The criminals who use this device (a variation of the old-fashioned "badger game"), are not often willing to go before a criminal court or a civil court because they know that many courts will see through the fraud, but of course the victim cannot be sure of this, and most often pays off.

There's another very strong reason for *not* coming to the defense of a victim who is under attack by a criminal. This is the so-called "good Samaritan" doctrine.

Let us say that you see someone pointing a gun at a helpless woman and threatening her. Acting in the intended victim's defense, you attempt to snatch the gun away. In the struggle, the intended victim is injured because the gun goes off by accident. Under the "good Samaritan" doctrine you can be sued by the intended victim, and the shocking fact is that the intended victim or her relatives may win the suit and that every penny you have and your salary for years to come may be taken to pay them off. Such suits are often motivated by the desire to collect large amounts

106

from the protector's insurance company. The intended victim is morally guilty, I would say, of a horrible and peculiarly vicious act, but nevertheless, he or she may win the suit.

The reasons for the existence of this good-Samaritan doctrine are not obvious but they're worth thinking about. It's true that many of the people who sue under such circumstances are morally despicable, but this is not always so. If the defender is stupid or not equipped to undertake the defense of another person, he may actually do more damage than the criminal himself intended. For instance, in a holdup, an ill-advised or ill-equipped bystander who suddenly tries to interfere may startle the criminal into pulling the trigger when he did not intend to do so. If an innocent person is injured or even killed, a civil suit may be justified since the defender could have avoided the injury simply by doing *nothing*. If you are not capable of taking effective action in defense of another person, I suggest that you do precisely that—nothing—except of course, that you should summon the police if that is possible. Ill-advised and hasty action may lead to unnecessary injury, and it may involve you in a serious lawsuit. This is not a reason for folding your hands if you can help, however. Though the law may not require you to defend the victim of a serious violent attack, you are morally bound to do so, provided you are sure that your help will be effective. Ignoring crime has been one of the causes of its dangerous increase, and you should do something if called upon even if the only thing that you can do is call the police.

After dragging you through this gallery of horrors, you may come to the conclusion that you should never use force in defense. That's a perfectly legitimate conclusion on moral grounds if you are a complete pacifist, but it's not a logical conclusion if you have some nerve and skill. It's wise to remember, however, that there are many things that you can do to preclude the possibility of a criminal attack.

Most ordinary housebreakers and burglars do not want to become involved in a physical attack. They'll do everything they can to avoid the occupants of an apartment or house even to locking doors behind them. In some cases, criminals have unloaded guns they found inside a home so that they could not be used by anyone in-

107

cluding the criminal himself. Actually, the average housebreaker or burglar will not attack anyone unless that person interferes with the criminal or unexpectedly panics him. This is another good reason for paying particular attention to good security hardware. If the criminal cannot enter the home, you'll never unexpectedly come into contact with the ordinary housebreaker or burglar and panic him into hurting you. When this does happen, it can often result in a bizarre and horrible crime. In a recent New Jersey case, a housewife was stabbed over forty times with a short-bladed table knife before she died in agony. No one really knows what caused the crime, but it's my guess that the woman returned home unexpectedly and found a housebreaker at work. In his panic, and perhaps because the woman cried out, the criminal snatched up the first weapon he could find and silenced her.

With most criminals, the slightest indication that someone is on the premises will frighten them away, and simply turning on a light or making some sort of noise is all you need to do if the criminal is outside the building or attempting to break into it. If, however, the criminal is already inside, an attempt to interfere with him or to trap him may cause him to attack even though he did not intend to do so. Other parts of this book contain material on avoiding this —it's probably the most common dangerous situation inside the home and undoubtedly results in a large number of murders.

You should, however, realize that there are dangerous criminals who don't mind using weapons or committing assault or murder. Most of them are mentally defective in some way or are bent on rape. Some are motivated by racial hatred. The use of a necessary degree of force in self-defense to repel an attack by this kind of criminal is generally justified by the law, but to avoid possible retaliation by the criminal or his relatives and to avoid lengthy, expensive, and possibly unjust court proceedings, it's best to reduce the possibility of such an attack to an absolute minimum.

Legitimate Self-Defense

For years, *The American Rifleman,* official publication of the National Rifle Association, has been publishing a monthly feature called "The Armed Citizen." It consists of stories reprinted from newspapers that tell how an armed private citizen prevented a crime of violence or apprehended a criminal. The fact that four or five of these items have appeared in the magazine every month for many years is in itself something to think about. Here are three of them quoted in full just as they appeared in the magazine:

In his Newark, N.J. home, Edward W. Williams, who was watching television, was alerted, first by his growling dog, and then by a woman's screams. He heard: "Don't let the man kill me . . ." Grabbing a rifle, Williams ran outside and saw a man hitting a woman and dragging her towards some tall weeds. Williams shouted for his wife to call the police and then trained his rifle on the man. He held the would-be attacker until police arrived. Newark Chief of Police Charles M. Zizza recommended Williams for an outstanding public-service award. (*Newark Star-Ledger*)

Charles Bonura was informed by his wife that an unidentified man had entered the Kenner, La., home of his 76-year-old mother next door. Bonura got his revolver and went to investigate. He found a thug attempting to strangle his mother. When the assailant tried to flee, Bonura felled him with one shot. It was later learned that the seriously wounded bandit was wanted by police in connection with a series of crimes. (*New Orleans Times-Picayune*)

An Atlas, Ill., mother of five, Mrs. Frank Rodhouse, returned home with her four daughters to face a shotgun-armed intruder. The man herded them to an upstairs room where he bound Mrs. Rodhouse. Slipping her bonds when the man left the room, she obtained a .38 pistol and three cartridges from a dresser drawer. Moving quickly downstairs, she got instructions from her 15-year-old son, who had also been bound, on how to load and fire the pistol. Returning to an upstairs room, she found the man preparing to attack her 13-year-old daughter. Mrs. Rodhouse pointed the gun at him and fired three times. As the would-be attacker turned toward her with raised shotgun, he fell at her feet mortally wounded. (*Pike County Democrat Times*)

In each of these cases, the defender acted to protect someone else, but *The American Rifleman* also reproduces many cases in which the defender acted to defend himself or herself in order to repel a violent attack of such a serious nature that extreme force was required. In these three cases, firearms were used in self-defense, but other weapons such as tear gas, clubs, and bladed weapons have been used effectively many times in recent years in similar cases.

One of the first things to notice about two of these cases is that they could have been avoided without the use of force. If Mr. Bonura's mother had provided her home with good locks and other security hardware, and had used the equipment, the criminal probably never would have entered her home and her son would not have been obliged to use force. In the third case, Mrs. Rodhouse might have kept the intruder out of her home by the same method, and if she had exercised care when entering the building, she probably never would have found herself and her children in the hands of an armed man. Mrs. Rodhouse would also have been better off if she had had competent instruction in the safe use of firearms.

In the first case, Mr. Williams acted as a good citizen should and went off his own property to aid a complete stranger. He behaved with good sense, however, and did not shoot because the circumstances did not call for it. If he had used his rifle, he might have found himself involved in lengthy court hearings of the type previously described. It's unlikely, but if the intended victim had been injured or even killed, it might have been claimed that it was due to his interference, and Mr. Williams might have been sued under the good-Samaritan doctrine. Nevertheless, Mr. Williams showed good judgment and he did what every good citizen should do provided he or she has the physical and moral resources to do it effectively.

There's another point about these three cases which should be noted. All three people did a public service because they put a dangerous criminal out of circulation, permanently in one case.

Mr. Bonura's case raises an important point. This courageous person went to the aid of a near relative, his mother. The fact that he was carrying a pistol undoubtedly discouraged the criminal from his attempt at murder, and saved her life. Mr. Bonura would have been entirely within the law as interpreted by every court in this country if he had been forced to shoot the criminal in order to make him stop his attempt to murder. He would have been obliged, however, to demonstrate that fact clearly to the law-enforcement authorities after the event. So far, so good—Mr. Bonura acted legally, and in fact he did what almost anyone would do under the circumstances. In fact, as a good son, he had absolutely no other choice. He could not simply stand there and allow his mother to be killed. The fact that he was armed with a pistol—a legal weapon in Louisiana—simply made him more effective; he might possibly have dealt with the criminal with his bare hands.

When Mr. Bonura shot the criminal when the criminal was attempting to escape, however, he was *in my opinion* taking an additional risk. It's true that he really did a public service because he wounded a dangerous person who was later captured by the police because of his wound. But let us suppose that the wounded criminal had succeeded in lying his way out of the situation. It's extremely unlikely that it could happen, but let's imagine that the law-enforcement authorities believed that the criminal was innocent of a murder attempt or any attempt at dangerous violence. Mr. Bonura would have been faced with lengthy, expensive court hearings and might have been convicted of a crime, though it's difficult to imagine that an appeal would have failed. You may approve of the fact that he used his weapon to prevent the strangler's escape, but there's no denying that there was some risk of legal prosecution. It may not have been possible in a small Louisiana town where Mr. Bonura was well known, but it's possible in many large cities. In general, as soon as the immediate threat to life is over, it's best not to use force to prevent most criminals from escaping—the risk of trouble later on is too great.

In the third case, there is absolutely no doubt. Mrs. Rodhouse was acting against a dangerous, armed criminal, intent on a felony of violence, and she shot and killed him in defense of her daughter, to prevent a horrible crime, and in her own self-defense since he tried to use his weapon. Mrs. Rodhouse also probably prevented a multiple murder. The criminal might have murdered everyone in

111

the house in order to silence them—such things have happened only too often. Mrs. Rodhouse was compelled to take a human life. She had absolutely no other choice and it is extremely unlikely that any court in the country would find that Mrs. Rodhouse acted unwisely, much less illegally. In fact, she deserves some kind of congratulation for her courage, and any prosecutor who attempted to trouble her would have a very short future in public life. You should decide now how you would act under similar circumstances. At the very least, you should make every effort to make sure that such circumstances do not arise.

"A MAN'S HOME IS HIS CASTLE"

It is often remarked that a man's home is his castle and that he has a right to defend it. But people who make this statement seldom go on to explain it, and all too often a misinformed citizen commits a rash act as a result.

My personal advice to you is to forget about this abstract legal doctrine. It has many shaky aspects and it cannot be made entirely clear. Instead, act only to prevent severe bodily harm or death. If the intended victim is a relative, some other loved one, or yourself, you really don't have much choice. Could you fail to resist murder, rape, kidnapping, or severe injury in such a case?

It's true that you are on somewhat safer ground when you act in your own home since American courts have consistently held that the right of self-defense (and defense of others) is stronger there than it is in the street. In that sense, your home may be your castle, but don't act unless it's a serious case. For instance, if someone is "attacking your home" merely by throwing rocks at it or stealing garden equipment outside the dwelling, you have no right to use deadly force against him. As long as there is no danger to life, the best remedy is to call the police and let them handle it. You can, of course, warn off the person, but very often that simply involves you in a useless argument that may lead to violence. In such a case, call the police and perhaps get a weapon ready for use if a mere trespasser or nonviolent thief suddenly becomes dangerous.

Your home is wherever you live, and that includes rented as well

112

as owned property, and it includes the owner or renter and his entire family. You have just as much right to act in self-defense in a rented apartment as you do in your own house, provided your rent is paid in full and your lease is in force. This even applies to boardinghouse rooms and hotel rooms. It is illegal to use deadly force if the attack will result only in damage to a building even if that building is very dear to you. You may not use deadly force to protect mere property, including your own home, if there is no danger to life. If you think about it for a minute, you'll see that there are only two crimes in which both property damage and danger to life are involved—arson and bombing. Certainly you may use force to stop someone from setting fire to your home or from planting a bomb or dynamite—not because the property might be destroyed but because those who live in the building (including yourself) would be in extreme danger.

The crimes of arson and bombing are so serious that prevention of them is regularly accepted as a basis for the legal use of extreme force in self-defense. Unfortunately, both these crimes are becoming more and more common in the United States as racial tensions increase. Even with these crimes, however, avoidance is sometimes possible.

If you claim that you used deadly force to prevent bombing or arson, will the claim stand up? Well, that's a matter for law-enforcement officials, judges, and jurors. You must demonstrate to their satisfaction that arson or bombing was intended. Your own sincere belief is your best support, and it will usually be accepted by an unprejudiced court. Of course, evidence such as an unexploded stick of dynamite, a bomb, or an unused Molotov cocktail helps, but such clear-cut evidence is not always available. If you are really sure that arson or bombing is intended, however, should you really worry about possible legal proceedings afterward? You have no choice except to see your home destroyed, and perhaps, your whole family killed. As with so many other self-defense cases, whether or not to act is a matter for accurate observation and good judgment, and you cannot acquire these valuable qualities from any book.

In a case of arson or bombing, must you warn the criminal

113

before you use violent means to prevent the crime? Unfortunately, there is no clear-cut answer to the question. The law does not usually require you to risk your life in order to give a warning to a very dangerous criminal. If someone is about to touch a match to a fuse of a dynamite bomb that will blow up your house and the people in it or is about to hurl a Molotov cocktail through the window of your apartment, you are not required to say, "Don't do that or I will use deadly force in order to prevent you from doing so." On the other hand, if you do *not* have good reason for using force and go ahead anyway, you may find yourself on the wrong side of the law. For instance, if you mistake a child throwing a firecracker for a fire bomber or a prankster for an arsonist, you will be in trouble. You may be convicted on manslaughter or some other charge commonly used by law-enforcement officials when they must prosecute because public indignation is overwhelming. It is strictly a matter for law-enforcement agencies or jurors to decide whether excessive force has been used, and it's best to exercise extreme care and good judgment.

Arson and bombing are two crimes in which it may be necessary to use force in self-defense outside the house or apartment. It's easy to see that your best defense against a dynamiter or an arsonist is to stop him before he can actually enter the home or plant a bomb against the outside wall or throw a Molotov cocktail through a window or against a wooden wall. It's extremely unlikely that you would be prosecuted for preventing such an action unless the courts in your jurisdiction are subject to prejudice of some kind.

FORCEFUL ENTRY

Another very frequent crime is often met with forceful resistance. It goes by several names, but most often it is called "breaking and entering", or burglary. Several other legal designations for this crime are used in different states. It simply amounts to breaking into a house, apartment, or place of business in order to steal or to commit some other crime. If this act is committed at night, it is almost always called burglary; if it is committed in the daytime, it is almost always called breaking and entering. In following the tradition of English law, many states make burglary at night a more

114

serious crime than breaking and entering in daylight, though this distinction is gradually disappearing since many more crimes of this type are now committed during daylight hours. In large cities, most of these crimes are now occurring during the day while people are usually away at work.

With the idea that "A man's home is his castle", many people are under the impression that they have the right to use force against a burglar or housebreaker without giving warning and with little fear of adverse legal consequences. This may be true in some jurisdictions, but do not rely on this idea too heavily. It's one thing to use force against an armed burglar breaking forcefully into your home at night—a man who is subsequently found to have a long criminal record. It's quite another thing to kill a twelve-year-old boy in broad daylight when the young housebreaker was not armed and had no criminal record. The defender is sometimes in considerable difficulty because it's not always possible to know how dangerous the housebreaker or burglar is, and this is more than ever true today when adolescents often commit very serious crimes.

Many people, because of strong moral reasons, are so adverse to the use of force in self-defense that they would actually allow a burglar or housebreaker to enter and take anything he wished without interfering with him in any way, and this has actually been done. A person who takes this attitude and acts on it, however, is undergoing considerable risk because the housebreaker may not be intent on stealing. He may, in fact, turn out to be a rapist, a kidnapper, a homicidal maniac, an arsonist, or a bomber. This is why the law of most states allows the defender of a home some discretion in defending it against illegal, forcible entry. The defender is not acting to protect his home or mere property—he is acting to defend himself or his family against possible death or severe bodily harm.

TRESPASSERS

This distinction between dangerous persons and those who are not is brought out by the law as it relates to trespassers. A well-established principle of the law is that deadly force may *not* be used against a peaceful trespasser—that is, a person who is simply walking on your land even though you have posted a "No Trespassing" sign or signs, or the "Posted" signs used in some states. The simple trespasser does not have any right to be where he is, but since life is not in danger, the use of deadly force is not permitted. In fact, if deadly force is used, the trespasser may legally use deadly force to defend himself and may be excused by the courts if he kills the property owner! To accomplish this, of course, the trespasser would have to prove that he did not commit a felony of violence after crossing the property line, and he would also have to prove that he was in fact acting solely to save his own life when he used deadly force and that there was no way in which he could safely retreat out of danger.

How does one deal with a trespasser? There are two possible courses. One is to telephone the police or sheriff. If at all possible, this is the best way to handle the situation. The property owner or renter is legally entitled to ask the trespasser to leave, and he doesn't have to be polite about it. This is very often done if the situation is only a matter of a mistake by persons who perhaps do not realize that trespassing is a minor crime (misdemeanor) in most states. If, however, the trespasser reacts to the request to leave with a refusal, it's best to turn away and call the police to eject him. Don't interfere with a trespasser who may turn out to be violent. It's simply asking for trouble. The trespasser, when asked to leave, may possibly react with violence if he is in fact a criminal or a demented person. If he attacks the property owner or renter, however, the incident becomes a matter of self-defense. If the force used by the trespasser justifies it, the defender may even kill the criminal, and will *usually* be cleared by the courts. It's important to remember that the defender in such cases does not act simply to defend property. He or she acts in self-defense against a criminal attack. Whether or not the defender has used a justifiable degree of force to meet the attack is a matter for the courts to determine, with all the disadvantageous possibilities that were mentioned previously. In all cases of self-defense, the force used by the defender must not be excessive in the light of the threat. Again, it's a matter of your own good judgment, but using deadly force against a simple trespasser is surely the worst possible judgment.

116

In some areas, many local officials and even private employees have been given blanket authority to enter onto private land, though in most cases, this does not include entering private homes unless a written warrant or court order has been obtained and it is shown to the building's owner or renter. Commonly, building inspectors, sewer and health inspectors, game wardens, dogcatchers, emergency gas and electric-company employees, fire inspectors, and other such people may enter private land, and the owner or renter has no authority to eject them, provided they are on legitimate business. Even if this kind of person is not on legitimate business as you interpret that term, it is best to call the police and let them handle the situation if there is no immediate threat of severe physical harm. Because of this expanded right to enter private land, it's extremely unwise to act hastily against trespassers. You may be dealing with someone who has the legal right to be on your property, and a criminal charge will be the result.

In rural areas, a farmer has a somewhat different problem with trespassers because he has considerable property away from his house—animals, outbuildings, barns, farm machinery, and so forth. A farmer may possibly need to bring a weapon with him when investigating a trespasser, particularly at night. In the country, it's sometimes difficult to get police help promptly. In the meanwhile a barn may be burned or cattle may be stolen. If the farmer takes a weapon with him when investigating a trespasser, he's well-advised to avoid using it if he possibly can do so. In fact, the only time when he can use a weapon legally is when the trespasser turns out to be using dynamite or a bomb, or makes a dangerous attack on an innocent person. In such cases, the farmer is preventing a felony of violence that is dangerous to life. In doing this, he subjects himself to all the dangers and expense of lengthy legal proceedings, though it's unlikely that he will run into serious trouble if he is a respected member of his community and acts in good faith and without malice.

In a city apartment or a suburban home, the problem of dealing with trespassers outside the dwelling is considerably simplified. The person who lives in an apartment has no property outside his dwelling. The suburban homeowner may have considerable property

117

away from the house itself such as a garage or an automobile that may be damaged or stolen. Does the suburban property owner have the right to use deadly force if this property is threatened? There may be legal jurisidctions that allow the use of deadly force under such circumstances, but in most places, the answer is no. Human life is not in danger if someone is breaking into a garage or stealing an automobile, and therefore deadly force should not be used.

The normal expectation in such a case is that the thief will be pursued by the police, arrested, and punished and that the stolen property will be returned. There is no reason for the property owner to use violence to protect mere property. In a practical way, this makes good sense, too. Usually, a homeowner's multi-purpose insurance policy covers property damage and may also cover theft, so there is little possibility of severe financial loss. Check your policy to determine if this is true in your case.

Since there is no danger to life and no danger of financial loss, why interfere with a thief who is committing non-violent larceny outside your dwelling? The law entitles every citizen to use the necessary degree of *non-deadly* force that will not cause severe bodily harm to prevent a serious crime (felony), but why take the risk? If you interfere with a thief outside your dwelling, he may turn out to be extremely dangerous, and if you do succeed in over-powering him, you may inflict severe bodily harm or even kill him —a kick, or a blow with the hand can be as deadly as any weapon, and it is extremely foolish to go after a thief outside your home with deadly weapons since you may find yourself with a weapons-violation charge against you. In this situation, of course, the property owner or renter is legally entitled to do just as the farmer does —investigate the situation and defend himself if the criminal or trespasser makes a dangerous attack, but why should you undergo the risk if there is no danger involved and you can handle the situation by staying inside your home and calling the police? Stay inside, keep your eyes open, call the police, and perhaps get a weapon ready in case the trespasser or criminal tries to break into your home, and wait out the situation. It's certainly the wisest course.

Again, deadly force may not be used to protect mere property—
that's a principle which holds true in all fifty states. Human life
(even the life of a criminal), is more valuable in the eyes of the
law than any property. You cannot use deadly force against a
simple thief though you can use non-deadly force. If a struggle
develops and the thief suddenly becomes so violent that your life
is in jeopardy and you cannot avoid the dangerous attack by retreat,
then and only then, deadly force may be used—not to recover the
property, but to defend yourself from death or severe bodily harm.
Therefore, never use weapons against a thief who is merely taking
property without offering violence. It's important to understand the
different labels used in these situations. Larceny is theft without
violence or the threat of violence. Robbery is forcing a person to
turn over valuables by threatening violence or by carrying out a
violent attack. Robbery, armed robbery, and burglary are more
serious crimes (all are felonies) than larceny. Larceny may be a
misdemeanor if the amount stolen is small (petit larceny) or a
felony if it is larger than a certain amount specified by state law.

The difference between larceny and the more serious or dangerous crimes such as burglary, robbery, and other felonies of violence
is that the law presumes that a criminal engaged in one of the more
serious crimes is really dangerous and allows the homeowner or
renter to use a greater degree of force in defense. On a practical
level, this makes the use of good locks and security hardware extremely important. Breaking and entering, and burglary are serious
crimes. Merely entering a private home or place of business is not.
Criminals realize this and hesitate to break a window or jimmy
a door in order to enter. Therefore, all sorts of dodges are used to
enter a home without physically breaking in. Criminals pretend to
be deliverymen, magazine salesmen, poll takers, and may even pretend to be tax collectors or assessors. This is often done to "case"
a piece of property for a crime later on, but these criminals are
not averse to stealing something on the first go-round if that can be
done without real risk.

Let us say that you have been careless in installing or using

119

security hardware and suddenly find yourself confronted by a man who is already inside your apartment or house. He may be a homicidal maniac or a dangerous criminal, but he may be a non-violent thief, or he may be a perfectly innocent though mistaken salesman. If you are tricked into allowing someone to enter your home because you believe he has a legitimate errand, you're in much the same situation. At the moment, the stranger is legally only a trespasser. If you allowed him to enter peacefully, and with your permission, he is not even a trespasser. The law regards him as your guest. Do you have the right to use force to eject the intruder even though you did not voluntarily admit him or because you were tricked into admitting him? The answer is a clear *no*. The person is merely a trespasser until he proves otherwise, and you have no evidence for believing that you or anyone in your family is in danger of severe bodily harm. All you can do is request the person to leave. If the person refuses to leave, a necessary degree of force (not including deadly force) may legally be used to eject him from your home. To avoid danger, however, it is much wiser to try to get away and call the police, and indeed you have no choice except retreat if you are physically incapable of using force or do not have the necessary equipment. You have no right to eject or refuse to admit a law-enforcement officer who has a written warrant from a court, or a law-enforcement officer who enters when there is a clear and evident necessity for him to do so in an emergency.

If the intruder does turn out to be a criminal, and attacks, you can then use the necessary degree of force to ward off the attack. If the attack is so violent as to endanger you or any inmate of the home, you may even kill the criminal. It becomes a case of personal self-defense against violent attack, and in meeting it you must act within the ordinary law of self-defense.

It is much better to make it difficult or impossible for the criminal to enter by using good security hardware and by exercising extreme caution about admitting strangers. I can hear some reader saying, "But that's obvious." It's fairly obvious, I admit, but the reasons for installing good security hardware and using it go beyond merely keeping trespassers and possible criminals out. The hard-

120

ware also reduces the need for force in self-defense to an absolute minimum and will keep you out of court. Always keep weapons or force of any kind in reserve as a last-ditch defense if security hardware fails. Never rely on violence as your first line of defense. One of the most dangerous things you can do is maintain a deadly weapon for defense without needed security hardware and avoidance procedures. This can bring on a situation in which you're forced to use your weapon hastily, mistakenly, and perhaps illegally.

Should you immediately use some sort of weapon to disable or kill a burglar or housebreaker who is trying to break through an outside window or door? I would not do so if I could possibly avoid it. The possibility of adverse court action in some jurisdictions is too great, and it's always best to avoid the chance of revenge by the criminal or his friends and relatives. Use your security hardware instead of force. Immediately retire to the security room, taking children and others with you, lock the door, call the police, and get a weapon ready. Get everyone away from the security-room door in case the criminal is armed with a gun. After making doubly sure that the security-room door is locked, call out to the criminal and warn him that you have a weapon and that the police are on their way.

I would make no effort to trap the criminal by remaining silent once the door is locked. It's too dangerous. If the criminal is still in the act of breaking an outside window or door, he will usually get out of there just as fast as he can when he hears your warning. If he has already entered while you were gathering up children and perhaps a few valuables, he'll probably jump out of the opening he has made just as fast as he can once he realizes that there is someone on the premises and that you are prepared and equipped to resist.

If, however, the criminal is really dangerous, he will try to break the second barrier—usually the locked door of the security room— by throwing his weight against it or by using tools against the lock or the hinges. If he does so, repeat your statement that the police are on the way and that you have a weapon. If the criminal continues to attempt to break through the barrier, I would have no hesitation about using deadly force against him. If you shoot him or use some other weapon at this point, I do not think that any law-enforcement agency or court would prosecute you unless the officials and courts in your locality are remarkably prejudiced. In fact, the danger is so clear and so immediate that you have no other choice.

The whole point of the security-room system is to allow you the greatest freedom to defend yourself without fear of disadvantageous consequences.

Let's say that you have not been careful about your security hardware but that you do have some sort of weapon in your home. If the criminal breaks in suddenly or silently, you will be forced to use the weapon hastily and without giving warning—this can lead to lengthy court hearings, though your action will *probably* be justified or excused by the courts. Let's say that you have rigged up good locks and other security hardware on all outside doors and windows but have failed to provide yourself with a security room or any means of putting a locked inside door between yourself and the intruder. This may force you to use a weapon while the house-breaker or burglar is working on an exterior barrier, and that may also lead to lengthy court hearings and makes retaliation by the criminal's friends or relatives much more likely. If you claim self-defense under such circumstances, your case is fairly weak because it's more difficult to demonstrate that life was in danger. In fact, there are some jurisdictions where the claim may not be accepted in all cases. Without a security room, warning the criminal that you have a weapon and will use it may work, and he may clear out immediately, but giving that warning may endanger your life since the criminal may attack. The law does not require you to give warning before using deadly force, provided the danger is very clear and immediate (usually there is no time to give warning), but you'll have to demonstrate to the law's satisfaction that there indeed was very great danger and that is much more difficult if only an outside barrier has been tampered with and perhaps not even broken.

There are exceptions to this, of course. If you actually see a person armed with a deadly weapon trying to break into your home, and it is impossible to retreat to a secure place, you may be forced

122

to deal with him immediately. Actually, you may have no other choice. If you are very sure that the intruder is a criminal and that he is armed and intends to attack, it's foolish to wait or even to warn him before taking forceful action. Few courts would cause any kind of legal trouble if deadly force were used to prevent *armed* entrance into a private home.

If the criminal appears to be unarmed, don't use deadly force to prevent him from entering. If, for instance, you see someone outside your window on the fire escape, don't use weapons immediately. At the very least, don't use a weapon until the criminal breaks a window or forces a lock to enter. Even this restraint may not provide enough evidence to support a claim of self-defense if there is no other evidence that innocent human life was in danger. Yet, if a barrier was forced, you have physical evidence that a criminal was trying to break in. Remember, however, that most housebreakers and burglars are not at all dangerous. Merely giving warning before the tool is used or the window broken will frighten them away 99 percent of the time. If you are six feet tall and the housebreaker is a puny teenager who does not have a weapon, and you use deadly force without giving warning, I assure you that there will be a lengthy, costly, troublesome investigation and perhaps a jury trial. If, on the other hand, you are an elderly woman and the housebreaker shows a weapon, deadly force can probably be used immediately without giving warning. The law does not require you to risk your life to give warning but it is better to do so if you can without risk. The basic principle is that the danger of severe bodily harm or death must be clear and immediate. You must use your own judgment. The law does not deal kindly with people who use deadly force foolishly even though they are mentally deficient, intoxicated, or just plain stupid. If you kill an innocent person or even a criminal who is not really dangerous, you will probably be charged and convicted of the crime of manslaughter—unlawful killing without malice. The penalty is usually a prison sentence, and a civil lawsuit is likely. The proper remedy with a criminal who does not threaten severe bodily harm or death is non-deadly force or avoidance.

Retiring to a security room leaves a thief free to take anything from the rest of the home, but it's unlikely that you'll lose much. Remember, you have called the police, and if possible, you have warned the criminal that help is on the way. Few criminals will stay around to search for valuables. A great loss is unlikely, and the loss may be covered by insurance.

LEGAL BASIS OF SELF-DEFENSE

The security room can be used as described above if you're alert and prepare for emergencies in advance, but there's no denying that sometimes you can be caught off guard even in your own home. In such circumstances, you may be forced to take much more active measures against the criminal. In an extreme case, you may even be forced to search through a home looking for the criminal if, for instance, children in another part of the home are in danger. There's also the possibility that you or a loved one may be attacked in the street or that you may run into a situation where you will want to come to the assistance of a complete stranger. For these situations, it's not possible to lay down hard-and-fast defense procedures. You must use your own best judgment in deciding what you will do within the law of self-defense, and you must come to your decision rapidly.

So far, we have been discussing situations in which the defender usually acts against an unknown person. If it should ever happen that a person you know—even a relative—attacks you, you may be obliged to act in self-defense. In these situations, it is more difficult to sustain the claim of self-defense. Prosecutors are always more prone to look for malice and murder in such cases.

In all these less-restricted defense situations, therefore, the defender is on less sure legal ground than he is when he acts on his own property against a criminal whose identity is not known.

To describe what you can and cannot do in such situations, I will quote from Clark and Marshall, *A Treatise on the Law of Crimes,* one of the finest authorities on the law of self-defense. Remember, however, that the authors are trying to generalize on the law of 50 states and the law does change from time to time and in ways that are sometimes difficult to understand. You should therefore

124

interpret their description of the law in the most conservative way possible. Applying these principles wisely and safely is your own responsibility. All the quotations below are from Clark and Marshall.

Non-deadly Force

... an officer or a private individual is not guilty of an assault and battery in making a lawful arrest in a lawful manner, or in detaining a person who is lawfully in his custody, or in suppressing a riot or affray or preventing a felony. He is guilty, however, if an arrest is made, or a person detained, without lawful authority, or if excessive force is employed.

This statement requires some explanation. First of all, any person has "lawful authority" to prevent a serious crime—that is, a felony. The various states, however, differ in their classification of crimes. Yet, you can be sure that the following crimes are felonies in all 50 states, no matter what exact legal label is used: murder, rape, robbery, burglary, kidnapping or abduction, arson, bombing, and all the more serious forms of physical attack with weapons and very severe physical attacks without weapons. In some states, a mild slap or blow is only a misdemeanor (minor crime), but if a person tries to injure another severely even though no weapon is used, the crime is a felony and this crime is often called aggravated assault or assault with intent to kill. One crime, breaking and entering, may be a misdemeanor or a felony, depending on the state in which it is committed, but this should not worry the person who acts as a householder, renter, or member of the household to defend the home against it in the manner described previously. If a dangerous criminal attempts to break into your home, and you are compelled to use force against him to prevent his entrance, the crime ceases to be mere breaking and entering, particularly if you have given warning. The criminal who persists in breaking and entering after having been warned is obviously dangerous, and if force is used against him, it is justified. As explained previously, the defense may include deadly force if that is the only way in which the criminal's entrance can be prevented.

125

When a man is assaulted, but not in such a way as to endanger his life or threaten great bodily harm, he has a right to defend himself, and, in doing so, to use any necessary force short of taking his assailant's life or inflicting great bodily harm; and, unless the force employed is clearly excessive, he is not guilty of assault and battery. . . . The force employed in repelling an assault must not be clearly out of all proportion to the assault. One who repels a simple assault by force that is clearly excessive and out of all proportion to the assault is himself guilty of assault and battery.

One who is assaulted by another, without fault on his part, is not bound to retreat before resorting to measures of self-defense short of taking life or inflicting great bodily harm. Nor is he obliged to wait until he is struck. He may prevent a battery.

Try to avoid the attack rather than striking first if you can possibly do so. If you act too quickly, it may not be possible to make your claim of self-defense stand up.

Clark and Marshall then add an excellent point for those who have violent tempers and are inclined to get into fights:

One who is himself the aggressor, or who intentionally provokes an assault, as by the use of abusive language, cannot escape criminal responsibility for blows given by him in the course of the difficulty on the ground that they were in self-defense.

In other words—if someone provokes a fight and then depends on self-defense to escape the consequences, he will probably be convicted of a crime.

Killing to Prevent a Dangerous Felony

It is a well-settled principle of the common law that any person, whether he be a peace officer or merely a private individual, may and should kill another, if necessary to prevent him from committing a felony attempted by force or surprise, [such] as murder, rape, sodomy, robbery, burglary, or arson. The homicide in such a case is not merely excusable, but it is justifiable. . . . It

126

is not at all necessary that the felony shall be directed against the person, habitation, or property of the person committing the homicide, but it is justifiable to kill in order to prevent such a felony against a third person, even though he may be a stranger. . . .

This chapter has already presented some advice about being cautious in coming to the aid of a complete stranger.

Either an officer or a private person, having authority to arrest another for a felony, may kill him if he cannot otherwise be taken, and he may do so when the party is fleeing, as well as when he is engaged in violent resistance. . . . When a felon [the person who committed a serious crime] has once been arrested, the officer or other person having him in custody may kill him, if necessary, in order to prevent his escape.

Take this point about killing a criminal in order to prevent him from escaping with more than a grain of salt. For reasons stated previously, it is more practical to let the criminal escape than to risk adverse legal proceedings and revenge by the criminal's friends or relatives. In some cases, however, it is difficult to imagine how the private person could restrain himself. If the criminal were fleeing after the rape or even the murder of a near relative or other loved one, could he really be expected to stand by and do nothing? In less serious cases, however, it's much safer to allow the criminal to escape rather than to use deadly force. In all cases, there should be no attempt to punish the criminal or to inflict severe bodily harm with malice because that would be equivalent to a lynching, which is murder. If force is used under these circumstances, and I insist that it is very risky, it should only be used to prevent the escape of an extremely dangerous criminal. If malice or a desire to punish can be proved, a verdict of murder is likely.

Since a homicide in prevention of a felony is only justifiable when necessary to prevent the felony, the doctrine does not apply to the prevention of felonies not attempted by violence or surprise. It is inapplicable to secret felonies like larceny.

In a case of embezzlement, for instance, the amount of money stolen may be large enough to make the crime a felony, but there is no danger to life or limb involved in this crime, and thus force may not be used to prevent it. The same applies to forgery, and all other non-violent crimes.

On this matter of not using force unless physical danger is involved, Clark and Marshall give some further guidelines:

> Numerous cases indicate that if a person is in peaceable possession of another's property, though his possession may be wrongful, the owner cannot resort to violence in order to regain possession, but he must resort to the machinery of the law. A man, however, may use necessary force to regain momentarily interrupted possession of his property, as where another wrongfully takes it in his presence, and refuses to give it back.

The familiar example is the pickpocket. You may not kill a pickpocket merely to recover something he has taken from you, but you may use a necessary degree of non-deadly force to recover your property. If the criminal then attacks you in such a way as to endanger your life or threaten severe bodily harm, the matter becomes one of self-defense, not recovery of stolen property. As a practical matter, it's best to let the pickpocket get away if restraining him would involve extreme physical danger. You must use your own judgment. Clark and Marshall sum up the point in one sentence: "An assault with intent to kill is not justifiable in defense of property. . . ."

Retreat

Earlier in this chapter, the author advised the reader to retreat from a criminal entering his home by retiring to a security room. Legally, the homeowner or members of the household have no obligation to do so—it's merely a matter of safer tactics. Here's how Clark and Marshall state the legal principle:

> A man is not bound to retreat from his house [or rented apartment]. He may stand his ground there and kill any person who attempts to commit a felony therein, or who attempts to enter

128

by force for the purpose of committing a felony, or of inflicting great bodily harm upon an inmate. In such a case, the owner or any member of the family, or even a lodger in the house may meet the intruder at the threshold, and prevent him from entering by any means rendered necessary by the exigency, even to the taking of his life, and the homicide will be justifiable. The doctrine, however, does not justify a homicide merely to prevent a trespass upon the habitation, when it is evident that there is no intention to commit a felony, or to inflict great bodily harm upon an inmate. Of course, in defending his habitation, a man must act upon appearances, and if he acts in the bona fide and reasonable belief that the assailant intends a felony or great bodily harm to an inmate, and kills him to prevent his entry, the homicide is not criminal though he was mistaken as to the assailant's intention.

Yet, for all the reasons cited earlier, it's better to let the intruder prove that he is dangerous by giving warning and putting an interior barrier as well as an exterior barrier between you and him.

In the street or public places, however, there is a need for retreat. First of all, let's deal with the situation in which the defender is not entirely faultless himself because he has voluntarily entered into a fight. Clark and Marshall put it this way:

Excusable homicide in self-defense differs from justifiable homicide in self-defense in that the parties are engaged in an affray or mutual combat, by reason of which both are deemed to be in fault, so that the homicide is merely excused, and not justified. It is called homicide *se defendendo,* on a sudden affray. The affray [which is only a fight dressed up in legal terminology] may arise in various ways. Where a person is assaulted without felonious intent, and engages in a combat with his assailant, in the course of which it becomes necessary to kill his adversary in order to save himself from death or great bodily harm, and he does so after *retreating as far as he can with safety,* he is regarded as being to some extent at fault, and the homicide is not justifiable but it is excusable.

129

From the point of view of the defender, however, there is little practical difference between justifiable homicide and excusable homicide, since neither act is punished. Earlier, excusable homicide was punished by fines or confiscation of goods, but this is no longer done.

Save for the duty to retreat, the slayer occupies the same status as in the case of justifiable self-defense. The affray may arise in various ways: from resenting and returning a blow, or from resenting insulting words, or from resisting a trespass on land or goods, or from resisting an unlawful arrest. None of these provocations justify or excuse a homicide, and some of them do not mitigate or reduce it to manslaughter. If, however, in any of these cases it becomes necessary for one of the parties to take the other's life to save himself from death or great bodily harm and he does so, the homicide is excusable, except as explained in the sections following.

Clark and Marshall then go on to explain that the homicide is not excusable

... if, at the time of the killing the deceased had thrown away his weapon and was turning away. But an intention to withdraw from the conflict in order to deprive a person assailed of his right to kill in self-defense must in some manner be known to him.

The danger to the defender must also be "imminent and immediate"—another way of saying that the force used in self-defense must not be excessive.

Clark and Marshall then outline the duty of the jury in such a case and in other cases of homicide in self-defense.

It is the province of the court [judge] to instruct the jury what the law is in relation to the right of self-defense. Whether, under the law as thus laid down, a necessity existed at the time to take life in order to save life or prevent grievous bodily harm, and whether the killing, under the circumstances of the particular case, was prompted by such necessity or, by some other motive, is to be determined by the jury.

130

In other words, you are ultimately thrown upon the judgment of the jury to substantiate the claim of self-defense.

I'd sum it up this way: if you get into a fight, always retreat out of it at the earliest possible moment that you can safely do so or you may find yourself facing a jury. Though the jury may find that a killing in such a fight is excusable, you cannot really depend fully on such a finding. Even if you must bear an insult or submit to a mild blow, it's best not to fight since the fight may lead to a killing and considerable legal trouble. The law relating to excusable homicide as a result of a fight is not so firm as the law governing homicide in prevention of a felony of violence. Stay out of fights, but if forced into one, retreat as early as possible if you can safely do so. In all cases where malice aforethought can be proved, the verdict will probably be murder in spite of a claim of self-defense.

Now we come to one of the most startling points in the law of self-defense. In some states, the defender must retreat before taking life in self-defense even if he was *not* at fault and was attacked by a criminal. Here's what Clark and Marshall say on this point:

> ... in excusable self-defense, in a sudden affray, the party threatened must retreat as far as he can with safety before taking his adversary's life (*some courts apply this rule to justifiable self-defense, where a person is feloniously assaulted, being without fault himself,* while others hold that retreat is not necessary in such a case).

In other words, some states require retreat from your attacker if you can safely do so even if you are not at fault and you are attacked by surprise. In the states that require retreat in all cases outside the home, you cannot stand your ground and take the assailant's life even though you are not at fault in any way. My own personal advice to you is *always* to retreat if you can safely do so inside your home as well as outside it. If a criminal threatens you but does not attack immediately, and you can get away from him, it's better to retreat even though you feel you can overcome him. It's too risky on a practical level, and you may find yourself in a complex legal situation if you are successful.

The retreat rule, however, *never* requires a person who is not at fault to retreat if he must risk his life to do so. For instance, if the defender in a knife attack manages to catch the attacker's knife arm and then manages to kill the criminal, the defender will almost always be excused provided he can demonstrate that there was no possibility of a safe retreat. And he should have no difficulty demonstrating the fact because letting go of the criminal's arm would leave the attacker free to carry out the attack. In many personal attacks, it is extremely dangerous to turn one's back on the attacker, and so it can often be said that there is no safe way to retreat. Again, it's a matter for the defender's own judgment.

I'd sum up the retreat rule as follows: In your own home, you are never required to retreat from a dangerous criminal attack before using deadly force in self-defense, provided the attack threatens severe bodily harm or death. Outside your home, you are required by some state courts to retreat if you can safely do so, even though you are not at fault and did not voluntarily enter into a fight. In all 50 states, you are required to retreat to avoid taking your opponent's life if you can possibly do so when you have voluntarily entered a fight, and deadly force may only be used in self-defense when retreat is no longer possible and you have been driven "to the wall." My advice: ALWAYS retreat if you can safely do so. Use weapons or deadly force only as a last resort, no matter what the circumstances.

Has all the legal language confused you? If it has, I'm in a position to offer you one rule that reduces all the complexities of the law to a single sentence. It was given at the beginning of this chapter, but it bears repetition: Take human life or use force only if an innocent person is in danger of severe bodily harm or death, and there is no other way to ward off the attack or safely retreat from it. If you follow that simple rule and stay out of fights, you'll be able to act with a good conscience and the smallest possible chance of adverse consequences.

Weapons Laws

We have been blithely discussing the law as it applies to the defender—his rights, his duty as a citizen, what is permissible, and what is illegal. Yet, everyone knows that in many cases, the law,

132

which should protect the citizen and give him a legal basis on which he can firmly act to defend himself, actually makes effective defense impossible by forbidding him to carry concealed weapons.

Take the case of Agripino Bonillo, for instance. Here's what happened to him as reported in the *New York World-Telegram* of March 29, 1966:

A father of 10 was beaten and kicked to death last night in the East New York section of Brooklyn as he frantically tried to defend himself from three young muggers.

But a trail of blood from a knife wound inflicted by the victim led police to arrest three teen-age suspects in the slaying.

Agripino Bonillo, 49, of 408 Georgia Ave., Brooklyn, was pronounced dead at Brookdale Hospital, where he was taken after police found his battered body in front of 311 Alabama Ave., only a few blocks from his home.

A few minutes later, in the emergency ward of the same hospital, police arrested . . . [three teen-agers, one 18 years of age, another 17, and the third only 14 years old].

Police said the youths had gone to the hospital to seek treatment of a badly bleeding cut on . . . [one of their faces].

The hospital had been alerted to watch for anyone suffering possible knife wounds after police found a trail of blood leading from the scene of the beating and followed it to . . . [the house of one of the alleged killers].

Bonillo was on his way home from work in a Manhattan restaurant when he was jumped by three youths. In trying to stave off their attack, police said, Bonillo pulled out a collapsible linoleum knife which he carried.

Fighting for his life, Bonillo slashed one of the attackers across the face with the short, hooked blade, but the youths battered him to the pavement and then stomped him to death, police said.

Bonillo's empty wallet was found on top of his body and his wristwatch, torn from his wrist was a short distance away.

Police theorized that the attackers fled to the home of one of the youths and attempted to stem the bleeding wound of the

133

injured member. When that failed, they took him to a hospital but police already had broadcast an alarm.

Bonillo lived in a seven-room apartment with his wife, Rose, and his children, ranging in age from 2 to 20.

Neighbors described him as a hard-working, peaceful man.

Bonillo was aware that he was in danger—he lived in an area that is infested with criminals. To protect himself, he carried a folding linoleum knife. This is a ridiculous weapon because the blade is short and hooked. It cannot be used to thrust and can only inflict a shallow slash. Yet, by carrying that ineffective weapon, Mr. Bonillo put himself on the wrong side of one of New York's weapons laws which prohibits carrying concealed any ". . . dangerous weapon with intent to use the same unlawfully." Of course, the police almost always act on the belief that anyone caught with a dangerous concealed weapon intended to use it unlawfully. If Bonillo had been discovered carrying this concealed weapon, he probably would have received a prison sentence. Yet, in his desire to protect himself, he went ahead and took that risk.

Yet, the weapon he carried turned out to be ineffective, and he was killed as a result. Even if Mr. Bonillo had only been carrying a long, straight fighting knife, he could probably have protected himself, and he would be alive today. Why didn't Mr. Bonillo have a more effective weapon? He was probably afraid to carry one because of the New York weapons law. If you know anything about how pistol permits are issued in New York and in some other cities, you realize that this man could never have obtained a permit to carry a concealed firearm. Permits are simply not issued at all to carry knives, clubs, brass knuckles, and that sort of weapon. In the City of New York and in many other places, the law-enforcement agencies say, in effect: If you are to carry concealed weapons of any kind, it must be a gun, but gun permits are not issued to ordinary citizens. Mr. Bonillo carried the ineffective linoleum knife because he thought it would probably not earn him a severe prison sentence if he were discovered with it. Or at least, he hoped that would be the case.

Carrying the ineffective weapon probably led to his death. When the three alleged criminals jumped him, he used the knife and they became so infuriated that they allegedly kicked him to death. And yet, many men and women have been killed in this kind of crime in spite of the fact that they offered no resistance.

What would have happened if Mr. Bonillo had succeeded in warding off the attack and police had intervened after he had slashed one of the alleged attackers? If the three alleged attackers had no criminal records, they probably would have succeeded in making it appear that Mr. Bonillo was the aggressor. After all, sometimes people do suddenly act without sense. Mr. Bonillo was armed, though ineffectively, and the alleged criminals were not. I'm fairly sure that Mr. Bonillo would have been sent to prison. It can happen, and it can happen to you if you defy concealed-weapons laws in effect in your community.

When a defenseless person is killed because the law did not permit effective use of weapons, I believe the state should help the family of the victim. In order to further public security in some areas, the law forbids almost everyone to carry weapons. This is probably a sensible law in a crowded, unruly city, but when someone is killed, the state or city with a concealed-weapons law owes the victim's family compensation. In effect, the state or city is sacrificing the victim's life for the general welfare by denying him the means to defend himself when he is away from home. At the very least, the city or state with concealed weapons laws should be obliged to grant a pension for the support of minor children, and the victim's Social Security account should be paid up in full. In 1966, the New York State Legislature passed a law granting limited payments to those injured or killed by criminals or to their survivors, though payments will not begin for some time and the law is not retroactive—that is, it does not cover crimes committed prior to enactment. Money payments of this kind, however, should not be used by the authorities as a justification for entirely depriving citizens of weapons in their own homes and places of business. To do so would amount to substituting money compensation for every person's right to self-defense with effective weapons.

Laws of this kind, however, would help to correct a strange social injustice. While the person who has killed is fed and housed

135

in prison and given the benefit of recreation and education programs, the family of the murdered victim usually struggles along on entirely inadequate relief payments or plain charity. The injustice of this situation is worse than many kinds of social injustice which receive headline treatment in the press every day.

Some countries manage this problem much more fairly. In Finland, for instance, a murderer is not executed. He is sent to an arctic workcamp for the rest of his life, and all his wages are paid to the victim's family. That sounds like better justice than the death penalty or a prison sentence usually cut in half by "good behavior" and parole. In England, the government is experimenting with a compensation system for the victims of violent crimes. The yearly budget is small, but the government has paid small amounts so that families could keep going without being driven down to intolerable levels because of some criminal's wanton act. The English government forbids carrying concealed weapons, but at least it is making an effort to compensate the defenseless victim.

If crime continues to increase at its present rate, we may be forced to reconsider concealed weapons laws and the way they are administered. The laws were originally intended to disarm the criminal but not the law-abiding person. In actuality, however, the licensing authorities are so cautious in issuing permits for concealed weapons that the average citizen must go unarmed when away from home. Perhaps we will ultimately decide to alter the administration of these laws to permit more law-abiding citizens to carry weapons. The only alternative in many crime-ridden cities is an enormous increase in the number of police, and most city administrations are unwilling or unable to bear the expense. If the licensing laws were administered with intelligence and a bit of courage, they could be used to create a volunteer, armed police auxiliary that would be very effective in deterring crime. If a law-abiding person with no record of crime passed a gun-safety test and another test of his knowledge of the basic law of self-defense, I see no reason why he should not be able to obtain a concealed-weapons permit. If even a small number of ordinary people were armed, it would have an immediate effect on the number of dangerous muggings and other personal attacks. Each citizen who obtained such a permit and carried a weapon with him would be, in effect, a law-enforcement auxiliary since he or she would be obliged to use the weapon only within the well-established law of self-defense.

Does all this sound far-fetched to you? Well, it isn't, because that's how most cities and states in the United States administer their concealed weapons laws. Any law-abiding citizen with no record of previous convictions can obtain a concealed weapons permit, and many people do so. Of course, if New York, Chicago, and some other cities reverted to this system, there would be a few accidents, but perhaps criminals would no longer feel free to rape, murder, and assault without much fear of resistance.

In fact, New York City—the locality with the strictest laws against concealed weapons—already has a large, well-armed volunteer defense force. These are the merchants and shopkeepers who obtain concealed-weapons permits from the police. The possession of a weapon capable of being concealed is forbidden in that city without a license, but a merchant or shopkeeper, or a businessman who handles large amounts of cash can easily obtain a permit. Liquor-store proprietors find it especially easy to obtain these permits. The businessman does not usually carry the weapon away from his place of business, but keeps it concealed inside his shop or store. In general, the merchant, shopkeeper, or businessman has exactly the same rights of self-defense in his owned or rented place of business as the homeowner or renter. The law, however, in New York City is so administered that the businessman can use a concealable weapon rather than a shotgun or a rifle. Despite the fact that hundreds of these permits are in force in New York City, the rights they grant are almost never abused. Every year merchants and shopkeepers prevent hundreds of robberies, and in dozens of cases, they have apprehended or killed dangerous criminals. It's rather strange that a merchant is permitted the use of a concealed firearm to defend his cash register while other law-abiding people must use their fingernails to defend their very lives.

The fact that there is growing public tolerance of the civilian use of weapons is demonstrated by the growing number of cases in which private citizens carry weapons illegally to defend themselves. For instance, there is the case of Miss Arlene Del Fava.

As she was returning to her home in Queens County (within New York City) from a visit to the World's Fair late at night, a navy enlisted man tried to pull her into the undergrowth on a vacant lot. He had picked the wrong victim, however, because Miss Del Fava took a switchblade knife out of her purse and stabbed him. The alleged attacker fled and Miss Del Fava stepped out into the street and flagged down a passing motorist. She insisted on being driven to a police station in spite of the fact that the motorist warned her that the weapon she had used was illegal. In fact, mere *possession* of a folding knife activated by a spring and a release button is forbidden in New York City. Carrying one is illegal under New York's Sullivan Act—the usual sentence being a year or two in prison.

The police charged Miss Del Fava with the weapons violation, and she was brought before a grand jury. Miss Del Fava testified that she had found the weapon in her new apartment when she moved in and had not purchased it, but she did not deny that she was carrying the prohibited weapon, and she did not deny that she had used it, and effectively too. The alleged attacker was forced to seek medical attention and he was arrested at the hospital.

The grand jury, composed of Miss Del Fava's fellow citizens, was advised that she had violated the weapons law. Note that there was no charge against her for defending herself. Apparently, the district attorney felt that her action in using the knife was entirely justified. He was only asking the grand jury to hold Miss Del Fava for a jury trial for the weapons violation. Of course, the proceedings of the grand jury are secret, but we do know that the jury refused to indict Miss Del Fava. In effect, the grand jury said— yes, we know she violated the law, she admits it, but we are not going to do anything about it. Isn't there something wrong with laws like that? Here you have a ridiculous situation in which a grand jury—a law-enforcement agency—deliberately ignored the existing law! Not one of those jurors would have failed to resist a dangerous criminal attack if effective equipment for such a defense were available, one suspects, and therefore the members of the jury refused to hold Miss Del Fava for trial.

138

One wonders, however, what would have happened to poor Mr. Bonillo if he had not been killed, but instead had been arrested and accused of slashing an adolescent with his ineffective linoleum knife. After all, Mr. Bonillo was a 45-year-old restaurant worker, not a pretty young woman. Probably, he would have been held for trial, and he probably would have been convicted of a weapons violation and sent to prison. The fact that he was kicked to death demonstrates in no uncertain terms that he had a desperate need to use deadly force in self-defense. Yet, if he had not been killed he might be in prison uniform today.

Both these cases illustrate another important point. If an illegal weapon—most often a concealed weapon—is used in legal self-defense, the defender may be convicted of a weapons violation, but he or she is not usually convicted of manslaughter, murder, or some form of felonious assault. In other words, the act of self-defense is legal even if an illegal weapon is used. The fact that the defender acted within the law of self-defense, however, must be satisfactorily demonstrated to the authorities or to the jury, and there's the rub. If the defender was carrying a weapon illegally, he or she is often held to be the aggressor, and that's another reason why these licensing laws should be reconsidered. Take the case of an elderly person who is attacked by an unarmed but powerful young criminal who attempts to "stomp" the victim as Mr. Bonillo was stomped. If the defender shoots the criminal with an illegally carried gun, it may be decided that excessive force was used and a manslaughter or even a murder conviction may result. But how else is a comparatively defenseless person to defend himself or herself against a dangerous attack by a criminal or a maniac?

No one can really offer a pat, ready-made solution to the problem, but some intelligent effort should be made to solve it or most law-abiding people will be forced to move out of this country's large cities because they are rapidly becoming very unsafe, particularly for women.

Of course, most laws prohibiting concealed weapons outside the home do not prevent the use of legal weapons inside the dwelling, except that in some areas it is illegal to possess a firearm capable of being concealed unless a license is obtained.

139

The reader may ask whether or not firearms may be carried outside the home if they are *not* concealed. In most states and cities, there is absolutely no law or regulation against carrying firearms openly. If you do so in most cities, however, I'm sure you will be arrested. The police, almost universally in crowded areas, will not allow anyone to carry a legal firearm through the streets, and they don't really concern themselves with whether or not it is loaded. Some charge can always be brought against any person who does this. Most commonly, the individual who carries legal firearms openly in an urban area is simply arrested for disorderly conduct (a very useful catch-all charge), and it is made plain to him, law or no law, that he is not to repeat his error. In one New York case, a man who deliberately tested the law by carrying a rifle openly on a crowded city street was arrested for hunting out of season even though there was no game for miles around. Since that time, New York City has added to its Administrative Code provisions that make it illegal to carry a rifle or a shotgun in any public place unless the weapon is in a closed case. If the weapon is loaded, the crime becomes a felony whether or not the gun was in a case. These new regulations do not affect those who have obtained permits allowing them to carry concealed handguns, and they do not affect persons who maintain loaded shotguns or rifles in their own homes. Other cities have similar laws or may enact them at any time. They are obviously intended to prevent armed combat during riots. All such laws violate the second amendment to the Constitution, but law-abiding citizens obey them even if criminals do not.

Pennsylvania has a law which prohibits anyone in the state from firing a shotgun without the specific permission of the governor. This law was passed to prevent people from carelessly firing shotguns up their chimneys in order to clear them of soot, but it's on the books, and it may be used at any time to prevent misuse of guns, though no one interferes with thousands of Pennsylvania shotgun hunters who take the field every year.

All over the country, there are many of these strange laws which can be used by the police to enforce orderly use (or non-use) of firearms. In some cities, it is against the law to fire a gun for any reason except legitimate self-defense. In other places, it is illegal to have loaded firearms in rented dwellings, though they can be loaded if a self-defense need arises.

A citizen often supposes that he can do as he pleases with firearms in his own home as long as he stays within local regulations and state laws and does not commit a crime. In many areas, however, you will be arrested if you are seen behaving in a foolish way with a gun in your house or apartment, or even if you are seen simply displaying a gun by a policeman standing outside your window. The formal charges will not usually be upheld in court, but that doesn't matter. All that interests the police is making sure that no misuse of guns occurs.

Foolish or premature use of firearms is forbidden by law. It is against the law to point or aim a firearm at a person unless you are acting in legal self-defense. Therefore, if you make a mistake, and perhaps threaten an innocent person by pointing a gun at him, you may be arrested and sent to prison. Actually, the same laws apply to threats made with knives, clubs, and other weapons, but penalties are more severe if a firearm is involved. Again, it's best to remember that deadly force may not be used (or even threatened) unless human life is in danger.

If you ever buy a gun for home defense, you should take a safety-training course, and you should check all local regulations very carefully. You should also get some experienced person to fill you in on how the laws are *actually enforced*. In these times of crime and social unrest, there is a constant clamor for new regulations and laws controlling sale and use of firearms, and it pays to keep up-to-date on new laws and regulations coming into effect in your community. The same may apply to the basic law of self-defense, though rapid changes in that body of law are less likely since the right of self-defense is so basic and precious that it is seldom tampered with on a short-term basis.

The reader may also be curious about the use of weapons in an automobile, since most Americans seem to spend about one-quarter of their lives in their cars. In general, when you're in your automobile, you are subject to whatever laws apply outside the home. In other words, weapons regulations apply with equal force to a person who is in a car and to one who is on foot. If you are in

141

an automobile, however, you also run into the hunting regulations of many states. These laws are aimed at preventing sportsmen from shooting animals from their cars. Therefore, most guns must be disassembled before they can be put into a car. At the very least, most states require that any gun transported by automobile must be unloaded and inside a case or box. In an automobile, your best defense against someone outside is locked doors and a ready touch on the accelerator.

I'd like to urge a very cautious respect for weapons laws. In the United States today, there is a constant agitation for laws that would really make it impossible for anyone to own any kind of firearm at all even for self-defense within the home. If there are a large number of cases in which firearms are carelessly used, such laws may be passed and then even the home itself will be largely defenseless. The American people will then be in the same situation as the English. In England, it is almost impossible for any ordinary citizen to own any kind of firearm for home defense. And yet, many English criminals are equipped with firearms and use them. The Englishwoman who lives alone and is incapable of using the less-powerful weapons such as clubs, is absolutely defenseless against the rapist and the maniac. Most American women, on the other hand, have the legal right to keep a gun at home and to use it in self-defense. If we lose this precious right through stupidity or carelessness, we will probably never regain it.

There are people in this country who advocate abolition of the right to keep and bear arms. For instance, a book entitled *The Right to Bear Arms,* by Karl Bakal, a New York City resident, strongly urges the complete prohibition of all hunting and also urges that civilian possession of firearms be prohibited, even in private homes. People who support this view forget that they owe a debt to the gun owner. The United States is a violent country with a high crime rate, but criminals almost always try to avoid entering private homes when they know someone is at home. Why is this? The criminal can never be sure that the householder is not equipped with a firearm. The doubt is too strong, and therefore the average criminal checks carefully before entering to make sure that the home is empty. If civilians were completely deprived of firearms (and only law-abiding people would give them up), the criminal would feel free to enter almost any home, and we could look forward to numerous attacks by street-corner gangs and other criminals who would no longer be risking their lives the moment they jimmied a window or forced a door. The fact that a neighbor maintains a gun and has the courage to use it protects even those who advocate the abolition of the civilian right to possess effective weapons. Remember that, if you are asked to support foolishly restrictive firearms regulations. No one who is familiar with current agitation for "gun control" laws could fail to believe that much of the comparatively mild regulation now proposed is actually an entering wedge for the ultimate prohibition of all firearms in civilian hands.

CHAPTER V

Weapons, Defenses Against Them, and the Security Room

A N official police pamphlet gives the following advice: "If awakened at night by an intruder, don't try to apprehend him. He might be armed. Do not panic. Lie still, observe carefully and at the first chance, call police." This is excellent advice for a person who can do nothing else, and anyone who devotes a moment's thought to it will realize that it should be followed if the intruder is already in the room and no weapon is ready at hand. Really, there's little else that can be done. But if the intended victim is awakened by the noise an intruder makes in another room or as he is breaking in, there's much that a person can do to preclude the possibility of physical harm.

In the street, it's best to submit to a robbery as long as the criminal makes no attempt to harm you. But in the home, it's probably always best to make determined resistance if you can do so. This is particularly true if you are alone and there is no possibility of summoning effective assistance. The intruder may possibly be only a thief who would flee at the first sign of resistance, but on the other hand, he may be dangerous. If you have a good chance of putting him out of action with little risk to yourself and you are sure that you are acting within the law of self-defense as discussed in Chapter IV, it's best to do so before he can do any harm.

Hand-to-hand defenses are always more effective in the street

144

or other public places. If you use them effectively, the criminal will often flee because he knows that police or people willing to assist you may happen along at any moment. In your own home, the very fact that you are indoors will prevent many people from entering to help you no matter how loudly you call out. Even in public places, many people hesitate to involve themselves in any form of violence. When you are indoors, few people will enter to help you. Almost the same reasoning applies to police. A policeman will assist the victim if he sees an assault or other crime in the street, but when it comes to entering a home, even the police hesitate. The disturbance may only be a family quarrel or it may only be a drunken person making a fuss, and there's the delicate matter of entering without a written warrant.

Your best defense is always avoidance, and nearly always, you can preclude the undetected entrance of a criminal into your home. Don't become careless even in the daytime. Keep doors, windows, and screens locked or fastened, but always be prepared to exit quickly in case of a fire. If you acquire the habit of security consciousness, few criminals will be able to reach you.

Selecting a Defense Weapon

Undoubtedly, firearms are most effective as defense weapons, but many readers will not wish to use them. Firearms have a terrible finality about them. Suppose you point a loaded gun at a dangerous criminal and tell him to raise his hands and stand still. You are threatening that you will fire unless he obeys. What will you do if the criminal does not obey but instead makes an armed, dangerous attack on you? A few people are skilled enough and controlled enough to ward off even a dangerous attack by using a gun as a club if they do not wish to shoot, though they have the legal right to shoot if they act within the law of self-defense. In this situation, most people have only one choice—fire the weapon. For this reason, it's best not to keep a gun in your home if you have any hesitancy about using a deadly weapon. Once you pick up a gun in self-defense, you must be able to use it. Otherwise, the weapon can be a source of danger. Use *any* weapon in accordance with the law of self-defense, discussed in Chapter IV.

145

The logical substitute for a firearm is a weapon that can be used to disable rather than to kill, and for this purpose, clubs and tear gas are fairly effective. Yet, are you to contend with a criminal who may be dangerous while you are armed only with these less effective weapons? For instance, if you try to disable a criminal with a club and you fail, it may result in serious injury to yourself. To a certain extent, you are taking your life in your hands if you use non-lethal defense weapons. It is the price you pay for unwillingness to take a criminal's life.

DOGS AND DEFENSE WEAPONS

The choice of weapons is yours, but by using a combination of them, you obtain a certain degree of flexibility so that you make your defense appropriate to the threat. The oldest combination is the dog and some weapon held in the hands. The shepherd and his flock were usually accompanied by a large dog, and this dog was a capable fighter against wolves as well as human beings. The herdsman was often armed with a crook, a club, or even a short sword. If a raider or thief threatened the flock, the criminal was risking his life. The dog served his master in two ways. The animal often gave warning of the thief's approach. Once he was detected, the dog participated in the defense. The thief, trying to fend off a powerful dog, had his hands full, and the dog's master could strike a blow with the club or a bladed weapon to finish off the intruder if the situation was dangerous enough to require it.

This combination of dog and weapon still does good service today. Most farmers have one or more large and capable dogs. They also usually have a firearm of some kind, most often a shotgun. Ordinary criminals usually avoid farms—the combination of a good dog and a shotgun is simply too effective. While the dog attacks, the farmer moves up close with his shotgun and then he makes his choice—call the dog off and hold the criminal at gun point, or if the criminal shows that he's dangerous and attacks, shoot and shoot to kill. In most suburban areas also the householder could use this tested combination. All that's needed is a shotgun and a large, well-trained dog. Probably, this simple combination of defenses is the very best.

146

Other combinations can be effective, too. If you combine a dog with a tear-gas projector, you can move in close to spray the intruder while the dog keeps him busy. If you hold a tear-gas projector in one hand and a police nightstick in the other, you're even more effective. While the dog occupies the criminal, you can use the gas, and afterward disable him with the club if the situation calls for it. In an emergency, you can even use a knife snatched from the kitchen drawer as long as the dog gives you time to get the weapon. A very good combination if you have no compunctions about using firearms, is a dog, a tear-gas projector in your left hand, and a revolver in your right. This gives you three degrees of force, each increasingly severe to meet any degree of emergency.

A powerful dog is a very frightening adversary, in the dark, particularly. Most people have an exaggerated fear of a "vicious" dog. Actually, most dogs have teeth that are too short to inflict dangerous wounds, and of course, a dog's nails are not dangerous. All one needs to do to defend one's self against most dogs is to fall to the floor and put clasped hands over the back of the neck with the elbows touching the floor, legs together, and stomach pressed firmly against the flooring. In this position, it's almost impossible for the dog to reach the throat or any other soft, vital point except the kidneys. Of course, the animal's bites will be painful, but it's very unlikely that he'll do serious harm. Nevertheless, the sight or sound of a large animal attacking at night will send most criminals into a disorganized flight.

If the criminal is informed about the standard passive defense against an attacking dog—falling to the floor in a protective position—the dog's master has a great advantage. Once the intruder is on the floor, it's very easy to control him or flee. If the criminal is armed, however, he will probably try to use the weapon against your dog. So much the better from your viewpoint—you'll hear the sound of the shot or see or hear the dog's reaction to the club or knife. At least, you are not the immediate target. While the criminal is using his weapon on the dog, you have the choice of fleeing or using your own defense weapon. Some people, however, fear dogs and would never be able to use one for defense. Other persons find it impossible to train animals, or they may live in circumstances that make it impossible to maintain a dog.

Fortunately, other combinations of weapons are effective. If, for instance, you use a tear-gas projector and a club, or tear gas and a knife, you're fairly well armed, and you have a certain flexibility. Tear gas loaded into shotgun cartridges is available in most states. You can use this in a double-barreled shotgun by putting a tear-gas shell in one barrel and using a lethal cartridge in the other or use a tear-gas projector in one hand and a pistol in the other.

By using a combination of a defense weapon and the security hardware in your home or place of business, you can put up such a formidable defense that you will be safe against almost any form of attack. But to use weapons in combination, you must know how to use each one effectively. You must also have some knowledge of the best defenses against each weapon.

In attempting to give a broad understanding of weapons in the following pages, the author does not go into great detail about each one. It's up to the reader to study the weapons he selects to assure safe and effective use. Rifle instructors, pistol coaches, skeet and trap instructors take no responsibility for the actions of their students when instruction is over, and the author of this book certainly does not. When you use a deadly weapon, you are completely on your own, and you must accept the consequences if you do something stupid or foolish.

Use weapons of any kind only if you have the ability to use them safely and effectively.

TEAR GAS

Police and the military use very large tear-gas containers which are either fired from special launchers or are deposited by hand at selected release points. These large units are not sold to civilians and are much too powerful for personal defense. If you already have a good 12-gauge shotgun or a .38 Special pistol, gas shells are available for it.

Special civilian tear-gas projectors are also sold.

These civilian projectors almost always work in the same way.

The loaded shell is either screwed into the apparatus or loaded into a firing chamber. The shell is hollow and the open end is sealed with hard plastic. The closed end contains a firing cap which is most often of the type used in a 12-gauge shotgun shell. The firing mechanism consists of a firing pin operated by a long coil spring. You simply pull a button-like spur backward with the thumb and then release it. A spring drives the pin forward into the primer cap. The cap explodes with enough force to push the plastic sealer out of the shell and the gas follows. Most of these tear-gas projectors can be cocked by pulling the spring back and shoving the spur into a slot which holds it until the user pushes the spur out of the slot. This can be done with a very slight motion of the thumb. Don't carry a projector in the cocked position. Cock the device only when you have good reason to think that serious trouble is on the way, and always remember to uncock the projector if the trouble evaporates by letting the pin go forward *very gently*.

A projector like the one in the illustration is available from Penguin Associates, Inc., Pennsylvania Avenue, Malvern, Pennsylvania. The projector comes in a plastic box with two shells and the price is $6.95. You can order new cartridges. Several other companies make these projectors including Hercules Gas-Munitions Corporation, 5501 North Broadway, Chicago, Illinois. The latter company has a projector which fires a very large shell (caliber .45) with a claimed range of 20 feet.

These tear-gas projectors are very handy little defense items, but too much reliance should not be placed on them for several reasons. Perhaps the most important is that they are one-shot devices. If one shell is not enough, reloading takes too long. If you do use this type of tear-gas projector, be ready to follow up with another weapon or get out of there fast. A good pistol and a tear-gas projector are an excellent combination. Sometimes it pays to have two of these small projectors. If one blast doesn't suffice, you then have the option of firing another.

People wearing glasses are not as susceptible to the effects of these projectors because the eyeglasses shield the eyes to some extent. But the gas also enters the nostrils and causes immediate

FIGURE 5-1: One-shot Civilian Tear Gas Projector.

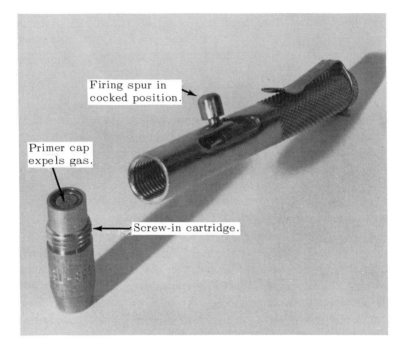

Firing spur in cocked position.

Primer cap expels gas.

Screw-in cartridge.

serious discomfort. The attacker is usually forced to close his eyes and keep them closed for 15 or 20 minutes and this allows you to take follow-up action or depart.

When the primer cap explodes, there is a noise equivalent to that of a .22 rifle. In some cases, this noise will help you to defend yourself. Many criminals are unfamiliar with this type of projector and they may think that you are armed with a small-bore pistol and that they have gotten a whiff of the powder gasses from the shot. The tear-gas itself is invisible just like the gasses from smokeless gunpowder.

A word of warning: some tear-gas projectors are made so that they will load rifle and shotgun ammunition since the shells are the same size. *Don't ever put regular ammunition in a tear-gas pro-*

jector. They are usually made of soft metal, and they will burst if fired with regular ammunition.

Don't fire these projectors directly into the face of an intruder unless you are absolutely sure that you are acting in legal self-defense. The primer cap exerts considerable force and the plastic sealing breaks into small pieces which may go into the eyes and cause blindness. The gas discharged directly into the eyes may also cause serious harm. Remember that you are legally responsible for any injury you cause to an innocent person. The safest method is to fire at the chest. The gas spreads enough to enter the nostrils and eyes.

These projectors are fairly effective inside buildings since the gas does not disperse. I still wouldn't use one against a person armed with a deadly weapon if he were standing only a few feet away. He might still be able to stab you or pull a trigger after he has received a full charge of gas. Used alone, these defense devices are really only effective against unarmed attackers.

Outdoors, the gas disperses rapidly. If there is a strong wind, some of the gas may even be blown backward into your own face. Actually, you will probably not get enough of it to incapacitate you, but it can be disconcerting for a few seconds. This happened to the author when he was testing one of the projectors and I can assure you that I was uncomfortable for the entire day. The effect is to dry the mucous membrane so that one feels as though he were suffering from a severe virus infection. If you use one of these projectors, remember that outdoors, against a strong wind, the effective range is only a few feet.

Don't drop these projectors. Most of them have rebounding firing pins. If they are dropped on a hard surface, the firing pin may spring forward and discharge the load. In order to test one of these projectors, I dropped it on a wooden floor. It fired on the third try. This can be highly embarassing, I imagine, if one is standing in line at the bank or waiting for a train in a crowded terminal.

These projectors, worn in the breast pocket like a fountain pen attract the curious. Someone sees a thick, metal, pen-like apparatus sticking out of your pocket and the more impolite may snatch it out. At that point, they will be even more curious, and flipping the

FIGURE 5-2: Tear Gas Billy.

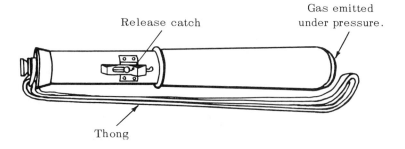

firing spur is easy. If you carry one of these devices, keep it completely concealed. If you insist on carrying it in your breast pocket, mask it with a handkerchief.

The Hercules Company, address above, also makes tear-gas ammunition for the .38 Special pistol and for all the popular shotgun gauges. If you use these shells in your gun, clean the weapon immediately afterward. The residue from the gas may corrode gunmetal unless it is quickly removed. The shells are quite expensive. The price ranges from 60¢ for *each* .38 revolver load to over $2.00 for *each* shotgun shell.

One of the most useful tear-gas projectors is a combination weapon—the M-29 tear-gas club or billy made by Federal Laboratories. This weapon is a sturdy hand billy that can be used as a striking weapon or to discharge gas. It contains a large tear-gas charge that is fired with a flashlight-type button. The gas is emitted in a spray and lasts three or four seconds in continuous discharge. This is an advantage in that a half-second of gas is usually enough for one individual. The spray can then be cut off and the remainder saved for a renewed attack. If a follow-up is required, the 9½-inch billy is heavy enough to strike a fairly effective blow. New tear-gas cartridges for this device can be purchased for $3.00 apiece. The weapon itself is priced at $33.00.

Tear-gas ammunition deteriorates with age. Most of such ammunition sold in the United States is dated in the same manner as some flashlight batteries. Dispose of the ammunition when the expiration date arrives. It's best to fire it outdoors so that it cannot be accidentally discharged after you put it in the trash bin. New, undated ammunition is probably dependable for three years.

Ridiculous as it may seem, some communities make the use of tear gas by civilians illegal. Be sure to check local regulations before you buy these shells or projectors. In some places, you must secure a license before you can purchase or use this type of defense hardware. This method of repelling attack was conceived because it is harmless as long as the user does not fire directly into the eyes. Even when that is done, serious damage is rare. With crime at its present levels, civilians, particularly women, need a powerful means of defense. New York City, for instance, is one of the most dangerous communities, and tear gas for civilian use is forbidden there except when a license is obtained, and that license is almost never granted. The woman who was raped and slowly stabbed to death by some degenerate in a Manhattan elevator early in 1965 would probably still be alive if she had had one of these projectors. Civilian use of tear gas is also illegal in Illinois and California, and other states may pass similar laws.

An official of a tear-gas manufacturing firm wrote the author: "It is unlawful to ship tear gas to anybody in the State of New York except to the Police Department. However, we can ship to surrounding states such as Massachusetts or Connecticut."

A young lady visiting New York City in 1965 was arrested by the police because a tear-gas projector was found in her hotel room. She was fined $25.00 and released. In most states, however, there is no law against these effective defense devices, which are particularly useful against the unarmed sex degenerate.

Since criminals are not usually interested in a purely passive weapon such as tear gas, there's little need for a defense against the device. In a civil disturbance or riot, however, you may sometimes encounter a situation where tear gas is widely used and you may get a whiff of it. For ordinary, old-fashioned tear gas, washing the face with a strong soap as soon as possible is usually quite effective, though you should get to a doctor as soon as possible.

153

To avoid the effects in the first place, it's usually enough to drape a damp cloth over the eyes, nose, and mouth.

The military are now using a new gas called CS, and a few civilian projectors also employ this compound though in small amounts. The effect is so strong that it causes psychological disorientation. One common symptom is an uncontrollable desire to run. A person who has been doused with this gas will run away even if he runs into a river or over a cliff, and there is no way to prevent this reaction once the gas has permeated the clothing. If a relative or friend is sprayed with this chemical compound and shows signs of extreme fright or terror, it's important to restrain him so that he will not injure himself by running against a wall or into a window. Hold the individual firmly or even tie him down; strip off the clothing. If possible, a shower under a very powerful showerhead helps to wash away the particles, but it will be some time before the victim will be able to regain control. Care by a doctor is essential if the symptoms continue, especially if the eyes have been seriously affected. Sometimes the gas causes psychological collapse, and symptoms include inability to avoid danger. Try to drag friends or relatives away from the gas-release point.

Bladed Weapons

You already have one effective weapon in your home—a knife. Since knives are essential tools, almost every home is equipped with an array of knives of different lengths and shapes. In many homes, a kitchen or carving knife is the only available defense weapon. Even if you do not intend to purchase a special defense weapon, it pays to know a bit about the effective use of a knife in self-defense since the need for a weapon may arise when you least expect it. Without this knowledge, a knife is quite ineffective because the untrained person almost always uses the weapon in a very awkward way. Used effectively, a knife is a very potent weapon, and a person armed with one is capable of taking care of almost all the criminal intruders he may encounter.

Because knives are necessary tools, there's no way in which legal authorities can deprive criminals of them. Actually, there's no way

154

in which law-enforcement people can deprive them of firearms either, but that's another matter. If you know how knives are used, you stand a better chance of developing an effective defense against them. At the very least, you'll be able to recognize the trained knife-fighter and distinguish him from the unskilled person who is actually rather easy to avoid or even disarm.

Most people of Anglo-Saxon, Scottish, Scandinavian, Irish, and German ancestry find knives repugnant. Persons of other racial or national strains usually do not have this same feeling. In the Japanese culture, for instance, a knife or a short sword is a very natural weapon. Though a Japanese criminal who uses a knife is prosecuted like any other felon, there's no special horror about his use of a bladed weapon. In the United States, on the other hand, stabbing or slashing another person or even "pulling a knife" in a fight is often regarded as a very despicable act. Many men have been beaten seriously because they used a knife in a brawl. Because of these instinctive feelings it's sometimes hard to teach a person to use a bladed weapon effectively despite the fact that it's a very useful defense weapon.

Figure 5-3 shows three methods of holding a knife—overhand, underhand, and what is often termed the "effective" grip.

The overhand grip is the one most often used by demented persons or the untrained. The blade protrudes downward from the hand. Almost invariably, the edge of the knife is inward. That is, the edge faces the knife-wielder. To strike, the criminal must raise his arm high in the air and he stabs downward at the target. To block a blow of this kind, it's only necessary to grasp that wrist as early as you can with an open palm and hang on. With all knife blocks, you must act quickly before the blow starts to develop speed and strength. If you do not, it may crash through your block. Almost everyone confronted with a man using a knife in this way will throw up an arm instinctively to block the blow and this is a good defense, but do it swiftly. If possible, use both arms in a cross so that the knifeman's forearm falls into the X formed by your forearms. If you are slightly built, this block will prevent an effective blow since you are using two arms while the knife wielder is

155

FIGURE 5-3: Methods of Gripping a Knife.

Overhand

Underhand

Effective

using only one. A photograph in Chapter VII shows this knife block used to stop an overhand blow with a club. With any knife block, you must be prepared to follow up. The best unarmed defense against a knife blow, after a successful block is a disabling kick. These kicks are also illustrated in Chapter VII on unarmed defense.

A knife held in the underhand grip is also ineffective. The knife crosses the palm at right angles and the blade protrudes between the root of the thumb and the forefinger. If you can administer a block or grasp the wrist, you can get in a kick or a blow and disable your attacker. The worst he can do to you if you hang onto that wrist is administer mild cuts to your wrist. Even this is not likely since it is extremely difficult for the attacker to move the knife back and forth so as to cut deeply. Several blocks for these blows are also shown in the chapter on unarmed defense.

A man who holds his weapon in the "effective" manner is usually a trained knife fighter, whether he has received his training in the Armed Services or has learned about knife fighting in criminal circles, probably from a relative. The point of the knife is directed straight at the target and the blade is held edge up. The knife forms a straight extension of the forearm and the weapon is usually held quite low, most often at belt level as shown in Figure 5-4. When a thrust is made, the arm straightens and the knifeman has the full benefit of the length of his arm and the length of the knife, something that's not true of the overhand or the underhand grip. The person using the knife selects the precise strike area and he drives his knife into it with considerable force. Since the blow is straight, it's almost impossible to block and it's almost never possible to grasp the wrist. Since the edge is up, and the knifeman is free to move his arm straight back, it doesn't make much sense to try to grasp his wrist. If you do, his reaction is most often a forceful backward movement that pulls his wrist out of your grip. The edge of the knife may then cut the web of your hand between thumb and forefinger and render it useless. To fight off a man using the "effective" grip, you need some object with which to block his blows or a weapon with which to disable him.

Under no circumstances should you resist anyone armed with

FIGURE 5-4: Effective Stance with Fighting Knife.

The left hand is used to parry or block. A thrust is made by straightening the whole arm. Note the effective grip with knife hand. If a criminal holds his knife this way, chances of successful defense are slight.

a knife as long as you feel instinctively that he will not use it. In an ordinary robbery, it's best to submit. Use blocks or any other form of resistance only if you are quite sure the intent is physical harm.

The ready position with an "effective" knife grip differs markedly from that of a fencer or a swordsman. In fencing or swordplay, the side of the body is presented to the opponent with the right foot forward and the left foot trailing. The ready position in knife fighting resembles that of a boxer. The left foot is slightly in advance of the right and the body is diagonally opposed to the target. The left hand is forward as shown in the illustration above. The left hand is not normally used to strike, but as a guard and to parry. If the knife fighter is opposed by another person armed with a knife, each individual may attempt to seize the opponent's knife wrist with his left hand or to parry blows with the forearm. Con-

FIGURE 5-5: Spanish Cape Defense Against Knife Attack.

With coat or jacket folded over the left arm, the intended victim has a slim chance of catching the criminal's blade in the cloth and swinging it aside. This defense must be followed up with an effective blow or kick such as a straight-arm to the lower throat.

siderable jockeying results. In southern Italy and Sicily, this form of fighting has been developed into a form of combat which has much sophistication and many complications.

To parry with the left hand, the knife fighter tries to knock aside his opponent's knife hand with a sideways blow while the thrust is in mid-flight. If this is accomplished, the man making the parry usually has an opportunity for a clear thrust since the original attacker finds himself in an overextended position. In the Spanish style of knife fighting, the guard hand is usually draped with a cape or jacket. If it's a rather long garment, the cloth is wrapped once around the arm, but some cloth is always allowed to hang down below the arm as shown in Figure 5-5. In the illustration, the garment is a raincoat, though a heavier topcoat or overcoat is even more effective. If the defender is skilled enough, he can oppose this hanging cloth to a knife thrust. When the attacker's blade pierces the cloth, he swings it aside to the left and thus gains an opportunity to strike himself. Even if the initial thrust pierces the cloth covering the defender's arm, a small wound usually results rather than a severe one.

The Spanish technique with a cape or other garment on the arm can be of value to an unarmed man or woman in defense, if a topcoat is being carried. If suddenly confronted by a man with a knife, try to oppose the left forearm. If it's an overhand or underhand thrust, you'll often be able to catch the blade in the cloth and immediately swing the thrust aside. If it's a thrust from the "effective" position, try to catch the blade as close as possible to your own forearm. In that position, there's not enough slack in the cloth to allow the knife to reach your body. If you have time, and the cloth of the coat is fairly thick, try to fold the coat once around your left forearm and hang onto the collar with your fingers. If it's a heavy overcoat, folding it over the arm is difficult, but usually the thickness of an overcoat will prevent a bad wound and may halt the knife entirely.

Stopping that attack is not enough—you must be prepared to follow up with kicks, effective blows with the hands, or a weapon. At least the block gives you a chance to make some sort of defense.

In the home, the best method of blocking a knife attack is to use a chair as shown in Figure 5-6. Of course, it must be a chair light enough for you to handle effectively. If you are unarmed, you must rely on the chair as your main defense. Hold it horizontally with all four legs directed at the criminal. If possible, point one leg at the eyes and keep another at the level of the upper stomach. As shown in the illustration, the back of the chair should be toward the floor so that the seat of the chair effectively shields your arms. Since the mass of the chair forms an effective block, rest assured that the wielder of the knife will not be able to reach you. His reaction, most often, will be to try to take the chair away from you with his left or guard hand. He will usually grasp a rung and jerk the chair toward himself. At this point, the slight person may lose heart because he or she feels that the chair can be easily jerked away, but this is not actually the case. Resist the pull at least twice. As the third pull comes, let the attacker have the chair by relaxing your resistance. In fact, go all out. When the criminal pulls, use the force he exerts against him—shove the chair forcefully forward,

FIGURE 5-6: Using a Chair in Knife Defense.

The attacker cannot possibly watch all four legs at the same time. If the defender can thrust a leg into the throat or groin, it may disable the attacker.

Note that the knife cannot reach its target if the defender holds it high to fend off a high attack and low to block a low thrust. The criminal will almost always attempt to pull the chair away.

Resist the first few pulls, but use the attacker's own strength against him with the next tug by thrusting the chair at him when he pulls. Aim a leg at throat or groin and follow through. If you time it right, the knifeman will go over on his back. Follow through with the chair and by kicking. Like all other defenses against deadly weapons in which the defender is not using a lethal weapon, this defense will succeed only in a small number of cases. It should be used only when there is no other choice.

161

guiding the top leg at the face or the throat. His strength plus your own will drive the leg so forcefully into him (with another leg probably in the stomach) that you will almost certainly force the attacker over backwards so that he will fall and relax his grip on the chair. At this point, drive the chair downward on top of him as powerfully as you can. Try to get a leg in the throat, stomach, or groin and keep shoving it hard. Most often, you'll put the attacker out of business. Never try to lift the chair away from him so as to swing it for a blow. The minute you lift the chair away, you're giving him the opportunity to squirm away sideways, get to his feet, and renew the attack. If possible, however, kick at kidneys, crotch or stomach while pinning the upper body with the chair. One good kick in the genitals will put out the attacker. Even though you may not be successful in causing unconsciousness or disabling the attacker, you'll often injure him so severely that you can get out of the room and lock a door behind you. This defense has often enabled an intended victim to escape and obtain a weapon. You must judge your moment very carefully, however. If the attacker shows very evident signs of confusion and grogginess, give him one last forceful jab with the chair and then run. Leave the chair where it is. Getting it out of the way will take him a second or two and that may be just enough to make escape possible.

In all these block defenses with chairs or other objects, the principle is the same. Use the object to confuse and block. If possible, use it also as a disabling weapon. Finally, leave the object with the attacker so as to encumber him. Even a large floor lamp or a footstool can be used in this way.

Though few people will make the special effort needed to obtain one, there is an effective fighting knife that can be purchased for a few dollars. It's shown in Figure 5-7 along with less effective types. This is an English Commando double-edged fighting knife that was used during World War II. Similar double-edged knives were issued to special forces of many nations. Keeping such a knife handy may save your life.

In using a knife for defense, always hold the weapon in the "effective" grip and thrust with it. The edge of a fighting knife should not be used to slash, since a slash wound will not usually

162

FIGURE 5-7: Three Types of Knives.

Left to right: Ordinary kitchen knife, two-edged commando knife, sportsman's sheath knife with single edge. Note large cross guard on commando knife.

incapacitate the criminal. The edge has only one purpose—it prevents the criminal from grasping your blade and twisting the knife out of your hand. If the criminal does manage to grasp the blade, jerk the knife quickly away from him and the blade will cut his hand and force him to let go. The double-edged fighting knife is, therefore, more effective than any knife with only one edge. A fighting knife should also have a fairly large cross guard to prevent your hand from slipping down onto the blade. Do not use a bayonet or a knife made with bayonet steel. Bayonets bend easily so that the soldier will not break his weapon. After being bent, a bayonet can be easily straightened, but this kind of steel is simply too soft to take a sharp edge.

Knives are good defense weapons if they are used with intelligence and combined with effective security hardware. If your *only* weapon is a knife, however, it is unwise to interfere with an intruder in your home. As long as that intruder keeps away from you, you are fairly safe. He is probably a thief and will not harm you unless you make some move to call the police or to apprehend him. If, however, the criminal is a rapist or is intent on some other form of dangerous physical attack, a knife will stand you in good stead. If the criminal is already in the room, secure the knife and remain quiet. If you are in bed and you have concealed the weapon near you, it's often possible to obtain the weapon without attracting attention. Lie still and wait. If the intruder comes close to the bed, and it becomes apparent that a dangerous attack or rape attempt is about to be made, it may be best to use the weapon. Whether or not to do so is a matter for you to decide in accordance with the law of self-defense as detailed in the previous chapter. If the criminal is armed, however, you must be extremely careful. If his weapon is directed toward you, it may be impossible to use your own weapon, but in this situation, using your own weapon may be the only way in which you can survive. It's up to you.

Using a knife in defense is very effective when the criminal is not already in the room. If you've provided yourself with a security room with a lock on the door and locks or locking pins in the windows, the criminal will be forced to make considerable noise when entering. If you act quickly, you may be able to get your knife ready and take up a defensive position before he succeeds in entering. Do this only if you have no safe way to escape by retreat, but if the criminal is really dangerous, and you must do so, stand alongside the opening and strike at the neck. This is one of the few times an overhand blow may be effective. Once you are quite sure that the criminal is really dangerous, you must overcome any repugnance you may have about using a bladed weapon. Strike forcefully since a superficial wound may only infuriate the criminal and cause increased danger to yourself and your family.

In other situations, the target area for an effective knife thrust should be the central trunk of the body above the navel but below the chin line. A knife thrust to the head is usually ineffective unless delivered with considerable force. A thrust in the lower abdomen or stomach is very painful and may ultimately kill, but it is not immediately disabling. To be effective, the blade must pierce a lung, the heart, or the large arteries or nerve centers in the neck. The best strike area is about the size of half a playing card, and is located above the stomach but just below the point where the two lowest ribs join with the blade angled slightly upward. If this area cannot be reached, thrust at the center of the lower throat just above the collar bone. In both these areas, there is no bone to block the knife and a hit will put the criminal out of action almost immediately. If neither of these targets is available, strike at the rib cage so as to pierce a lung. This is not as effective as hitting the other two areas, but a deep wound there will probably cause unconsciousness in a second or two. Ribs may block the blade, so it must be thrust forward with considerable force. If possible, the knife should be held with the flat of the blade parallel to the floor when striking anywhere in the rib-cage area. In this position, the blade will pass more easily between two ribs if the criminal is standing upright.

This information on good strike areas for knives is not very pleasant, but it should be carefully considered because you may be forced to use a knife in an emergency whether or not you find bladed weapons repugnant.

In the street, the most common criminal weapon is a switchblade knife. These weapons are big clasp knives equipped with a spring mechanism that opens them with a snap when a release button is pressed. Almost all switchblade knives are also equipped with a lock which holds the blade rigid once it is open so that the edge will not fold back on the user's hand. Switchblade knives are fairly good weapons, but they have defects. Commonly, lint or thread from clothing gets into the switchblade's spring or into the lock mechanism so that it will not function properly. In one case, the knife will not spring open. In the other, the blade will not stay rigid. With the switchblade, the handle must be as long as the blade. If the blade is six inches long, a good length for a fighting knife, the handle will protrude an inch or more behind the user's hand. The extension easily becomes entangled in clothing and sometimes the intended victim has been able to grasp this extension during a struggle and turn the weapon away from himself. A sheath knife carried on the belt is a much more effective weapon, but few criminals use them since they do not wish to be encumbered with the sheath. It is good evidence in court if they're caught with it.

The ice pick and the straight razor are criminal weapons that should not be used for defense. Both are really quite ineffective when used against a person who knows how to protect himself.

The ice pick is commonly used by criminals because its spike-like blade is easily concealed. The wooden handle is often cut away so as to make it smaller. The weapon's blade is pushed inside a seam in the clothing and the handle is concealed under a lapel or inside a pocket. The ice pick is ineffective for two reasons. The blade is of such a narrow diameter that it is difficult to inflict a killing wound. Since the blade has no edge, the intended victim can often grasp it and twist the weapon out of the criminal's hand. All the standard defenses against knives work well against ice picks because they have no sharp edges.

The straight razor has one disadvantage as a weapon because it has no striking point. Criminals usually hold the handle of a straight razor in the overhand grip. Then a fist is formed and the blade is folded over the fingers in front of the knuckles, edge out. The criminal punches with this weapon, using uppercuts and jabs. Most often, he will aim at the trunk of the body or the neck. Frequently, he will throw roundhouse punches in order to make long cuts. Since many of the blows are straight toward the target, they are difficult to block. After a hit, the criminal will often slide the weapon along the surface in order to make a very long cut. This is an extremely vicious form of attack and it often inflicts gaping, spectacular wounds, but these wounds seldom kill because they are not deep.

Since the blows are hard to stop, it's best to use a chair or other object to block and then to kick. Because the weapon does not penetrate deeply, a coat wrapped over the arm is effective in fending off this form of attack. Don't try to catch the blade in the cloth, however. Interpose the forearm directly in the path of the blow to block it. If the intended victim has some training in boxing, he often thinks that the attacker is merely using his fists in the conventional manner since the razor is surprisingly difficult to see.

166

Many boxers react by putting up their hands as in an ordinary fist fight. When the first cut comes in, the mistake is only too apparent.

If approached by any person who seems to want to fight with his fists, try to look at his hands to check for the straight razor, brass knuckles, large signet rings, short knives propped between the fingers of the fist with the handle in the palm, or a shoemaker's awl held in the same way. Never box with anyone holding anything suspicious in his hands. If forced into such a fight, use every possible means of forceful defense. Don't box, even though the criminal makes boxing motions—it is your least-effective defense. Use a weapon, kick, or use the edge of the hand in a karate blow.

The Club

A policeman's nightstick is quite useful if it is combined with effective security hardware. As with the knife, it's best to use the club when a dangerous criminal is in an awkward position climbing through a window or other narrow opening.

Police nightsticks or batons are sold by many military surplus dealers and can also be purchased in many police-supply stores. For indoor use, buy one that is between 16 and 26 inches long. A shorter club deprives you of some reach and one that is longer than 26 inches is awkward to handle. Longer police batons—up to three and four feet—are intended for outdoor use in riot control. These longer sticks are usually wielded with two hands, and this makes it impossible to hold another weapon in the other hand.

I would not purchase a short, lead-loaded flexible club. These are known as blackjacks and they are intended to be carried in the pocket and are therefore much too short for anything except a sneak attack.

A baton with three or four ounces of lead in the end is deadly. Some police batons intended for riot-control are deliberately made of light, easily shattered wood. The theory is that the stick will break if it is used with too much force and that therefore it will not usually kill. These sticks are used when the police merely wish to control disorderly people. In self-defense, on the contrary, you act only when facing a dangerous criminal, and these breakable sticks should be avoided. Unfortunately, many dealers do not know

167

about this type of stick and will sell them as ordinary nightsticks. Therefore you should test any stick that you buy by hitting a tree forcefully with it several times. If a non-breakable stick is not available in your area, a good bench carpenter can easily turn one for you on a lathe. White oak, teak, or rosewood are the best woods, but any heavy, close-grained hardwood will do. Test the stick even if you have one made especially for your use. Some pieces of timber will split even though the surface shows no sign of weakness.

Police sticks have a heavy leather thong attached at a point just in front of the grip. Many people loop the thong around the wrist. This should be avoided. The thong is very strong and if a criminal succeeds in grasping the baton, he will often be able to jerk you off your feet. To use the thong properly, it's only necessary to put the loop around your thumb as shown in Figure 5-8. With the doubled thong leading across the back of your hand, grasp the handle of the stick and the thong in your palm. This gives you the necessary whip provided by the extra tension of the leather or web thong, and yet you can let go of the baton if that proves necessary. In a dangerous situation, let go of the weapon entirely and the thong will slide off your thumb. Of course, if this happens it's best to get out of there as quickly as possible since the weapon may be used against you, but at least, you're still on your feet and can do so. If you have a second follow-up weapon and the criminal is very dangerous, this is the time to use it.

The primary strike area for a wooden stick is the head and the back of the neck. Sufficiently hard blows in either area will completely disable or kill the criminal. Sometimes, however, these target areas cannot be reached, particularly if you are facing an alert criminal. In such circumstances, blows to the bony parts of the forearms, the elbows, the wrists, the kneecaps, or shins will cause sufficient pain so that the criminal will be thrown off balance and then a more effective blow can be struck. Sometimes, it's possible to swing a longer stick in a downward sweeping arc so that the tip catches the criminal on the rise in the genitals, though this is actually an easy blow to block. As a surprise tactic, use the stick to thrust. The "effective" grip of the knifeman is the best. Direct a forceful thrust at the base of the throat or at the area just below

168

FIGURE 5-8: Looping a Police Nightstick.

The thong should not be looped around the wrist. If this is done, the stick may be grasped, and it's possible for a person to pull the user right off his feet because he cannot let go. The loop should go around the thumb as in the top illustration. Then turn thumb down and grasp stick. Bottom illustration shows proper use of thong—to give leverage and a firm grip that can be released merely by opening the hand. A club or riot baton is particularly effective if used against an intruder who is halfway through a broken window or shattered door.

the center of the rib cage. Sometimes, these thrusts can be gotten home when a wide swing is impossible because the criminal has his arms up ready to block the blow. Usually, these thrusts will not cause unconsciousness, but they will discomfort the criminal so much that a follow-up can then be directed at the head or neck.

Police manuals are full of methods of using a stick to strike disabling blows that will not kill. For instance, a blow that breaks the collar bone will completely disable the arm on that side. You can also thrust a club at the face to throw a criminal off balance. With the thrusting weapon only a few inches away from eyes, the bridge of the nose, and the teeth, all but the most determined criminals will retreat. These methods of using a club are very useful for police who are attempting to control people who are not really dangerous. In addition, the police always have firearms available as follow-up weapons. But, in defending yourself, it's best to avoid such tactics except when forced to use them because more vital areas cannot be reached. You should use weapons of any kind only against dangerous criminals. Therefore, there is no need for harassing techniques intended to make the criminal retire. If the criminal is really dangerous, you want to put him out of action as quickly as possible. Remember that a blow to the head requires considerable force to kill. Usually, it will only cause unconsciousness, but as with all other *self-defense* weapons, you must be prepared to use them forcefully if a really dangerous situation develops.

Defense against clubs consists of blocks and follow-ups much the same as those used against knife attacks. Defense against clubs is easier because the weapon is not as deadly. As with knife defense, try to block *before* the blow acquires sufficient force to break through your guard. Both forearms held in a cross will stop almost every blow if applied early enough. This defense is shown photographically in Chapter VII. The defense with a coat wrapped around the arm or a chair used as a block are also very effective. As with knife attack, it is sometimes possible to grasp the weapon. In this case, twist it against the user's thumb and you will easily remove it from his hands, as shown in Figure 5-9. As with any other defense against weapons, you must be prepared to follow up quickly with a disabling blow.

170

FIGURE 5-9: Club Defense—Twist Against Thumb.

These photographs show one club defense. Again, this type of defense should only be used if the intended victim can find no other way out of the situation. Against a knife or club, always twist against the thumb. You are using two hands and arms against the attacker's thumb, and even a slight person can disarm a heavyweight, *if* the weapon can be grasped. Note that the defender's right thumb is *down* because of her cross grip. In a really dangerous situation, this defense can be used against a knife even though the palm may be cut. For other knife and club defense, see the chapter on unarmed defense.

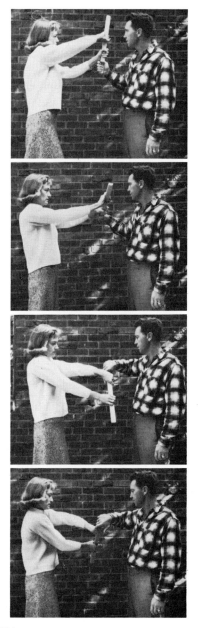

The Electric Baton

A new weapon is being sold to civilians as a defense device. The electric baton is a club or police billy made of metal which contains two or more batteries and shock electrodes. By closing a switch resembling the ones used in flashlights, the user can administer a painful electric shock.

This is a police weapon and should not be used for self-defense no matter what claims the advertiser makes. In self-defense, you do not need such a device because you should call the police in situations not involving physical danger. If, on the other hand, you are up against a really dangerous criminal, the electric shock baton is not powerful enough to disable him. The pain of the shock is only as severe as a bee or wasp sting, and it will not disable even though some advertisers claim that it will. On the other hand, if the person against whom it is used has a bad heart, it may kill when the legal circumstances do not justify it. In addition, some people have a tremendous natural tolerance of electric shock, and the mild current may not affect them in any way. It would be somewhat disconcerting to jab an intruder with the electric shock rod only to have him calmly remove the weapon from your hands and clout you over the head with it. The shock does not pass through heavy clothing. If the shock is not felt, you are merely poking someone with a stick—a procedure that will probably cause injury to yourself. The electric baton is a specialized device intended for use in situations that do not arise in legitimate self-defense.

The Molotov Cocktail

A weapon new to the American scene made its appearance during the racial disturbances of 1964 and 1965. It consists of a bottle half full of gasoline with a twist of cloth inserted in the neck. Just before the weapon is thrown, the cloth is ignited and the missile is aimed so that it bursts against a hard surface. When the gasoline fumes reach the smouldering cloth after the bottle breaks, a flash of flame results which may ignite a wooden building. The missile will also ignite even if the bottle does not break since the gasoline

172

runs out of the neck and reaches the burning cloth if the bottle falls in a horizontal position.

The best home defense against the weapon is a brick or brick-veneer wall, metal-framed windows, metal roof trim and rain gutters, heavy window screening, and if the building is wooden, asbestos or other fireproof shingles. In other words, every exterior surface should be constructed with fireproof materials. If you have some choice of the place where you live, look for this form of construction, particularly if you are taking up residence in a racially-troubled city. Negro householders especially need this form of protection, since Negro homes are often burned in the riots. So far, the rioters have paid most of their attention to commercial establishments, but many private homes have been burned to the ground, and undoubtedly these attacks are very dangerous to those who live near commercial establishments.

Do everything you can to fireproof the exterior of the building in which you live. For instance, some buildings have brick exterior walls but they have exposed rafter ends and wooden rain gutters. These should be covered with fireproof materials and the wooden gutters should be replaced with aluminum or fiber glass. Every effort should be made to clean up leaves, broken lumber, and other inflammable trash that tends to accumulate next to the walls of buildings. It's also wise to remove stones and other large, hard objects lying close to the house since this may prevent many of the missiles from breaking. Remove inflammable window curtains—use fiber glass fabrics if curtains or drapes are desired. Wooden doors should be covered with sheet metal at least $\frac{1}{16}$th of an inch thick.

Even if you live in a house or apartment building with fireproof exterior surfaces, there's still danger that the Molotov cocktail may be hurled through a window or door. This is particularly true in extremely hot weather when doors and windows are left open and only thin copper, aluminum, or plastic screens cover the openings as protection against insects. A heavy bottle or mason jar filled with gasoline often breaks through light screening, particularly the new lightweight screens constructed of plastic filaments. Rocks, bricks, and other heavy objects may be used to pierce the screen and then a Molotov cocktail can be hurled through the opening.

Warfare in Israel demonstrated that the best protection against grenades and Molotov cocktails is heavy wire screening, or still better, pierced-metal grillwork over every opening. Keep the glass windows closed behind such screens in times of danger since the flaming gasoline may spill out of the bottle and spray into the room if the glass window is open. One of the better materials is heavy galvanized wire screening with one-quarter inch mesh. This should not be used with a wooden frame since the wooden sash material may take fire. In the United States, screens with metal frames are not normally manufactured with heavy screening of this type. To protect your windows and doors, you should wire the heavy screening over the light insect screening. If you do not have metal-framed insect screens, they're a worthwhile investment if you have the slightest reason to expect this form of attack. With a heavy metal snips, cut a piece of heavy screening to fit nicely over the ordinary insect screening. Use copper bell wire, aluminum wire, or even steel to weave the heavy screening to the light insect screening all around the edges. Then wind the binding wire through both sets of screens and take several turns right around the aluminum frames. Take a turn through both screens and around the frame every half inch or so. You need considerable strength to ward off heavy objects. Binding the wire around the frame may not look very pretty, but it may save your life. After the emergency is over, you can investigate neater ways of fastening the heavy screening to the frame.

The heavy screen unit should be mounted in the window so that it can be easily removed from the inside. In the event that fire does start inside the building, you may find it necessary to exit through a screened opening. Secure the window with hooks and eyes so that the hooks can be knocked out of the eyes from the inside but cannot be reached from the outside. This type of screening will keep thrown dynamite bombs out of a building too.

If you cannot cover the exterior of the building with fireproof siding or shingles, fireproof paints provide some protection, though they will ultimately peel under strong heat. Several coats will at least inhibit the fire. Liquid fiber glass used for covering boats and

174

fiber glass fabric is a worthwhile investment. In covering a house with fireproof material, work from the foundation upward and also start near any very hard surface and work away from it. For instance, if one part of a wooden wall incorporates a few feet of decorative stonework against which a bottle would break, cover the wood near the stonework first.

If you can keep all windows screened and the glass closed behind the screens during troubled times, you're increasing your degree of protection, but this is impossible during the summer in hot areas. Room air conditioners, however, make it possible to seal the house entirely.

In areas where riots may occur, however, it's best to have 10 or 12 ordinary water pails filled with sand placed at various points around the house. The sand should be fine-grained and free-flowing so that it will spread when dropped on a burning surface. God forbid that you should ever need them, but God forbid also that your family should be harmed because you don't have them. If flaming gasoline flows over a flammable surface, the best remedy is smothering the flame with sand. To do this, fling the bucket of sand onto the *base* of the flame. You should also have a long-handled hoe which can be used to spread the sand over the burning surface. By using the hoe to work the sand from place to place, you can smother flame over a large area.

If the walls ignite (unlikely with plasterboard or lath-and-plaster walls), try to fling the sand against the root of the flame. Of course, you can't work with a hoe on a vertical surface, but the flung sand may smother the flame. If this doesn't work, one recourse is to try to smother the flame with a mattress or several heavy blankets folded together. Press the bedding against the flame and hold it there until the fire is extinguished. This will also work on a floor if sand is not available. If the cloth pad ignites, you may possibly be able to throw it out of a doorway before it can cause serious damage.

Never use water to fight a gasoline fire. The water merely picks up the burning gasoline and floats it across a flat surface to another place where flames will again break out. The only effective use of water is from a high-pressure hose that puts out such a tremendous volume that it smothers the flame through sheer force. Ordinary water pressure in the home will not usually accomplish this unless the amount of flaming gasoline is very small. After the gasoline itself has burned out, however, water can be used effectively.

Chemical fire extinguishers are effective against gasoline fires, but they must be large and they must operate at quite high pressures. The best fire extinguisher for this purpose is a large commercial type intended for chemical and petroleum fires. These extinguishers are usually equipped with a sealed pressure cylinder and a hose with a cut-off nozzle under the control of the operator. With this type of extinguisher, you can put out a certain amount of liquid or foam to extinguish a small fire and then cut off the flow, reserving the rest of the charge for a second or third outbreak if more missiles are thrown. Ordinary chemical extinguishers of the acid-and-base type are one-shot affairs. Once you activate them by turning them upside down, the entire contents spray out of the hose and there is no way in which you can turn them off so as to retain part of the charge. If an extinguisher does not have a hand-operated cut-off nozzle, it's usually a one-shot apparatus.

Even if you do buy a large, commercial, chemical fire extinguisher suited for gasoline fires, it's probably best to keep a few buckets of sand available for that awful moment when the chemical runs out. A pile of sand in the cellar or yard is very reassuring even if you have the best extinguisher.

To sum up defense against Molotov cocktails:

1. Fireproof exterior surfaces.
2. Remove inflammable trash around the house.
3. Remove inflammable curtains and drapes.
4. Cover all openings with heavy wire screening heavily fastened to metal sash.
5. Provide yourself with one or more large-capacity, heavy-duty chemical fire extinguishers, several buckets of sand, and a long-handled hoe.

It is a tragedy of our times that most of the private homes burned in the recent riots have been occupied by Negroes. Middle-class Negroes who can afford to live in single dwellings need good self-protection equipment against the Negro arsonist because a rioting mob does not always discriminate when destroying property.

Another type of arson is becoming common. Recently, Newark, New Jersey and Darien, Connecticut, have had several cases. In these crimes, a full garbage or trash barrel is used as a weapon. In the Newark cases, the trash barrels were set afire and placed on the wooden porches of Negro homes. In Darien, the smouldering trash barrels or garbage cans were placed near the wooden walls of white, suburban dwellings. Whether these crimes are the work of misguided teenagers or insane people is not known, and at least a few of these crimes may be committed by racists. Of course, the criminal hopes that the authorities will believe that the trash was set afire by accident, and no one knows how many cases reported as accidental fires are really cases of arson. To guard against this type of crime, don't put your garbage or trash outside your building until a short time before it is due to be picked up. If, however, this type of crime or other forms of arson are happening in your home community, the equipment described for use against Molotov cocktails can be an excellent investment.

TACTICS, THE SECURITY ROOM, AND WEAPONS

It is apparent that bladed weapons, clubs, tear gas, and several other weapons are much less effective than firearms.

In spite of the effectiveness of guns, the author does not advocate the widespread use of firearms in self-defense by persons who do not know how to use them safely. If you have no firearms-safety training, and feel you must have a gun for safety you should take a course in gun safety. These courses are briefly described in the next chapter.

The less effective weapons may also be dangerous to the user because they are less capable of putting a really dangerous criminal out of action quickly. It's a fact that these less effective weapons are actually more dangerous *to the criminal*. To use a knife or a club, for instance, the defender must be close to the criminal. If the defender fails to use his weapon effectively, the criminal has the opportunity to grasp the weapon or the user's arms or body. Acting in self-defense, the only recourse then is to use the knife or club

177

in the most forceful manner possible, and the criminal may be injured or killed.

With a gun, the defender can keep his or her distance from the criminal's reach. The sight of the gun will immobilize most criminals, and if you're several feet away, there's little chance of an attack unless the criminal is also armed with a gun. In using a firearm, always keep away from the criminal. Never move up close enough so that your gun barrel could be grasped. Even when holding a gun on a criminal, never attempt to disarm him or search him for weapons. The best procedure is to order the person to face away from you and to place his folded hands on the back of his neck. Keep your distance, get someone to call the police, or hold your weapon in one hand and use the phone yourself. As long as you maintain your distance, you've fairly safe.

With the other weapons described in this chapter, you cannot "cover" a criminal at a distance. These weapons can only be used as last-ditch devices to disable a dangerous person who is attacking. If you rely on the less effective weapons, you are confined mostly to inactive defense. You must rely mostly on security hardware for protection and use the weapon when the criminal is crawling through a window or broken door. If at all possible, you must take the criminal at a disadvantage.

If you use the less-effective devices, it's extremely important to plan your defense. For instance, if there are children in the home, you might lay out a set plan of action as follows. When you first become aware of the criminal: (1) Gather up the children and retire to the security room. (2) Lock the door behind you. (3) Make your defense weapon ready for use. (4) Place yourself beside the door or window through which the criminal might possibly enter but out of the line of fire. (5) Telephone the police (a long extension cord is helpful). (6) Warn the criminal that you have a weapon and that the police have been called. These security steps will work only in certain circumstances. Your own particular situation may call for modifications, but you should be aware in advance of what you will do if faced with an intrusion by a criminal.

You can, of course, threaten an intruder by telling him you have a gun, speaking from behind the locked door of the security room.

But, if circumstances call for it, you can also move out of the security room with a gun and *seek out* the criminal. If, for instance, you have not had time to move children to the security room or to lock the door to their room, it may be necessary to move through your home looking for the criminal. If you have a dependable firearm and know how to use it, you can do this with some confidence. With the less-effective weapons, it is very dangerous to approach a criminal. He may be more heavily armed than yourself and may be more effective with his weapon. With a gun, however, you are absolutely sure that you have the most effective weapon available. In your own home, you are at a great advantage against a criminal. You know every turning and every corner. You probably even know which boards in the floor squeak and which treads in the staircase make a noise when someone steps on them. It is possible, therefore, to undertake active defense with a firearm, though you should do so only in extreme circumstances.

No set of tactics for the use of weapons in defense will fit all circumstances, but a few hints may be helpful. Bear in mind that you must plan your course of action *in advance* to meet the exact circumstances.

Don't turn on the lights near you if you feel that someone is entering your home. If you do, you let the criminal know that you are aware of him, and if he is really dangerous this may result in an attack. The nearby light usually illuminates you and leaves the criminal in darkness. Often, you will be unable to see him, but he will have a very clear view of you, probably against a bright light. A remote light, under your control, may be a solution. Locate a light with a long cord at some distance from your bed and splice a switch into the cord close to the bed. When you hear a noise at night or think that trouble may be developing, click the switch and the light will go on some distance away, perhaps in another room. This will attract the criminal's attention to that location and may even frighten him off. At least this move will give you some time in which to lock doors or to get a weapon ready. It's still better to have the weapon ready first and then click on the light.

In the event that you are obliged to go looking for the intruder, take your time unless children or others are threatened in another

179

part of the house or apartment. Remember that you can move fairly silently and surely in the dark through your own home. The criminal is likely to make a considerable amount of noise and may even become entangled in your furniture, the washing machine, the baby's playpen, or any of the other numerous booby traps in the average home.

Place yourself in an unlikely position and wait there. For instance, if you hold your weapon ready and wait in the corner of a room with walls at your back, you can only be approached from one direction. Stay still and wait. The criminal will be obliged to move about the house in the dark unless he wishes to turn on a light. If he does turn on a light, you can easily use a firearm against him, provided the situation is dangerous enough to justify that action in self-defense. Even with less effective weapons, he'll be obliged to approach you at a disadvantage unless, of course, he has a gun. Sometimes people have followed this passive course of defense only to find that the criminal quietly retired when he found that his intended victim was alert and ready to use a weapon.

If the lights remain out and you hear the criminal moving about, he may stumble on you, but you'll be able to hear him approaching—a considerable advantage. In the daytime, remaining still may also be advantageous. It's surprising, but a person lying full length on the floor or even standing still in a corner is quite difficult to see unless his or her clothing contrasts sharply with the surroundings. Movement is the real telltale, as any veteran of armed combat will tell you. As long as you remain quiet with your weapon, you'll probably see the criminal before he sees you. The principle is always the same—never move against a criminal unless you are forced to do so. Stay still, weapon ready, and let him come to you if escape is not possible.

At night, however, you may sometimes be forced to go looking for the intruder, particularly if there is danger to sleeping children. Many people would use a flashlight in such circumstances. If you think about it for an instant, you'll realize that a moving flashlight pinpoints your location for the intruder. Avoid using the light if possible. If forced to use one, make sure that you hold it away from your body. Hold the light in your left hand, your weapon in

180

FIGURE 5-10: Methods of Holding a Shoulder Gun and Flashlight.

At left, stock is held under the arm and firmly clamped against the side. At right, butt is braced against hip while flashlight is held away from body to deceive attacker as to the defender's actual position. Both methods should only be used by those who are sure they can withstand the recoil of the gun. The weapon is a double-barreled shotgun with 22-inch barrels.

the other. Turn the light on for short intervals and move as soon as you turn it off. If the criminal is armed with a gun, he'll fire at the light, thinking it marks your location. If you're holding it at arm's length when you turn it on, he'll probably miss, though most criminals are such poor marksmen they often hit several feet away from the point of aim.

If you're using a handgun, it's easy to hold it in your right hand and your light in the left. Even with a shotgun or rifle, however, you can hold the light in one hand, well away from your body, and manage the gun entirely with the other hand if you're strong enough and in good physical condition. Place the butt against your hip as shown in Figure 5-10 and hold the pistol grip of the shoulder gun firmly with your gun hand. If the weapon is a short-barreled shotgun equipped with a rubber butt plate, it can be fired quite accurately from this position with little discomfort. The spread of shot from this type of gun (see next chapter) makes extremely accurate marksmanship unnecessary, and the rubber recoil pad cushions the recoil. Turn the light out and dodge away after each shot.

If you hear an intruder outside your home, don't go looking for him. As long as he's outside the building, you're comparatively safe unless, of course, there is a riot in progress or arson and bombing are possible. With an ordinary criminal, remain indoors, get your weapon ready, call the police, and wait. If the criminal makes a determined attempt to break in, use your weapon, if possible after giving warning.

During a riot when Molotov cocktails and even explosives may be used, your defenses must be more active. How active is up to you, determined by the law of self-defense as described in the previous chapter. A strong effort may be made by several persons to break down your defenses, and it's very difficult to use weapons from inside the building since there will be many blind spots. Going outside your home when armed in order to defend it against arsonists and bombers, however, is very dangerous since it may involve you with a crowd of rioters, and it may also lead to disadvantageous legal hearings of the type described previously. Yet, if someone is attempting to burn your house down or plant a bomb under it, I wouldn't worry too much about being prosecuted for the use of weapons in defense. You really do not have much choice if there are innocent people inside the building, even though there may be trouble later.

Afterward

Weapons should not be used except in the most desperate circumstances when you have *no other choice*. Yet, once you have used a weapon, you will probably be obliged to go through one or more hearings to establish the fact that you really did not have any other choice, that in fact, you were forced to use a weapon in order to prevent death or serious bodily harm.

The police usually keep fairly detailed records of incoming calls. If that record contains a notation that a call for assistance was received *prior* to the use of weapons, the claim of self-defense is stronger. To further establish self-defense, it's very useful to have a photographic record. Of course, you won't be operating a camera at the time of the trouble, but immediately afterward, it's an excellent idea to take a few photographs, particularly of broken windows, smashed doors or other forced openings through which the criminal entered or tried to enter. If the criminal was carrying a weapon, burglar tools, a Molotov cocktail, or explosives, take several pictures of them, preferably with the criminal in the same pictures. Under no circumstances touch the implements or the criminal, since the police are very touchy about disturbed evidence. File the photographs away for the time when the hearing comes up. They may stand you in very good stead.

When the police arrive, tell the story of your actions in detail, truthfully, and frankly. Once the story is told, don't allow searching questions to throw you off. Police are justifiably anxious to test the statements made under such circumstances, and if you allow them to fluster you, they may become extremely doubtful about your statements. If newspaper reporters appear, tell them the same facts and cooperate with them to the fullest possible extent. As a favor, ask the reporters to refrain from publishing your address. Try also to prevent publication of photographs of yourself or of any member of your family. It's best to prevent anyone from taking such photographs in the first place, and the best way to do this is to remain in a dimly-lighted position when speaking to reporters. If you see a flash camera, of course, it's best to step behind a door or some other obstruction.

Most newspapermen know that many crimes have a non-monetary motive; instead, the criminal acts out of a feeling of hatred for the intended victim's race or nationality, though he also hopes to pick up a few valuables while working off his hatreds. Newsmen realize that many rapists are in reality working off hatred for a racial group through sexual assault. Therefore, newspapers have recently begun to refrain from publishing the home addresses of policemen involved in the repression of riots or action against such groups as the Ku Klux Klan. A private citizen who uses weapons in defense needs the same protection afforded the law-enforcement officer, and a decent newspaperman will cooperate if you state your case intelligently. At the time of the hearing, your name and home address may appear in a newspaper, but by that time tempers have usually cooled. Nevertheless, I would consider moving to another address after an affair of this kind on the off chance that there may still be bad feelings. The use of weapons in self-defense involves some serious consequences, and the repeated warnings in this book, that they should be used only when there is no other choice, are to be taken very seriously.

In many jurisdictions, a hearing before a coroner's jury or a grand jury will determine the circumstances under which you used weapons. In many towns, this hearing amounts to ten minutes of testimony and an almost automatic verdict of self-defense provided that is the actual case. In other jurisdictions, the hearing is more lengthy and testimony is more complicated. If you are involved in one of these hearings, present your testimony truthfully and if you have acted in accordance with the law, a verdict of self-defense is assured. It's extremely important to obtain a verdict of self-defense since you may be sued for damages or even prosecuted under the criminal law if it is determined that you used weapons prematurely, stupidly, or with criminal intent. Again—use weapons only when you have no other choice.

The police will probably seize any weapon used in self-defense as evidence for the hearing. They have the legal right to do so, but this leaves you defenseless until the weapon is returned as it *must* be. For this reason, it's best to maintain a spare or two in the home. If *all* your weapons are seized, even though such actions by the police are not legal, buy another as soon as you can. You do not wish to be defenseless at this particular time.

PREVENTION OF ACCIDENTS

Dangerous weapons may constitute a hazard to the members of your family if they are not carefully maintained and used. Yet, you should remember that many homes are already equipped with dangerous weapons—knives, hedge clippers, meat cleaver, hammers, crowbar, pickaxe. In many homes, particularly in the suburbs, a firearm that's well cared for and kept out of the hands of children is often the *least* dangerous implement in the home since it can be kept unloaded.

If you practice to achieve proficiency and speed with your weapon, you may use it too quickly when an innocent person appears unexpectedly. This type of accident is well illustrated by this case, reported by the Associated Press in May, 1966:

> Indianapolis, May 9 (AP)—An 18-year-old high school girl who arose before dawn to quiet the family dog was shot to death in the kitchen today when her father mistook her for a burglar. ... [the girl] cried, "Oh, Daddy!" then collapsed and died. Her father ... was sobbing beside the body when the police arrived. ... [he] said he had heard a noise in the kitchen, saw a figure silhouetted against the back door, and fired.

To guard against this type of accident, you should try to maintain a fairly orderly household. In particular, you should always know where your teen-age children are and what they are doing so that they do not unexpectedly crawl through a window late one night after an illegitimate absence. To protect children, it's a good procedure to be aware of their activities under any circumstances. Make it clear that it's best to arouse the whole household when returning unexpectedly, particularly at night. In fact, make it an unbreakable rule that this must be done by ringing the doorbell or knocking loudly. The teen-ager's own latchkey may be a badge of maturity, but it shouldn't be given to unreliable adolescents. In times of extreme danger, it's worth your trouble to arrange a family signal. This sounds melodramatic, but it's a very useful device if you are to use weapons when they are needed most desperately. A particular whistle or humming sound, known only to members of your own family can prevent a tragedy. Remember that if you are involved in riots similar to the ones that shook Los Angeles, New York, Chicago, Springfield, Newark, and other cities in recent years, you may need to set up a system of family self-protection almost as complicated as that of a small military organization. Probably

185

you will not need to do so, but if circumstances require it, make sure that you do.

If you take the proper precautions, weapons can be a source of security for yourself and your family. If you do not, they can be a constant source of worry. Learn to live with your weapons as necessary tools of the household. It was not so long ago that no home could long exist without adequate defenses, and this is rapidly becoming true again in many communities. Don't use deadly weapons unless you must, but if you must, use them knowing that you are acting strictly in legal self-defense. If you ever have to do so, you will have a clear conscience, and you'll also have the very great satisfaction of knowing that you contributed something to the defense of the country against criminals and degenerates who are just as dangerous as any foreign enemy. Self-defense by the citizen is an American tradition, and it is worth preserving.

CHAPTER VI

Firearms

IT is not enough to "... buy a gun and keep it at home ..." as one popular writer advised recently, following an atrocious rape-murder in his city.

If you buy the wrong gun and do not know how to use it safely, you will be more of a menace than most criminals. Some firearms are designed for long-range shooting, and their great range and power of penetration make them hazardous for use in self-defense.

This book does not advocate use of firearms by persons who do not have adequate training, but there are millions of Armed Services veterans who do have gun-safety training, and courses in gun safety are regularly sponsored by the National Rifle Association, a private organization of gun owners and sportsmen which is recognized by the Federal Government. This organization has 775,000 individual members and more than 12,000 affiliated rifle and pistol clubs. The organization is so well respected that the Congress, through the National Board for the Promotion of Rifle Practice and the Director of Civilian Marksmanship, authorizes the issue of ammunition to clubs affiliated with the NRA and enrolled with the Director of Civilian Marksmanship.

The purpose of the Civilian Marksmanship Program, and the cooperation between the Government and NRA, is the development of marksmanship proficiency among law-abiding citizens as an aid to the national defense.

187

I strongly urge you to join the NRA if you have little knowledge of firearms. In order to join, you must certify that you have never been convicted of a crime of violence and you must pledge that you will fulfill the obligations of good sportsmanship and good citizenship. Each candidate for membership must be recommended in writing by a member in good standing, a public official, or a commissioned officer in the United States Armed Forces. If you wish to join, send $5.00 to the National Rifle Association, 1600 Rhode Island Ave., N.W., Washington, D.C., 20036. The association will send you an application for membership which must be filled out and returned.

The advantages of membership are many. The organization will introduce you to local gun clubs, and these clubs are usually anxious to acquire members recommended by the association. Joining a local gun club will give you access to a target range and other facilities which may include the services of an instructor. The NRA also trains firearms instructors. These NRA Certified Marksmanship Instructors give courses in firearms safety and rifle, pistol, and shotgun marksmanship. A person interested in self-defense should first complete an NRA firearms safety course before undertaking marksmanship training.

The training given to members of the Armed Services and to those who take the NRA course, however, does not include much on the civilian use of firearms in legal self-defense. Therefore a brief treatment of the subject is given here. If you are not a veteran with adequate gun-safety training, take the NRA course first and then go on to apply the instructions in this chapter. Armed Services veterans will find that they are unfamiliar with much of this material since the military uses automatic and semi-automatic weapons that are not suited to self-defense, and much military training is devoted to good marksmanship at long ranges. Self-defense shooting is usually done at ranges of only a few feet.

Principal Types of Firearms

Shotguns, rifles, and pistols are generally available to civilians, though in many areas you must have a license to carry a concealed firearm or even to possess a pistol in the home. Possession of shotguns and rifles is legal everywhere in the United States—a right guaranteed to us by the Federal Constitution, though in Philadelphia, the shoulder weapon must be registered with the police as previously noted. However, a group of Federal laws is enforced in a way that makes it illegal for the civilian to possess fully automatic firearms (machine guns), shotguns with barrels shorter than 18 inches, and ordinary rifles with barrels shorter than 16 inches. In measuring the length of a barrel, a cleaning rod is inserted and shoved all the way back to the closed breech. This is an important point since the shorter the barrel, the better the weapon for self-defense. Fully automatic weapons continue to fire shot after shot as long as the trigger is held back. In other words, you may not possess a machine gun, a machine pistol, or fully automatic firearms of any kind.

A modern rifle fires a single solid projectile each time the trigger is pulled. The weapon is called a rifle because it has spiral grooves cut into the inside of the barrel which spin the bullet so that it remains stable in flight. A pistol, of course, is merely a short, rifled weapon intended to be used in one hand. For this reason, it is often called "handgun." There are two kinds of handguns—revolvers and automatics. The familiar cowboy pistol is a good example of the revolver. It has a rotating cylinder into which the cartridges are loaded. The cylinder is rotated to bring cartridges behind the barrel one at a time for firing.

An automatic pistol should actually be called a semi-automatic weapon since the trigger must be pulled for each shot. However, after a shot is fired, the force of recoil brings a new cartridge from the magazine into position for firing. In other words, with an automatic pistol the shooter merely pulls the trigger and the weapon automatically inserts the next shell in the firing chamber.

Weapons fired from the shoulder can be either manually operated like a revolver or they can be automatic. That is, one can purchase automatic shotguns and rifles that fire one shot for each pull of the trigger, or one can buy rifles and shotguns that require the shooter to work the mechanism to bring each new shell into firing position.

The shotgun does not have rifling in the barrel because it is almost always used to fire a charge of small shot rather than a single, solid projectile. Shot is available in many different sizes from dust-like particles to loads consisting of only nine lead balls. Shotguns are quite often referred to as smoothbores because they do not have spiral grooves in their barrels.

The Shotgun—Most Effective Defense Weapon

Many people jump to the conclusion that a pistol is the most effective defense weapon because it is short and handy, but a shotgun is also quite effective. In the hands of a rather inexperienced shooter, a shotgun is actually more effective than any handgun because it fires a charge of projectiles rather than a single bullet. The charge of shot covers a fairly large area and therefore expert marksmanship is seldom required. If you load a shotgun with cartridges containing several large balls, you're using a very effective weapon. A hit with even one or two of the nine balls in a 12 gauge, 00-buckshot load, for instance, will disable or kill. With a handgun, you must make a vital hit with that single projectile. It takes time and practice to develop enough skill at one-handed shooting to aim and fire a handgun effectively. With the long, wooden shoulder stock of a shotgun, you have a weapon that is more easily aimed even if you use it with only one hand while holding a flashlight or some other defense device in the other. The greater length gives the eye and the hand more perspective and therefore the weapon is easier to aim. Not that you can simply point a shotgun in the general direction of the target and pull the trigger. The spread of shot is not that wide, but with a shotgun you do have a much better chance of hitting than you do with any weapon firing a single bullet.

Shotguns are available in many different calibers from .410 gauge to 10 gauge. You need a fairly powerful shotgun if you're to use it in defense, but you do not want a weapon that's too powerful to handle. A 10-gauge shotgun is simply too much for most women and many men to handle. It's large, heavy, and the recoil of a shot is quite punishing. The smaller gauges such as the .410 and the 28-gauge may be useful in an emergency, but they're really

190

too small. Twenty gauge, 16, and 12 are effective for defense. The 12 has the largest bore diameter of the three (about three-quarters of an inch), and I would recommend it as the best choice for defense. If you're buying a new gun, buy a 12 gauge. If you already have a 20 or a 16, and like the weapon, stick with it since guns of these gauges are only slightly less effective.

It's sometimes thought that the recoil of a shotgun is too much for a woman or slight man, but many slightly built women are very good clay-pigeon shots with big-bore shotguns and fire hundreds of shots in a single day. If you are slight, make sure that your defense gun is equipped with a rubber recoil pad on the butt. Any gunsmith will install one for a few dollars. It reduces the jar from a shot to a soft push. You should also learn to hold the gun firmly so that it does not slam back hard against you. In buying a defense gun, steer clear of the ultra-lightweight weapons intended for sportsmen who carry guns long distances and therefore do not like heavy weapons. Lightweight guns kick more. The heavier the gun, the less recoil, and if you hold a fairly heavy 12-gauge gun firmly and use a recoil pad, you will hardly notice the recoil. However, physically incapacitated people should not use big-bore guns.

A 12-gauge gun has a bore diameter larger than a 16 or a 20, and therefore more shot can be loaded into it—an important consideration when you are firing buckshot loads containing a limited number of balls. In addition, the larger capacity of the 12-gauge cartridge allows more tear gas to be loaded into the shell. In the United States, many more varieties of loads are made for the 12 than for any other gun.

Almost any 12-gauge shotgun will be excellent for defense, but if you have time to shop around or to have the weapon altered, there's a special type that's exactly right for self-defense, and you should make an effort to obtain this type of gun.

For quick handling, the shotgun should have a short barrel. Inside the home, the chief difficulty in using a long weapon rather than a pistol is encountered when the shooter turns a corner. The muzzle of the weapon should precede the shooter around the corner and the gun should be kept level so that it is always ready to be fired. If the weapon is too long, the tendency is to point the gun toward the ceiling or floor when negotiating corners and turnings. Most sporting shotguns are manufactured with barrels from 26 to 30 inches long, far too long for effective indoor use.

In buying a shotgun for self-defense, therefore, try to get a riot gun like those manufactured for the police. These guns usually have 18- or 20-inch barrels and most of them have rather short stocks. Remington, Winchester, and almost all the other major arms companies manufacture them. Sales clerks may hesitate to order one of these weapons for a civilian, thinking that these weapons are reserved for police organizations. This is not true under present regulations, but the clerk may simply refuse to order the gun. If this occurs, order a "slug gun" with a 20-inch barrel. Almost all major sporting-weapons companies make them.

Slug guns are designed to fire single, large rifled slugs for deer hunting, but can also be loaded with a charge of shot. They're used in states which forbid rifles for hunting because the killing range of a rifled weapon is so great that they are dangerous even in rural areas. The rifled slug for deer hunting carries effectively for about 100 yards because it has spiral vanes cut into its sides so that it spins in flight. In other words, the rifling has been transferred from the barrel to the projectile. The slug gun, equipped with its short barrel, is a good weapon for home defense. You'll almost always be firing a charge of shot through it rather than a rifled slug, but the weapon is very effective at close range with these loads.

The shotguns described above have one short barrel. The double-barreled shotgun is in some ways superior to it. They are, however, always manufactured with tubes that are too long to be effective for self-defense indoors, unless they are shortened. Don't attempt this work yourself since it takes a considerable amount of skill even if you do have a hacksaw and a vise. Go to a gunsmith. State laws about shotguns are very vague. Many of them simply prohibit "sawed-off shotguns" and never mention a barrel length. If you cut down a shotgun yourself, you may be accused of having a sawed-off shotgun even though the barrel is still fairly long. At present, the federal law is the controlling statute, however, and it sets the minimum at 18 inches as evidenced by the fact that many

192

guns for deer hunting are manufactured with this length of barrel. If you take a double to a gunsmith, ask him to shorten the barrels to 20 inches—give the law the benefit of two inches to be on the safe side. Also ask your gunsmith to put the front sight back on the new muzzle.

The stock of the shotgun should also be as short as possible, but if the stock is too short it may be regarded as transforming the shotgun into a pistol—a smoothbore weapon capable of being concealed and against the law in many areas. Remember that you do need a certain amount of length in the stock in order to control the weapon properly. For shooting at short ranges, in self-defense, the length of the wooden stock should be equal to the distance from the *inside* of your elbow to the trigger—the front trigger, if the gun is a double. Put your right hand on the stock and curl your finger comfortably around the trigger and try to place the rear end of the stock against the inside of your elbow when your arm is crooked at a right angle. You'll find that almost every gun is much too long, and this includes many of the riot guns manufactured for police use. Have a gunsmith cut the stock off at the right length and re-install the butt plate that goes against your shoulder. If you intend to use a rubber recoil pad, remember that they're quite thick.

Your defense shotgun should be as short as the law allows, and it should also fit you. If you're rather short, you can handle a gun with a total length of only about 36 inches. Taller people, particularly those with long arms, need a longer gun.

The Pump Shotgun

The pump action is also often called a "slide" or a "trombone" action, since the shooter uses it in much the same way as a musician uses a slide trombone. The right hand goes on the pistol grip in much the same way that it grips a handgun. The butt goes on the shoulder, and the left hand grips the wooden forearm underneath the barrel. This forearm slides back and forth and imparts mechanical energy to work the action of the gun. To fire several shots, it's not necessary to remove the stock from the shoulder or from under the arm where it has been braced. Merely work the slide and pull

193

the trigger after each cycle when the forearm is as far forward as it will go.

Pump shotguns load through a port under the gun in front of the trigger guard. Four or five cartridges (depending on length) are shoved up into the port and forward against the pressure of a spring plunger into the tube underneath the barrel. Of course, they are loaded with the front end of the shell pointing toward the muzzle. After the magazine is full, the slide is pulled all the way back and then shoved all the way forward. To move the slide for the first loading, you must shove it forward about $\frac{1}{16}$-inch in order to unlock it. This is a built-in safety feature that prevents firing the gun when the slide is not forward with the action tightly locked. Moving the slide all the way back and all the way forward moves a shell from the magazine to the firing chamber in the rear end of the barrel. A pull on the trigger fires the gun since the safety does not come on automatically. If you wish to load your pump-action shotgun to the fullest capacity, load the magazine, work the slide to fill the firing chamber, and then shove another shell into the magazine. For quick firing of many shells, most pumps are very convenient since you can fire a shot or two and then load more through the loading port, if a pause in firing occurs.

Federal migratory wildfowl laws prohibit use of shotguns with a capacity of more than three shells for hunting ducks and geese. Therefore, the manufacturer inserts a wooden rod in the magazine of pump shotguns so that only two shells can be loaded into it. This gives the gun a capacity of three—one in the chamber and two in the magazine. For defense use, remove this rod or plug. It only requires a little jiggling to remove it, usually from the front end of the magazine.

In most pumps, the safety is a cross-bolt that runs through the root of the trigger guard just in front of the trigger finger. If you want to put the safety on after having loaded a shell in the chamber, use the right thumb to push the cross bolt all the way to the right. When ready to fire, push the cross-bolt all the way to your left with the tip of your index finger. The right index finger then drops back quite easily to the firing position. Ordinarily, you will store your defense gun with a full magazine but no shell in the chamber. With the magazine loaded, leave the safety off. You don't need it when you don't have a shell in the firing chamber. Almost all pump shotguns have this type of safety, though a few have safeties on top of the weapon within reach of the right thumb.

After a shell is fired, working the slide ejects the empty cartridge case through the ejection port on the top right of the weapon just behind the rear end of the barrel.

There's one other exterior control on a pump shotgun—the release catch. Let us say that you have the pump gun loaded to full magazine capacity stored in a convenient place. Trouble arises, and you snatch up the gun. Your first action normally would be to pull the slide all the way back and push it all the way forward to load the firing chamber. Let us say, however, that the trouble evaporates. You now wish to get that shell out of the chamber in order to render the gun harmless.

The gun is locked up tightly and ready to fire. In this position, the slide cannot be worked in order to open the action—a safety arrangement that prevents discharge when the weapon is not fully closed. In this situation, you should first put on the safety so that the trigger cannot be pulled accidentally. Now you must empty the tube magazine so that you can later work the slide and get that shell out of the chamber. With almost all pumps, the magazine must be empty before you can unload the chamber. Press the magazine-port cover into the gun. All the shells will slide out of the magazine under pressure of the magazine follower-spring, perhaps with a little assistance from you.

After the magazine is empty, open the action by using the small release catch, usually located on the left side of the gun near the trigger guard. Push the catch in, and you'll feel the gun "relax." The action is now unlocked and slack, and you can open it by pulling the slide back. The lock opens and the mechanism pulls the shell from the chamber. Grasp it with your fingers, remove it, and the gun is empty.

Both the firing chamber and the magazine of the weapon are now unloaded, and even though you pull the trigger, nothing will happen. Are you absolutely sure of that? To make sure, point the muzzle at soft ground or at a very thick wooden floor or wall (never stone), making sure that there is no one on the other side, and pull the trigger. If there's a dull click, the gun was really empty. If not, you made a mistake, but no one was injured.

It is unsafe to keep most weapons with a shell in the firing chamber, so it's wise to make this final check. It is also unwise to keep the firing mechanism of any gun cocked when storing the gun for long periods. Therefore, point the gun where it could not possibly do any harm and pull the trigger to make sure it's slack whenever you put your gun away for a long period. You do not want the springs to wear out because they're under constant tension. For the same reason, it is not wise to store any weapon that has a spring-activated magazine with a full load of shells. The magazine spring may wear out. Unless you make a practice of unloading and loading your weapon every month or two, perhaps by firing it at a practice range, load the magazine only at half its capacity so that the spring will not wear out.

Don't worry too much about the workings of the pump shotgun. Actually, it's a very simple weapon. It's much simpler to use than a gasoline-powered lawnmower or the washing machine. If these directions don't make the pump action entirely clear, you'll certainly be able to understand it easily when you're holding a pump shotgun in your hands. These directions are based mostly on the Winchester Model-12, a very popular pump shotgun. Other pumps have slightly different working parts. Any NRA instructor will explain a gun's workings.

The pump action is much simpler than the automatic, and is therefore more dependable. You want a very dependable gun for defense since you may stake your life on it. The automatic is packed with springs and small parts and gets out of kilter much more easily than a pump. Automatics are not as safe as pumps. With an automatic weapon of any kind, you do not have to work the mechanism to bring each shell into firing position. Under stress, it is all too easy to fire another shot when you do not intend to do so. Leave automatics to those who know how to use them. A pump is fast enough.

196

The Double

After discussing the rapid fire possible with a pump, it may seem contradictory to recommend the double-barreled shotgun. The double, however, has the simplest action of all. It merely breaks open after you move the unlocking lever to the right with your thumb. As the gun opens, fired shells are forcefully ejected by spring-loaded ejectors or are pulled from the chambers by an extractor so that you can grasp them with thumb and forefinger and pull them out of the gun. The force you exert in opening the gun also cocks both firing pins, and the safety comes on automatically. The shooter drops two shells into the barrels and snaps the action closed. To fire, he simply clicks off the automatic safety, usually by shoving it forward with his thumb, pulls one trigger and then the other.

There are so few parts that a good double hardly ever gets out of order. In fact, the locks of most doubles are sealed with the idea that they will remain that way for the entire life of the gun. Most owners of double-barreled shotguns never think of oiling the locks of their weapons because it's not needed, and indeed, the average double cannot be oiled because there are no openings to the cavity containing the firing pins, springs, and other moving parts. The double can be stored for many years without attention and will still fire when needed. Even the pump action gun requires fairly frequent care because it has many more moving parts.

The double is also a bit safer than the pump for those who are not used to firearms in that the action really opens when the gun is broken. The shooter can clearly see into both firing chambers and down both barrels to make sure that the weapon is unloaded and the tubes unobstructed. With a pump, you have to be more careful to make sure that the gun is empty.

Pump or Double?

The great advantage of the pump is that it has a 4 or 5-shot magazine so that the shooter can put out quite a volume of lead if it is required. Its rapid-fire capabilities make the pump extremely

197

attractive to the police. The double's advantages are even greater simplicity, dependability, and safety.

In most defense situations, the intended victim does not need more than two shots since dangerous criminals who enter homes usually do so alone. If you can't do anything with two shots, you might as well conclude that it's not worth trying. If you're in a defense situation where you may encounter more than one criminal, buy a pump gun. If your primary problem is defense against possible entry by one person, and if you are rather unfamiliar with weapons and a bit nervous about using them, the double may be the best choice.

The double delivers that second shot very quickly. As many hunters will tell you, there's no faster gun than the double when firing a follow-up shot. Even a pump cannot keep up with the old-fashioned double with two triggers. The index finger pulls the forward trigger and then quickly slips back to the second trigger. And if you become familiar with the operation of a double, it really doesn't take so long to open the gun, eject the empty cartridge cases, and insert two new shells.

If you buy a double with two triggers, you are actually holding two weapons in your hands at the same time when you pick up your weapon. This type of gun has two barrels, two firing chambers, and two triggers. You can put two different kinds of loads in the weapon at the same time, and you will have an instantaneous choice of either load. In effect, with one weapon, you have a weapons combination that is highly effective. For instance, you can load a tear-gas shell in the right barrel and a killing load in the other. If you encounter a situation where the tear-gas is needed, touch off that barrel and hold the other load for later developments or for a follow-up. If on the other hand, you encounter a dangerous situation needing the shot load, you can fire it first. You can also load a long-range buckshot cartridge in one barrel and a short-range birdshot cartridge in the other and use either instantly. Of course, you must remember which trigger operates which barrel. In doubles, the forward trigger usually fires the right barrel and the rear trigger fires the left.

Steer clear of doubles with only one trigger. These guns fire one barrel first and then the other as the shooter pulls the single trigger twice. The order cannot be changed. Alternatively, these single-trigger guns have a selector button which enables the shooter to choose the barrel he wants. If you're not too familiar with weapons, these arrangements are too complicated.

Of course, you can load tear-gas shells into a pump gun's magazine, but this arrangement is not as flexible as using two different types of shells in a double. With a pump, the shooter would load several shot loads into the magazine first and follow them with a tear-gas shell. The last shell loaded is the first shell fired. In a dangerous situation, however, the shooter would be obliged to fire the tear-gas first or eject the tear-gas shell unfired before a lethal load could be used. The fastest procedure would be to fire tear gas and follow up quickly with a shot load since this would not involve fumbling with the release catch. For quick selection of different loads, the double is best.

The Hammer Double

In discussing the double-barreled shotgun, we've been talking about the modern, hammerless gun. These weapons do not have external hammers cocked by the thumb. The firing pins cock when you open the weapon to load it. These hammerless doubles have one disadvantage from the safety point of view. You cannot safely store a hammerless double with shells inside the gun. The pump is fairly safe in this respect since you can keep the magazine loaded but refrain from putting a shell in the chamber. With the pump, you can fire fairly quickly simply by working the slide for that vital first shot.

The situation is quite different with a hammerless double. When you open the gun, the firing pins cock automatically. You insert the shells and close the weapon. Though the safety comes on automatically in almost all modern doubles, the weapon has shells in the firing chambers and the firing pins are under spring tension. It is all too easy for a child or inexperienced person to pick up the weapon, push off the safety, and fire the gun. Almost all modern shotguns have dependable safety mechanisms, but it sometimes happens that a safety does fail when a gun is mishandled. For instance, dropping a weapon when loaded and cocked is dangerous since the sudden jar may cause the safety to release and may also release the firing pins. It hardly ever happens, but it's best not to drop loaded weapons of any kind on hard surfaces. In fact, it's best not to keep most weapons with shells in the firing chamber or chambers.

If you do decide on a double, and buy one without external hammers, you will be safer if you keep it unloaded. This is all right as long as you have fairly effective locks and other security hardware in your home. It's only in an extreme emergency that you will need the gun, and you will probably have plenty of time to load the weapon. If you have good security hardware, the intruder will make a lot of noise. If the shells are near the gun, you will have time to open the lock, drop two shells into place, close the weapon, and click off the automatic safety.

If you are not in this secure situation, and still want a double, perhaps because you are somewhat timid about operating the more complicated pump gun, buy a gun with external hammers. Loading and firing procedure is as follows: push the release lever or latch to the right and open the weapon, drop in two shells, close the gun, cock the hammers with the right thumb and then pull the triggers.

The gun has no safety as such. Instead, the hammers have a safety half-cock. When you first handle one of these guns, investigate the hammers with the gun unloaded. You'll find that both hammers have a halfway position. Place your thumb on one hammer without putting your index finger on the trigger and pull the hammer slowly back. Halfway, or a little less, to the rearmost position, you'll feel a slight click. At this point, release your thumb. Do the same with the other hammer, and both your trigger mechanisms will be in the safety half-cock position. The triggers will not funtion. In addition, the hammers are not back far enough to fire the shells even if the mechanisms should release through a sudden jar—unless, of course, the shock is very great and the force is applied in a way that disturbs the hammer mechanism.

When the gun is loaded and in the half-cock position, it can be fired very quickly if a sudden emergency arises. All you need to do is snick back the external hammers a short distance and pull the trigger. You do not have to break the gun open and load the shells into the chambers. The gun can be kept with the shells in the chambers because the firing pins are not under strong spring tension.

These doubles do have one safety disadvantage, however, which they share with most guns that have external hammers. When using the gun, avoid catching the hammers on cloth, twigs or some other object so that they are moved backward. This may cock the gun without your knowledge, and this is *very dangerous*. Also, by some freak, the hammer may fall forward past the safety half cock if the tension is suddenly released. This is an unlikely event when using the gun indoors since obstructions can be easily avoided. It is the hunter using the weapon in thick scrub who has to be constantly aware of this hazard.

A short, old-fashioned double with external hammers was a favorite weapon with shotgun guards on stagecoaches and with frontier law-enforcement officers. This type of gun reposed behind the counter of almost all stores, banks, and places of public entertainment not so long ago in American history. The weapon's simplicity and dependability made it almost foolproof, and the user always knew he could get off two quick shots. Against an armed, dangerous criminal, two shots were about all that could be fired.

Unfortunately, the double with external hammers is no longer manufactured in the United States. As far as the author knows, only the Bernardelli Company of Italy is now making doubles with hammers. This gun sells for a little over $100, and it would be a fine investment in home defense if your situation calls for this type of gun. Hammerless doubles are made by several American firms and all of them are dependable. The cheapest sells for about $75. Unless you know a great deal about guns, always buy a new weapon. Don't stake your life on a second-hand gun.

SUMMARY

If you decide a gun is essential for self-defense, buy a 12-gauge gun, either a pump or a double. If you're in a situation that may require quick firing of many shots, buy a pump. In the more usual situation, particularly if you are not too familiar with weapons, buy a double and get one with external hammers if you think you need to keep the gun with shells in the chambers.

Incidentally, the pump is rather noisy when a shell is worked into the chamber. The slide action makes a peculiar click-clack. Once one is familiar with the sound, it is recognizable anywhere. Hearing this noise, particularly in the dark, will frighten off many criminals. If the double is equipped with a mechanical extractor for dead shells rather than noisy spring ejectors, it makes hardly a sound when you load it. Snicking back the hammers on a gun that has them is almost noiseless. This has advantages too if you're up against a very dangerous person. Again, the choice is yours. It does no harm, however, to keep two guns in the home since this gives you greater flexibility. A good choice would be a double with hammers for quick use and a pump-action shotgun for any situation requiring rapid discharge of many shells.

Shotgun Chokes and Loads

Hunting shotguns are constricted toward the muzzle so that the shot will stay together in flight as long as possible. This achieves a tight pattern, which is useful in long-range bird hunting. For almost all defense firing, you'll need as wide a spread as possible. The constriction in the muzzle of a shotgun is called choke. For defense, you want a gun that has no choke at all, and such a gun is said to have a "cylinder bore," or to be bored "true cylinder." All riot guns and slug guns are bored this way, so they are fine for defense work. If you have a double-barreled shotgun shortened to 20 inches, the shortening will remove the constricted portion of the barrels.

Shotgun shells are loaded with many different sizes of shot ranging from No. 12 (the size of dust) to No. 2 (a little smaller than an air-rifle pellet). Larger than these birdshot loads are buckshot intended for deer hunting. Buckshot ranges in size from No. 4 (the smallest balls) to 00 buckshot (the largest balls). The favorite police load for a shotgun is a 12-gauge shell 2¾ inches in length after it is fired and the tube is unfolded, loaded with 00 buckshot. This type of shell contains nine lead balls with a diameter almost the same as an Army rifle's bullet. That it's an effective load is demonstrated by the fact that firing one of these shells is equivalent to shooting most U.S. Army rifles nine times—at short range, of course. If you fire five 00 buckshot loads rapidly from a pump shotgun, you have sent 45 large lead balls on their way to the target. Most military sub-machine guns are equipped with magazines that hold only 20 or 25 cartridges.

The 00 buckshot load would be your best choice if you may be shooting at distances up to 100 feet or 33 yards—the length of the average building lot. At shorter ranges, the destructive power of these shells has to be seen to be believed. For ordinary defense shooting, however, you can use any buckshot load in an emergency. All buckshot loads intended for deer will do nicely at fairly short range. The larger the individual ball, the greater the distance at which a load is effective. Birdshot loads are not dependable at longer ranges when shooting at a dangerous criminal.

If your defense situation would involve firing inside a building with very light, plasterboard or fiberboard walls or crumbling plaster walls, use extremely small birdshot, say No. 8 shot or No. 9. These shot sizes are commonly used by skeet enthusiasts to break clay pigeons. Skeet shooting is done at close range, and if you order skeet shells, you'll be buying the right load for this type of very close-range defense shooting. One skeet shell contains about 600 pellets, and the damage they do at very short range is tremendous. At about eight feet, the shot covers an area of two or three inches and the material inside the circle is completely destroyed.

Skeet shells should not be used for defense at distances greater than about 10 feet. This load is useful in a last-ditch defense situation, say when defending a locked door or window against a dangerous criminal who is trying to break through it. Since skeet shells have a low-velocity powder load, almost anyone can use them with little or no discomfort. Because of the low velocity and the small size of the shot, a load of this type will usually not penetrate reasonably thick walls unless the gun is fired only a few feet away. In defense shooting of any kind, however, you owe it to your neighbors to give some thought to what lies on the other side of a wall, floor, or ceiling.

At close range, your gun pointing must be fairly accurate. As stated above, the spread at eight feet or so is only two or three inches with a cylinder bore. At 20 yards, the spread is about 30 inches. The 00 buckshot load is lethal up to 100 feet or 33 yards, but much beyond that, the nine balls soon lose velocity and ability to penetrate, though you should still be careful about accidental hits at longer distances.

When living on a farm or estate with considerable property, you may need a load that works well at long distance. For this, purchase shotgun shells loaded with rifled slugs intended for deer. They are effective at distances up to 300 feet, that is 100 yards, if your aim is good enough. To use these single, solid projectiles in a shotgun, you'll need extensive practice. If you're a good shot, this load gives you something like the fire power of an old-fashioned blackpowder musket. To use rifled slugs effectively, you really need a shotgun equipped with rifle sights—most slug guns intended for deer hunting have these sights.

If at all possible, you should investigate how your shotgun patterns and penetrates with the load or loads you intend to use for defense shooting. To do this, set up a wooden backdrop or use a soft bank of earth. Large cardboard sheets or paper sheets covering the soft material will give you a good idea of the spread of the shot at various ranges. If you live in a crowded neighborhood where firing practice shots is impossible, you should be using skeet loads with small shot; since these cartridges are only effective at distances up to 10 feet or so, it's really not necessary to check on shot dispersion or penetration. Only by actually firing the weapon, however, will you become familiar with its capabilities, and this familiarity is the only thing that will give you confidence when using the weapon. With any small-birdshot load, it is very important to remember that you cannot inflict a disabling wound at any great distance. Never fire at a criminal unless you can knock him down with the load and put him completely out of action. Avoid firing at a criminal as long as you can safely do so, but if you must fire in self-defense, always try to preclude any possibility of harm to yourself or to your family.

204

Rifles

Since all rifles fire a solid projectile intended for long-range work, I'd avoid using one in ordinary defense shooting for home protection. A rifle may possibly be needed for long-range firing on a farm or an estate if one is being fired at, at long distance by a criminal. It's very unwise to fire at a criminal at long distance even on your own property unless he is shooting at you. If the criminal is not shooting, and you fire at him, the law may regard you as the aggressor since you are not shooting in self-defense. Ordinary trespassing is only a misdemeanor, and you may not use deadly weapons to prevent it. In every situation where there is time enough to call the police, try to do so. Take no action with weapons unless you are acting in self-defense as defined in Chapter IV.

For this type of shooting, you should use a rifle with a low-velocity cartridge with little power to penetrate since you do not wish to injure persons at great distance by accident. Yet, you require a weapon with a fairly fast action since you may just possibly be required to fire shots rapidly at short range with the gun. For this reason, avoid bolt-action rifles that require you to lift the bolt with your right hand, pull it back, shove it forward, and lock it into place by pulling it down for each shot. The bolt-action rifle was the most popular type of gun used in World War I, and it is intended for long-range shooting when the user has plenty of time to aim.

For defense shooting at moderate ranges, I would select a rifle with a rather short barrel—that is, a carbine. My choice would be the .30/30 Model-94 Winchester lever-action carbine, any short-barreled Marlin lever-action carbine chambered for .30/30 shells, or the Remington pump-action Model-760-C (carbine), chambered for the .35 caliber Remington cartridge. The .30/30 and the .35 Remington cartridges are fairly low-velocity loads and they have round-nosed bullets made of soft lead, so they will not penetrate or ricochet very dangerously.

The operation of a pump-action rifle is much the same as that of a pump shotgun, except that this Remington rifle loads with a clip—a drawer-like metal box that slips into the gun through a loading port in the bottom of the weapon. The shooter loads the clip with shells and then pushes the loaded clip into the gun. Shells are moved into the firing chamber by working the pump in precisely the same way as one uses a pump-action shotgun.

The lever action is worked by moving the lever with the right hand. This lever forms an extension of the trigger guard. The action can be worked very rapidly and the gun can be kept at the shoulder while many shots are being fired.

All three weapons loaded with the ammunition mentioned above are quite accurate at distances up to 200 yards, but remember that they may kill someone by accident at distances much greater than that—a mile or more in fact.

Never use military ammunition of any kind in a defense situation. Military bullets are full-metal jacketed, not soft-nosed lead. These bullets are intended to kill at very long ranges and they have great penetrating power and ricochet excessively. The military want a bullet that will bounce around and kill as many enemy soldiers as possible even though the rifle was not aimed at them. In defense, you want to place your shots very carefully and you want to avoid hitting people by accident. You should also avoid a .22 rifle or any other weapon firing a very small, lightweight bullet. The .22 is intended for small-game hunting and target practice. It is simply not effective for defense. Like all other ineffective weapons, it may wound and infuriate rather than put the criminal out of action. Even with a .22, however, the dangerous range may be as much as a mile.

As with shotguns, you should be very careful to unload rifles when you leave your home. With the Remington pump-action rifle, pull the clip out of the gun and then make absolutely sure the chamber is empty just as one does with a pump-action shotgun. To unload the Winchester or Marlin lever-action guns, you must work all the shells in the magazine through the firing chamber by moving the lever back and forth without pulling the trigger. Make sure that the last shell has come out of the gun by working the lever several extra times. Of course, you should click off the trigger after removing the last shell to release spring tension. Because any rifle has

206

great power to penetrate, it's extremely important to point the gun in a safe direction when you do this.

HANDGUNS

For defense shooting, you need a fairly powerful handgun. The .22 target pistol is, of course, not powerful enough. Weapons with a bore diameter of .45 of an inch (the caliber of most U.S. Army pistols) are too big for most people. I'd buy a .38 Special revolver, a Smith and Wesson or a Colt. Other firms make satisfactory .38 Specials, but unless you know enough to select a good one, rely on these excellent makes.

The .38 Special has many advantages. It's a powerful gun for close-range shooting, and most policemen carry them. Also, a variety of .38 caliber loads is available for this gun. A "Special" is special because it takes shells with long cases that load a lot of powder and give the bullets a great deal of punch. But you can also buy less powerful shells for this gun that have less velocity and recoil if the .38 Special proves to be too much for you. For instance, there's the old "long Colt" .38 and the .38 Special, mid-range Wadcutter. Use the long Colt for close-range defense shooting. (It works in Smith and Wessons too.) The Wadcutter is not a defense cartridge and should be used for target shooting only. With Wadcutters, the velocity is low and the shape of the bullet is intended to cut nice, neat holes in paper targets. Almost everyone should be able to use the .38 Special cartridge without discomfort for a few shots, but the shooter can always drop back to the less powerful long Colt for defense and the Wadcutter for targets if the big shell does prove too powerful. When you buy any handgun, ask the dealer to specify all the cartridges that it will handle so you can make a logical choice for various types of shooting. Fairly effective .38 Special tear-gas loads are available.

A six-shot .38 Special revolver of the Smith and Wesson and Colt type is an extremely simple gun. The cylinder wheels out to the left for loading. There is no firing chamber, as such, since each shell is fired in its chamber in the rotating cylinder as it comes in front of the hammer. Because you can look right through the cylinder when it's in the open position, it is very easy to tell if the gun is loaded or not.

For defense shooting, it's best to buy a revolver with a four or six-inch barrel. Greater length is not needed, and the longer barrel only gets in the way when speed is required. A gun with a one or two-inch barrel is adequate when used as a defense pocket pistol. You should not be firing at long range if you are firing in self-defense.

There's a wide variety of Colts and Smith and Wessons in this category and almost any new .38 Special revolver manufactured by either of these companies will be satisfactory if you make it a point to avoid extremely heavy guns. For home defense, you should avoid specially manufactured "airweight" guns made to be carried in the pocket. These guns have a lightweight-alloy frame and other parts are pared down to assure very light construction. Such guns are difficult to control when fired.

Almost all revolvers fire in two different ways. When loaded, the gun may be fired simply by pulling the trigger. The trigger pull rotates the cylinder and also cocks and releases the hammer. This is called double-action shooting because the trigger pull does double duty. Since the strong trigger pull is inclined to throw the aim off, it should only be used at very close range. For long-range shooting, the hammer is cocked with the thumb and then the trigger is pulled. Only a light pressure is required to release the hammer if the gun is used in this manner, which is called single-action shooting. Guns that fired single-action-only were formerly the only type of revolver available. The old Colt Frontier "cowboy" pistol is a single-action weapon. Some modern manufacturers have revived single-action guns for those who prefer their simplicity and strength. Since a defense weapon should be capable of rapid fire, avoid the single-action pistol unless you are willing to devote a fair amount of time to training yourself in its rapid use.

The double-action revolver, as manufactured by Colt and Smith and Wesson is quite safe. Both weapons have built-in safety blocks that prevent accidental discharge if you drop the gun on a hard surface. With some other revolvers, the gun will fire if you drop it upside down on a hard surface. The hammer strikes the floor and the firing pin is driven forward into the cartridge. With Colts and Smith and Wessons, this is almost impossible, but try to avoid dropping loaded weapons. The blocking mechanisms are only mechanical contrivances, and it's always better to depend on yourself than to rely on springs and mechanical blocks.

Aside from the internal blocking mechanism, this class of handgun has no other safety mechanism. Do not cock the gun when storing it or carrying it in a holster or pocket. You do not need a safety when the hammer is not cocked. If you do cock the weapon and wish to let the hammer down because the situation is no longer dangerous, hold the hammer very firmly with your right thumb and pull the trigger. Then allow the hammer to come forward, controlled by your thumb, to the at-rest position, but do so very gently. Of course, you should be pointing the gun in a safe direction when you do so.

One modern .38 revolver varies markedly from the standard double-action type described above. This is the Smith and Wesson Centennial which is chambered for the big .38 Special cartridge. It's an excellent defense weapon because it has an extra safety feature. The back of the grip is equipped with a safety mechanism that must be pressed firmly into the gun before the action will work. You must grasp the pistol in a tight shooter's grip before you can pull the trigger. This safety device makes the gun extremely safe for people who are comparatively unfamiliar with firearms. The gun has no external hammer whatever, and must always be fired double-action simply by pulling the trigger. Aimed shooting at distant targets is therefore quite difficult with this weapon since you cannot use a light trigger pull. But if you wish to have a weapon ready, and one that is almost impossible to fire by accident, this is the gun for you. Kept in a concealed position beside your bed, it is always ready for instantaneous use. You can also be fairly sure that a small child will not have the strength or a hand large enough to press in the grip safety and pull the trigger at the same time. Since there is no external hammer to catch on clothing or holster, this gun is also an excellent pocket pistol as long as the shooter does not try to hit targets at a long distance.

209

Be extremely careful in firing the .38 Special cartridge. The bullet will penetrate $7\frac{1}{2}$ inches of pine board when fired at a fairly short distance. This bullet will easily penetrate the exterior or interior walls of almost all wooden buildings.

I would not buy an automatic pistol for home defense. Most of these guns have extremely complicated mechanisms and therefore malfunction more often than revolvers. In addition, most cartridges for automatic pistols are manufactured with hard-coated heads so that they will work through the automatic's spring mechanism without deformation. These coated cartridges have much less shocking power than the soft-nosed cartridges made for revolvers. In fact, the average automatic-pistol cartridge is in the same class with full-jacketed military rifle ammunition. Such ammunition has too much penetrating power and tends to ricochet in all directions. Soft-nosed lead bullets expand when they hit and therefore tend to knock the criminal down so that even if still capable of it, he finds it difficult to aim and fire a weapon. Jacketed bullets tend to pierce without exerting much knock-down power. Stick to a revolver unless you really understand what you're doing with an automatic.

Gun Safety

If you wish to maintain a defense gun safely, you should be conscious of standard safety practices.

You should always handle a gun with the conviction that it is loaded and ready to fire. When practicing, never point the weapon at anything you do not wish to shoot unless you have previously opened the weapon to make absolutely sure that it is empty, and even then, don't point it at a living target. If someone hands you a gun and assures you that it is unloaded, open the action anyway. Don't take another person's word on something that may mean the difference between life and death.

Before firing any weapon, always make sure that the barrel and the action are unobstructed. Open the action and look through the barrel to make sure that it's clear. Even a comparatively small object in the tube will cause the barrel to burst when the weapon is fired. After you're sure that the gun is clear and unloaded, work the action at least twice and pull the trigger to make sure that it is

210

functioning smoothly. If the gun works quickly and easily, you're ready to load. If it does not, clean it thoroughly and find out what is wrong.

Carry your gun carefully so that the muzzle is always pointed in a safe direction in order to avoid hitting anyone if you trip and pull the trigger.

Always be sure of what you are shooting at.

Never climb a tree or a fence or any other obstruction with a loaded gun in your hand, unless the seriousness of the defense situation forces you to do so. You may stumble and fire the weapon by mistake. Instead, put the safety on, and place the weapon flat on the ground with the muzzle pointing away from you. Climb the obstruction and then reach back for the weapon. Never lean a shoulder weapon against a tree or wall. It may fall to the floor or ground and go off.

Be careful about bounce and penetration. Never shoot at a flat, hard surface or water—the bullet may ricochet. When firing, near or inside a building, give some thought to what may be on the other side of the wall since some cartridges have great ability to penetrate. Using a shotgun eliminates bounce and penetration to some degree.

Don't use firearms if you have been drinking, and don't keep deadly weapons in your home if you or any member of your family drinks to excess or is subject to emotional instability of any kind.

Make sure that your gun is maintained in good working order. When you purchase any weapon, buy the right size cleaning kit for it and clean the barrel thoroughly after each use. With a revolver, clean the cylinder's chambers too. Even if you don't use it, make it a point to clean the weapon thoroughly at least once a month—oftener in damp climates. Go easy on the oil. A drop or two is enough. Too much oil leads to the accumulation of dust and lint and it may clog the action.

These safety practices are a somewhat expanded version of the "Ten Commandments of Safety" circulated by the Sporting Arms and Ammunition Manufacturers Institute.

The list also includes one "commandment" which reads: "Carry only empty guns, taken down or with the action open, into your

211

automobile, camp, or home." This is a good rule for the sportsman, but it must be carefully considered if you wish to maintain
an effective defense weapon.

If you are to have a gun ready for self-defense in your home,
you'll often want to keep it loaded, and it may even be necessary
to keep a shell in the chamber. There's only one instance in which
you can afford to keep an unloaded defense weapon. As mentioned
above, you must have a carefully planned system of locks and
barriers. In this situation, you guarantee yourself time enough to
load your weapon if a crisis develops. As the criminal tries to
break in, you have time to retreat to the security room, closing and
locking doors behind you. Even one locked door or grating will
give you time enough to load your gun, if the ammunition is stored
close to the weapon. If you have devoted enough effort to making
your position secure, you may be able to follow the commandment
which prohibits keeping a loaded gun inside a building. This is
obviously the best course. If you install the proper locksmith's
hardware, you probably will never be obliged to use the gunmaker's
product.

When the author was a child, his family kept two loaded
weapons. One was an old-fashioned, double-barreled, hammer shotgun loaded with two charges of buckshot. It hung on two wooden
pegs on a beam in the middle of the living-room ceiling. Most
modern homemakers would have thought it a charming decorative
antique. The other weapon was a loaded .45 caliber revolver that
always reposed in the drawer of a table which stood alongside the
head of the house's bed. Woe betide the small child who made any
attempt to touch either weapon. I was suitably disciplined just once
at the age of six for this offense, and I never went near either gun
again until I reached the advanced age of 12. At that time, the
head of the house made a determined and successful effort to teach
me about guns for hunting and also declared me in on the duty of
home defense. And I used that shotgun once to very good effect
at the age of 16 to defend a female relative against a drunken
soldier who was not too drunk to recognize a 12 gauge set of muz-
zles when they were pointed at him. But that's another story. When
I was a small child incapable of reason, the guns were always kept

212

out of my hands. When I was old enough, I was taught to use weapons safely and effectively.

I think the message is plain. Keep guns out of the hands of children unless they are old enough and trained to use them properly. Every capable adult in the home should be able to use the defense weapon or weapons effectively and it's worth a little effort to make sure that they can. Children should keep their hands off weapons unless under the immediate supervision of an adult. If any member of your family is untrustworthy, you have no choice but to keep the weapon unloaded and to conceal or lock up the ammunition. Even if all members of the family are reliable, it may be best to load only the magazine of the weapon and keep the chamber unloaded. Surely you have enough intelligent understanding of your family to be able to judge the situation properly. If you do not, have nothing to do with firearms.

It's also important to maintain weapons so that they cannot be used against you. If a housebreaker enters your home when you are away, you do not want him to find a loaded gun on the premises. It may be used against you if you return unexpectedly. For this reason, it's very wise to unload your weapon when you leave your home. Make it a matter of habit. You undoubtedly lock the doors and make sure the keys are in your pocket or purse when you leave your home, and you do this without much thought. Make it a habit also to open your weapon and drop out the cartridges. An old friend of the author's, for instance, kept a loaded .38 in a table drawer beside her bed. When she left her home for any extended period, she'd unload the six cartridges from the revolver and take them with her. Most often, this meant dropping them into the glove compartment of her car. There was no other ammunition in the house, and she was fairly sure that the weapon could not be used.

It's also possible to conceal the ammunition. One of the most convenient devices is to drill a series of holes in any wooden surface just large enough to accommodate the cartridges. For instance, a three-quarter inch hole takes a 12-gauge shotgun shell. Drill the holes in the top edge of a loose-fitting drawer, the back of a thick table top, or on the rear edge of a bookcase upright—any place that's not obvious and yet is easy to reach. Drill the holes just deep enough so that the rear end of each cartridge protrudes enough to be grasped. When you leave your home, take a minute to unload your gun and insert the shells in the hiding place.

To conceal an entire weapon, particularly a shoulder gun is somewhat more difficult, but it's by no means impossible. For a shotgun, any long space will do. For instance, most walls consist of upright 2 x 4 studs covered on both sides with plasterboard or lath and plaster. The four-inch-deep space between both surfaces will accommodate a long gun placed between two studs. Open up the surface and put in suitable pegs to hold the weapon. Cover the opening with a picture or a bookcase mounted on concealed hinges so that it can be easily swung aside. The long scroll in a heavy frame with a rigid backing is an excellent cover since it provides an elongated vertical shape that looks perfectly normal, but many other coverings will suggest themselves. I know one person who keeps two loaded revolvers in an opening behind a hinged medicine cabinet in his bathroom. It's the only room with a lock on the door in his very small apartment.

The object covering the cavity should be closed with a snap latch that's easily opened from a concealed position. One dodge is to make the opening latch accessible through a small hole cut through the back wall or side of a hinged cabinet. The hiding place is opened by reaching *inside* the cabinet. A firm snap latch on the covering object gives the hiding place a surface that appears to be permanently hung on the wall so that it would not occur to anyone to look there. Thieves often make it a point to look behind wall hangings and pictures for concealed valuables and safes, so you must make an effort to hide the weapon behind or in something that would not normally be moved or opened. Opening up a newel post or heavy picture frame or furniture works quite well. You can also hinge one tread on a stairway and hide a weapon under it as long as you have some means of snapping the tread closed so that it will not rise if someone catches a toe under its edge. Hollowing out a wooden object always regarded as solid makes an excellent gun cache, provided you're skilled enough to make a closing which is difficult to discern, snaps shut firmly, and yet is easily opened if you know how.

Even simple hiding places requiring no special construction whatsoever are quite effective if you devote a little time to thinking about them. For instance, you can tape a revolver to the under surface of a table or bureau top, or you can put pegs high up inside a closet on which to hang your gun. The trick to developing an effective hiding place for your weapon is to place yourself in the position of a thief who has entered your home. If you do this, many hiding places for weapons will suggest themselves which are not logical places in which a person would ordinarily conceal valuables. For instance, a revolver inside a plastic bag can be hung inside the water reservoir of a toilet, and it can be fired without even removing the weapon from the bag if the plastic is flexible enough and the trigger guard is large. Simple hiding places of this kind, however, may fool a thief but they are not proof against the exploratory drive of a child. Children will pry into every place in the house sooner or later. If you are trying to keep a gun away from a curious child, it's best to have a good hiding place with a snap or pin lock.

Even if you do conceal your gun in a hiding place, it is best to unload the weapon if you leave home for a vacation or other extended absence.

PRACTICE

Learning to use a firearm usually involves three phases: (1) Familiarizing yourself with loading, unloading, and the method by which the action is worked. (2) Slow fire at stationary targets. (3) Quick, instinctive firing. For defense shooting, you don't need superb marksmanship, but you should be reasonably accurate, and you should be able to fire quickly.

Familiarizing yourself with your weapon is most important. You must be able to load, cock, and fire your gun without thinking about it or fumbling. In fact, you really should be able to do all this in absolute darkness or without looking at the weapon, as for instance, when you are keeping your eyes on another person or a doorway or window. It's not as difficult as it sounds. With the weapon unloaded, work the action to familiarize yourself with the manner in which it functions and pull the trigger a few times to

215

make sure you know how the gun feels when the firing pin is released and so that you know how much pressure it takes to pull the trigger.

Be careful not to pull the trigger on an empty chamber too often. If you do, the firing pin may break off because it is falling on empty space. If you wish to practice pulling the trigger without actually firing the gun, put a dead shell (empty cartridge case) in the weapon. Don't use the same case over and over again since the pin will gradually punch away the metal. With one dead case, about 25 practice pulls of the trigger is the maximum before a new dead case is needed.

Any NRA instructor will show you how to load and unload your weapon and how to work the safety catch if your gun is equipped with one. Be very careful when practicing loading and unloading since it's sometimes easy to fire a shot when you do not intend to do so. Follow the requirements of the NRA Home Firearm Safety course.

After you're completely familiar with your gun, you're ready for your first few practice shots. Go to a supervised range at first, and shoot there. If you have developed a real interest in weapons, it may be worth a few dollars to join a local sportsmen's group. You can also fire a shotgun at numerous skeet and trap ranges that are springing up around the country. The Winchester-Western company sponsors many of these ranges. Skeet and trap are both clay-pigeon games in which the shooter fires at clay discs thrown into the air by a catapult. Since the pigeons move very rapidly, the shooter must fire quickly before they get out of range, and this sort of shooting is excellent practice for defense firing. Your defense shotgun, however, has too wide a pattern for most trap fields, though it will work fairly well at skeet because it does have a wide spread. On most clay-pigeon ranges, the management maintains a half-range catapult for those who are just starting out. These catapults throw the pigeon at a very slow speed. Hire the instructor for an hour or two and use your defense shotgun in a few practice sessions. Don't be discouraged because you don't do very well. Remember that the clay pigeon is only a small, thin disk; it's much harder to hit a moving clay pigeon than it is to hit a man-sized

216

target. The fact that you must fire rapidly, however, will help to train you for defense shooting. If you become interested in clay-target shooting as a sport, you may find that you'll want to buy a special trap or skeet weapon, and at most ranges, they can be rented for a dollar or two. A day at the clay-target range is most pleasant.

To practice rifle or pistol shooting, try to get out into the country and simply fire at tin cans at varying distances in an area where shooting is not prohibited. After you have mastered shooting at stationary targets, try shooting at objects that move toward you. The best way to do this is to use inflated rubber balloons as targets. Drive a short stick into the ground 25 or 30 feet from yourself, and upwind. Tie a light string to the balloon and drape the string over the head of the stick so that when the string is released, or flipped off the stick, the wind blows the balloon toward you. If you can hit a balloon moving wildly across a field, you'll be able to hit any intruder. Targets moving away from you are not as useful since real defense shooting should never involve a retreating target.

If you live in an area where ranges or open land are difficult to find, you can still practice instinctive gun pointing without fear of hurting anyone. Remember that defense shooting is most often done at ranges of only ten or twelve feet. Quite often, the range is only two or three feet, so you do not need lengthy practice at formal target shooting. In fact, this form of firing may be harmful. Most professional rifle and pistol instructors will teach you a method of putting a bullet into a nice, neat, black bullseye in bright light when you have plenty of time to fire at long range. The pistol instructor wants you to use your handgun to make good scores in slow-fire target matches. The emphasis is on shooting single-action. Cock the hammer, aim carefully, hold your breath, and squeeze off the shot. This form of firing is really not useful in defense since most often the defense shooter fires at targets moving toward him in poor light. Very often, defense revolver shooting is double-action —point the gun and pull the trigger quickly and forcefully. If you can get out in the open and practice on tin cans, firing double-action at short range, or at balloon targets, you'll probably be getting better defense practice than you would at most formal target ranges. In most cases, the range frowns on informal double-action shooting, so you may be forced to improvise. The same goes for rapid-fire rifle practice. You're not interested in becoming a long-range sniper.

One of the best ways to practice indoor shooting without using live ammunition is to use a small, pencil-size flashlight. With a shotgun, put the flashlight inside the firing chamber wrapped in masking or adhesive tape to hold it steady. The barrel is long enough to concentrate the light in an area roughly approximating the spread of your shot in a cylinder barrel. With a pistol or rifle, tape the light under the barrel. Make sure that the center of the circle of light is on target by shining the light against a wall about 10 feet away. Then look over your sights and make sure that the point-of-aim is dead center in the circle of light. You can always make adjustments by twisting the light inside the tape with which you attach it to the gun barrel.

Make sure your gun is not loaded. With your gun held at your side, pick out a man-sized target anywhere in the room—a big lampshade, the center of a panel in a door, the back of a chair. Now close your eyes tightly and put the gun on target instinctively and quickly. Open your eyes only after you have squeezed the trigger. If the center of the light is on target, you're pointing your gun effectively without even seeing the gun's sights. You'll be surprised how quickly you can point your weapon if you don't look at the sights, and the fact that you can do so instinctively, without seeing the target or taking deliberate aim, will give you real confidence if you are ever forced to use your weapon in earnest. This form of practice is advantageous because it takes place right where you would be doing your defense shooting—your own home.

Special practice ammunition is available for the .38 Special revolver. These shells have plastic bullets and there is no powder charge. The small amount of primer material in the primer cap is used to push the wax bullet out of the gun. They're good for close-range target work. This ammunition makes about the same amount of noise as a child's cap pistol. Use this ammunition to practice on targets around your home, though it's probably best to fire these shells in the cellar since the bullets may damage lamp shades and other delicate objects. After using ammunition with plastic bullets, clean the gun very thoroughly since the residue from the exploded primer caps may corrode the inside of the barrel.

In practicing defense shooting at close range, don't aim carefully. Grip the gun firmly in your hand or hands, throw it up quickly and pull the trigger. You shouldn't even see the sights or be very conscious of them. The pistol or shoulder weapon becomes a natural extension of your arm or arms, and you point rather than aim. Practice instinctive pointing while lying in bed, sitting in a chair, walking around the home, opening doors and turning corners quickly. Do this often with a light-equipped shotgun, rifle, or pistol, and you'll soon develop all the proficiency needed for defense shooting. In fact, you'll be better at it than the average policeman or soldier since their training usually emphasizes formal, slow-squeeze, long-range firing.

After you have had sufficient indoor practice of this kind, it's a good idea to make a few special trips to fire your gun with live ammunition. If you don't do this, the blast and recoil of the weapon may surprise you no matter how well you have learned to point your weapon.

As the least-important part of your practice, fire a few shots once in a while by actually looking at the sights, and aiming. In rare self-defense situations, you may have enough time and light to aim, and you should know how to take advantage of them.

Many women and slightly-built men would do well to practice two-handed shooting when using handguns. One popular grip for persons who find their revolvers a bit too heavy and powerful is to hold the gun firmly in the right hand and then grip the right wrist with the left hand to steady the gun as each shot is fired. For support and steadiness, many shooters take advantage of any rest they can find—desk top, window sill, tree branch, and so forth. Don't let the gun touch the hard surface. Rest your arm or elbow on it for support. If the gun actually touches a hard object, it will bounce away from it when fired and throw the shot off. This applies to shoulder weapons as well as handguns.

With shoulder weapons, the shooter should practice one-handed firing so that the gun can be used while holding another implement

219

such as a flashlight in the other hand. Brace the stock high up *under* the shoulder and clamp the end of the butt under your arm with a firm grip. By holding the pistol grip of the shoulder stock firmly with your right hand, you'll find that you have adequate support to fire most shoulder weapons with one hand. The butt can also be braced against the hip. The slight, small-boned person should not try this form of shooting with a big-bore weapon.

You do not need complicated peep sights or telescopic sights for your defense weapon. After all, you're not a long-range expert. The ordinary sights installed at the factory will do. On rifles, pistols, and most single-barreled shotguns, these consist of a simple blade or post as the front sight and a notch (usually V-shaped) in the rear. Put the blade or post in the center of the V with the top of the post level with both sides of the V. Then center the top of the post on your target and pull the trigger. Most double-barreled shotguns do not have any rear sight whatsoever. With these weapons, you simply use the front sight as an indicator. Put the bead or post on target and then center the bead on the top rear silhouette of your gun's frame, and you'll be aiming precisely enough. But this type of aimed fire will be rarely used in defense. For most defense shooting, you should be completely unconscious of the sights.

All this may sound complicated and time-consuming, but practice is important. It gives you confidence with your weapon and confidence has two benefits. It makes you more effective with your weapon and it is safer because you will not fumble and hesitate. There is no more dangerous person than the nervous, excitable shooter who doesn't know how to handle his or her gun.

Yet, even if you don't get in much practice, try to select an appropriate weapon, maintain it in good condition, and at least try to familiarize yourself with how it is loaded and fired. If your defense problem only involves a small apartment, this is probably enough.

DEFENSE AGAINST FIREARMS

Unless you are extremely skilled at judo, karate, or other sophisticated systems of hand-to-hand fighting, there is really no effective defense against a person armed with a gun. Police and special military forces sometimes are taught methods of snatching or twisting a loaded firearm out of an aggressor's hands, but it takes considerable practice to learn them. A few of the simpler methods are treated in Chapter VI on unarmed defenses.

In the usual case, it's best to comply with the directions of anyone who threatens you with a firearm. In an ordinary robbery, you stand little chance of being injured as long as you obey the criminal. In rare circumstances, you may encounter a situation in which you know the criminal intends to kill you with a gun. In these circumstances, and in these circumstances alone, you may find that it is necessary to use the following defense.

If the criminal is using a weapon with an external hammer, you may be able to prevent a shot by holding back the hammer. If the weapon, usually a revolver, is cocked (hammer all the way back), try to insert your thumb or index finger between the hammer and the frame of the weapon. This can best be done by grasping the weapon with the whole hand, fingers around the criminal's fingers. Jam your thumb into the space under the hammer. With smaller weapons, your thumb may not fit into the space, but in that case you simply jam the hammer back.

To use this defense, you must move very rapidly, and you must be extremely sure of yourself. Even then, your chances of success are very slim, so the defense should never be used unless you are in very desperate circumstances. Try to take advantage of an instant when the criminal's attention is diverted. If you're right-handed, step quickly out of the line of fire to the left and at the same time swing your right hand in a swift arc toward the gun, grasping it so that your thumb falls in the right place immediately. As you grasp the weapon, you'll be out of the line of fire and though the criminal may get off a shot, you may be able to block the hammer so that others cannot be fired. As soon as you have controlled the gun, follow up by kicking at the genitals or use your other hand to gouge or strike a disabling blow. Hang onto that gun! As long as the hammer cannot fall, the gun cannot be fired. If the hammer is down when you first see the weapon, the criminal intends to fire double-action. In these cases, the defender has a better chance than when the weapon is cocked. He has a bit more

221

time since the hammer must rise first when the trigger is pulled before it can come forward to fire the shot. Try to jam the hammer back as soon as you grasp the gun. The criminal's instinctive pull on the trigger may raise the hammer just as your hand arrives in position.

An automatic pistol poses an even more difficult problem. Hammerless automatic pistols have a recoil mechanism that loads another shell from the magazine each time the gun is fired. When the gun goes off, the whole top rear of the weapon and the barrel slide all the way back, sometimes as much as an inch, and a new shell rises from the magazine in the grip. When the slide is all the way back, the firing pin cannot be moved—a safety feature of almost all automatic pistols. When you are sure that harm is intended, it may be possible to sweep your hand in suddenly while stepping out of the line of fire, grasp the slide and hold it all the way back with your hand. It's a very difficult maneuver, and it is extremely dangerous. After you are holding the gun's slide, you must quickly disable the criminal because it's almost impossible to hold the slide back if he keeps moving the gun away from you. Normally, however, the tendency of the gunman is to push the weapon toward the intended victim so that the criminal's own effort tends to keep the slide back if you can hold it firmly. Almost all automatic pistols have deep notches cut in the slide where the shooter grasps it in order to pull it back when loading. If you are compelled to use this defense, try to grip the gun on this series of grooves, thumb on one side of the weapon, forefinger on the other.

There is no easy defense against a shotgun or rifle that is cocked and firmly held. You cannot interfere with the weapon unless it has an external hammer, and that is rare in modern weapons. If you must, try to knock the muzzle aside and hold it away while you kick to disable the criminal.

When you are using a firearm yourself, it's important to maintain your distance so that these defenses cannot be used.

CHAPTER VII

Unarmed Personal Defense

THIS chapter consists mostly of photographs arranged in a series which will give you a good working knowledge of the common unarmed defenses against armed and unarmed attacks. The first part of the photographic treatment consists of releases—methods of breaking arm grips, bear hugs, and other common grips. In some of these photographs, a comparatively slight woman is shown releasing herself from the grip of a quite heavy man. You may find it difficult to believe that she or any other slightly-built person could actually do the same if the opponent were really a criminal bent on serious attack. Yes, you are quite right. Many of these releases and some of the more active techniques will NOT work all the time and against all opponents. The photographs *are* carefully posed in order to show how the releases, grips, blows, or kicks should be used. No attempt has been made to make the photographic portrayal overly realistic.

These releases and other methods of fending off an attack will not work if the opponent is also trained or experienced in this form of combat. For instance, a young lady cannot expect to fend off any person who has received good training in judo or karate. A slightly-built clerk will have little success against a tough street fighter who has learned to use fists, elbows, knees, feet, and the top of his head (for butting). But if you must put up some sort of defense when unarmed, the defenses shown in the photographs are the easiest to learn and the most effective. Your best hope of success, however, is when the attacker is comparatively inexperienced or untrained or when you have taken him by surprise.

Weapons are always much more effective than the methods shown in this chapter, and I personally see no reason why a person should confine himself to unarmed defenses against criminals if a weapon is legally available. The law of self-defense makes it clear that the citizen has the right to use a necessary degree of force to protect himself or herself. If you are in doubt on this point, however, see Chapter IV. It seems that many persons really do believe that weapons are not to be used in defense under any circumstances, no matter how dangerous the attack.

Today, therefore, courses in judo and karate and other sophisticated forms of personal combat are increasingly popular in larger cities where there are large numbers of female office workers living alone in dangerous circumstances. What do these courses in Oriental forms of combat offer the participant?

A legend has been built up about the various forms of Oriental hand-to-hand combat which often attracts people who are unwilling or unable to use weapons in self-defense. It is often said that if you study the methods of the Japanese, you will be able to defend yourself against all comers. This is pure nonsense. The Japanese methods of combat were developed primarily to permit the unarmed peasant to defend himself against disorderly soldiery. In some areas, notably Tibet, these forms of defense were developed by monks who were forbidden to use weapons by their religion. They developed particularly murderous methods of fighting with hands and feet. Long ago, the Japanese established prison colonies on outlying islands and forbade the prisoners all use of weapons. Many prisoners were not confined but lived on the land as agricultural laborers. Since they could not use weapons, but often fought, they too developed extremely effective methods of unarmed combat.

It remained for the Japanese to put many of these forms of fighting together in an ordered system of combat. And yet, in Japan

(*Text continues on page 241.*)
224

FIGURE 7-1. If the attacker grasps you by the wrist, always work...

Against the thumb. The entire power of your arm opposes only that single thumb. If the thumb is underneath, circle your forearm swiftly downward and outward.

Keep it moving, and you'll feel his thumb give way.

When the thumb gives, pull backward, and you're free. Follow up by running before he can recover, or if the attacker is dangerous, follow through with a disabling kick or blow.

If the attacker's thumbs are below your wrists, your arms move down and out as in pictures. With the thumbs on top of your wrists, your arms move upward and not down. Experiment with a partner and you'll find out why this motion changes depending on the location of the attacker's thumbs.

FIGURE 7-3. Here's another way to break a one-handed grip if the attacker's thumb is on the bottom. This release is useful if the attacker is very strong. Perhaps the simple, against-the-thumb circle shown previously did not work and he managed to keep his grip. Then use this one. It opposes the power of both your arms and the weight of your upper body to his one-handed grip.

Make a hard fist with your captured hand. Reach forward quickly with your free hand and...

...grasp your captured fist firmly with your other hand.

Now pull backward and upward and your wrist will break through his fingers.

This is another non-painful, non-disabling release. Run if possible after all such releases. If the attacker is really dangerous, however, follow through with a disabling blow or kick while he is off balance after a forceful release.

227

FIGURE 7-4. Breaking a front choke is easy if the attacker stands fairly far away.

Clasp your hands but do not interlace your fingers.

Form a wedge with your forearms by keeping your elbows apart.

Drive this wedge forcefully upward between his elbows. His grip will fly apart because his thumbs cannot hold against the full force of both your arms. If the attacker is really dangerous, you may be justified legally in making a vigorous follow-up. From this position, drive the doubled fists into nose and mouth and make a kick with the knee to the lower abdomen. Do both instantly, and you'll put the attacker out of action.

FIGURE 7-5. A grip from behind under the arms is sometimes difficult to break because the defender cannot reach
the attacker's hands. To break this grip, make the attacker
stand farther away by inflicting pain. Lift one leg. . .

...and scrape the outside edge of your shoe forcefully down his shin.

Drive your spike heel or the back edge of a flat heel into the instep. He will step farther a-way. Repeat on other side. Alternate quick-ly to confuse him.

Suddenly twist your body around to one side. He will resist and push against your motion.

Now straighten your arm and bring arm and shoul-der forcefully forward. Spin your body force-fully forward, keep mov-ing, and. . .

...you'll spin right out of his grip.

FIGURE 7-6. A choke from the back is easy to break if you keep your head. Pry up both the attacker's little fingers and hold them in the palms of your hands.

Bend them outward and upward. He'll relax his grip.

As his hands come free, step quickly forward, let go, and run or twist to the side and face the attacker for a follow-up.

FIGURE 7-7: The Same Sort of Release Is Often Used with a Bear Hug from the Rear.

Form a fist and extend the first joint of your second finger. Make your fist as hard as possible and you'll find the extended joint forms a very firm, sharp projection.

Drive the joint into the back of the attacker's hand between two tendons. The pain is intense and he'll let go, but he may keep a grip with the other arm. If so, spin forcefully on your heel away from that arm and you'll break free.

FIGURE 7-8. Three ways of fending off a frontal attack. These blows are dangerous, and may cause death. Use only when there is no other way to escape.

Front spear to lower throat just below Adam's apple with tips of the rigid, straightened fingers.

If the attacker is closer, the elbow aimed right at the Adam's apple is effective. Use when the attacker bends over you. Try not to contact chest with elbow.

If the attacker is on top of you, but your hand is free, drive the extended knuckle shown in Fig. 7-7 to the throat just above Adam's apple. Slow pressure will force a release; a forceful blow may kill.

FIGURE 7-9. "Stay-away," kicks and scrapes. The knee in the lower abdomen may cause permanent injury or even death—use only in an extremely dangerous situation. The others are painful, but will not disable for longer than a few seconds. Be prepared to follow up.

Distant kick to kneecap may disable leg. Your leg is longer than his arms, spin away onto other foot after one kick and then kick again with other foot or use some other long-distance method. Keep him away. Kick with *side* of foot.

In knee kick, use attacker's arms to support yourself, if possible. Try to take him out of action with one kick.

In knee scrape, start just below knee and scrape his entire shin. Wind up with...

...powerful stomp to instep. If he's really dangerous, follow up with throat spear Fig. 7-8 or the knee kick. This close-up shows use of spike heel in instep.

233

FIGURE 7-10. These follow-ups may inflict severe, permanent injury or even death. They should be used only in situations that endanger your life.

Karate chop with edge of stiffened hand to side of neck may rupture large artery, but will almost always cause unconsciousness. Practice with a partner, both backhand and forehand, but "pull" your blows just before impact to prevent injury. All strike areas shown here are good targets for a club.

"Rabbit punch" with fist, shown here, or edge of hand can fracture vertebrae. It almost always causes unconsciousness.

Backhand chop with edge of hand to bridge of nose inflicts severe pain, may cause fracture and unconsciousness. This blow requires swift follow-up if not immediately effective.

Kidney punch with extended knuckle (See Fig. 7-7) causes severe pain. Attacker almost always collapses. It may also cause eventual death. Use blows to attacker's back after you have released yourself from his grip and know he will reattack, never against a person who is running away.

FIGURE 7-11. Defender, left, parrys attacker's blow with his left hand, and...

...follows up with a...

...finger spear to throat. Don't use dangerous karate blows and kicks unless the fist-fighting attack is quite dangerous or you may violate the law of self-defense.

FIGURE 7-12. Defender blocks double-arm grab with double

parry, shoving both the attacker's arms aside.

He follows up immediately with a double karate chop to large muscles in lower neck on both sides. If strong chops are used, both the attacker's arms will go numb.

Follow up with knee kick if attacker is dangerous.

FIGURE 7-13. Hip throw is used to slam attacker onto the floor or sidewalk.

If the attacker uses a bear hug or grasps you around the neck...

...circle his body with your right arm and cross your right foot in front of his feet, placing it beyond his right foot. Grasp him solidly with both arms...

...and throw him, using your hip as a fulcrum. No follow-up is usually required, but if it is, kick with the the point of the shoe at the head and neck. If the attacker is really dangerous, don't let him get up again. This method should be used only when you are sure you are acting legally in self-defense.

FIGURE 7-14. The flying mare is one of the most damaging throws. It should be used only to counter an extremely dangerous attack.

Capture attacker's wrist.

Use both hands, and begin to bring his arm over your shoulder while you begin to turn your back.

Bring arm over shoulder with his palm up.

Throw him right over your own shoulder. He will actually jump with his legs to help you since his elbow is bent the wrong way. As he goes over, hang onto the wrist and bang him onto the floor or sidewalk. The flying mare can easily kill.

238

FIGURE 7-15. It is theoretically impossible for a man with a gun to shoot a defender who whirls on him and shoves the gun aside with arm and body as shown below. The attacker's reaction time is not fast enough to allow him to pull the trigger in time. Nevertheless, use this defense only when the defender intends to kill. Most people are right-handed, and therefore the defender should spin clockwise to work against attacker's thumb. It's natural to glance over your shoulder when first approached – determine which hand is used. If the attacker is left-handed, spin counterclockwise to work against left thumb.

Without telegraphing action, spin rapidly, keeping in contact with gun muzzle.

Use arm to force gun aside and keep spinning.

Catch wrist with your left hand.

Gasp gun barrel with right hand and force upward...

..until grip is broken. Knee kick to lower abdomen is best disabling move now.

If weapon is a shoulder gun, spin must be very forceful and must work against thumb of attacker's forward hand.

FIGURE 7-16. In club and knife defense against overhand and underhand blows, try to stop the blow before it develops

force. Here, an X-grip with the forearms catches the club itself because of the attacker's posture.

If the club and arm form one straight line, it may be better to catch the wrist, and against a knife, that method is always best. The best follow-up from this position is usually a kick with the knee to the lower abdomen. In this case, the defender would move toward attacker and use left knee in one motion.

there are many different methods taught by many different schools and associations rather than one uniform style of unarmed combat. Before World War II, however, the Japanese Armed Forces taught many of these techniques to large numbers of soldiers. The purpose, of course, was to give the small-boned, slightly built Japanese a feeling of confidence or even superiority when in combat against larger, much more heavily built opponents. The legend of Japanese superiority in unarmed combat was carefully nurtured by the Imperial Government and it is still alive today in the minds of many instructors who teach this form of fighting in schools in the United States.

And yet, when the *average* Japanese soldier met the *average* American soldier in combat, even at the outset of the war, the heavier Westerner usually held his own with a combination of superior weight and strength coupled with determination and untrained application of fists and feet. Later, as Americans began to put the Oriental forms of combat to good use, mostly through the efforts of dedicated Marine Corps instructors, the Americans actually became superior to the Japanese in unarmed combat. Professional boxers sum it up this way: a *good* big man can beat a good little man any day. All other things being equal, weight and size count a great deal.

If you are going to use unarmed defenses and you have little heft or strength, your only hope lies in surprise and your opponent's lack of training. Fortunately, few ordinary thugs go to judo school or study sophisticated Oriental combat methods from books, though some thugs are very effective in ordinary street fighting. For this reason, the attacks pictured in this chapter are usually very elementary. If the attacker used the sophisticated methods of attack taught in armed-forces combat schools and did so by surprise, very few people would be able to defend themselves against him. For instance, one of the attacks shown in this chapter is a simple grip on the arms from behind. A trained man would never use such a simple, comparatively ineffective grip. There are numerous ways of tackling a person from behind by surprise that give him no chance whatsoever to defend himself.

Most of the defenses portrayed in this chapter are useful only against rather inept aggressors—drunks, overly-excited suitors, ambitious but weak teenage thieves, and so forth. These defenses are easily learned from photographs. If you are really interested in knowing a fair amount about unarmed defense, you should take a course under a competent instructor.

The author well remembers an exhibition put on by a Marine Corps instructor who had extensive experience with Oriental methods. Several untrained men who had no knowledge of Oriental forms of combat were given the opportunity to attack the instructor who sat on the floor with his back turned. The attacker was standing and had the option of choosing the precise moment of attack, and the attack could come from behind if he so desired. In spite of the fact that ten men attempted to kick, gouge, strangle, or strike blows one after the other, the instructor succeeded in throwing every one of them and pinning them in positions in which he could easily have killed them if he desired to do so. But this man had years of experience and seemed to have an almost occult sense of when the attacker was approaching and what he intended to do. He reacted instantaneously and effectively the instant *before* the attacker touched him even when the attack came from behind! To develop such a superb faculty, the individual must go through years of training and he or she must be a finely coordinated person. The Japanese often say that such a lightning-like ability is developed only by long years of *religious* contemplation and *spiritual* training, not by mere exercise in combat techniques. Don't believe that a quick course in a school will give you the means to defend yourself against all comers. False confidence is very dangerous indeed. Remember what happened to the average Japanese soldier when he became acquainted with the average American.

ORIENTAL CONTRIBUTIONS TO UNARMED DEFENSE

The Orientals have contributed a great deal to the art of unarmed self-defense. First of all, the Japanese taught many Americans to use all the "dirty" forms of combat—eye gouges, kicks to the groin, blows to the back of the neck, knee kicks to the stomach and many more. These are typically the small man's methods of overcoming a larger person. In certain ways, however, the Oriental

242

methods were also used by Americans. Merchant seaman, loggers, agricultural laborers, longshoremen, were familiar with them long before so-called "Oriental" forms of combat became the familiar term. The logging camps of the American West Coast, for instance, probably harbor more and better kickers than all Japan or even France, which is also known for fighting with the feet. If you're wearing heavy logging boots with hobnails or spikes, they're a natural weapon. The Japanese made it possible, however, for the average American to believe that such tactics should be used.

If you are ever in desperate combat with a criminal who is bent on doing you serious harm, and there is no other way out of the situation, don't attempt to fight him with tactics governed by the Marquis of Queensberry rules for sport boxing. Use every disabling kick or blow that you can muster. Be careful with kicks, however. A trained fighter knows just when to come through with a kick, but an amateur may kick at a moment when his opponent can block. If this happens, the kicker may find himself standing on one foot with his ankle held by his opponent. It's a very dangerous situation especially if the attack is taking place on a sidewalk or other hard surface. The kicker can easily be thrown by twisting his foot.

The Japanese also practically abolished the fist. Instead, the bottom edge of the hand is used in a "chop"—a downward blow that concentrates force in a small area. The American, English, Irish, and Scotch use of the fist in fighting is not followed by any other nation except those that have taken up boxing as a sport in modern times. The fist is actually a rather clumsy instrument for applying force. The size of the front of the fist is so great that it distributes the force of the blow over a large area and lessens its effectiveness. This is the reason why a boxing contest of the bare-knuckle variety often took such a long time. It rarely ended in a knockout because the combatant found it extremely difficult to put the opponent out of action with a blow. Instead, he was slowly worn down to exhaustion and then finished off with several blows. Bare-knuckle boxers were also fearful of breaking their fingers and therefore did not strike as hard as boxers who wore protective coverings on their hands. A karate chop, if delivered to a sensitive area, will disable or kill instantaneously.

To administer a karate blow, cup the fingers very slightly so the muscles on the edge of the hand are tensed and hold the thumb away from the rest of the hand. Experiment a bit, and you'll soon find the position in which the lower edge of your hand is most rigid. The long, thin, blade-like edge of the hand, when applied with force to the back or side of the neck, the throat, the bridge of the nose, and to various nerve and muscle centers in the extremities and the trunk will often either put the attacker out of business right away or will paralyze him to such an extent that a more effective blow or kick can then be delivered. Some enthusiasts toughen their hands by soaking them in brine every day or by plunging them into buckets of sand over and over again. They even break thin pine boards in order to build up a tough, hard ridge of callous on the edge of the hand. This is not necessary if you are simply using Oriental methods of fighting for self-defense. If you notice that a man has hard ridges on the bottom edges of his hands, however, he's not a person you should go out of your way to quarrel with.

The word *jujitsu* is variously translated, but most often it is said to mean the use of the opponent's own strength to injure or defeat him. For instance, in a very simple example, let us say that someone grasps you by the wrist and attempts to pull you off your feet so that you fall to the floor. Your natural response is to resist the pull by pulling in the opposite direction. If you let this go on long enough and the attacker has more strength and weight, he will inevitably succeed in throwing you. The capable fighter will instead resist the pull at least once and then suddenly give way and assist the attacker by pushing in his direction. He may also aim the weight of his body at the attacker and jump toward him with all the power of his legs. If accurately timed, this move will force the attacker over onto his back with a crash that will often put him out of action. Timing is the essence of this aspect of Oriental fighting, and masters of the art often defeat the opponent by an adroit use of his own strength applied when the opponent least expects it.

The Orientals also taught Western combat men much about the

human nervous system. The rules of Western wrestling as practiced in most countries forbid "punishing" holds. In other words, Western wrestling involves only the skillful application of bodily strength in ways that will not permanently damage the opponent. Not so with the Oriental form of combat. Learned Japanese instructors probably know as much about the human muscular and nervous system as many medical men. For instance, imagine for a moment that you have clamped your arms around an opponent's waist but that his arms are above yours and that the opponent is capable of putting up a good unarmed defense. Now place the tip of your own thumb under your own jaw inside the bone and far back toward the place where the jawbone meets the neck. Press inward and upward *very gently* and consider the sensation that you feel. You are touching a very delicate nerve center. If the opponent really forced his thumb into that soft concentration of nerves, you would be forced to let go immediately or you would faint from the effects of the extreme pain. These nerve centers are located all over the body. Remember that attacks in these areas can inflict severe permanent damage. If you practice such defenses with a partner, do so very gently. Several of these defenses are shown in the photographic portion of this chapter.

In European and American wrestling in the ring, the two combatants wear only trunks and shoes. All holds must be applied to bare skin. In the Oriental form, the contestants wear loose-fitting pants and jackets, and many holds are applied to the cloth. Actually, the Oriental form is much more realistic since self-defense normally involves fighting a fully clothed opponent. You can usually apply force more easily if you grasp the opponent's clothing rather than bare, slippery skin.

The art of falling is also taught to every student of Oriental unarmed fighting. The floor of the judo studio is covered with mats and the student is expected to be able to fall at any time and from almost any position without undue damage. He is also taught to recover quickly. Many experts are as skilled as circus tumblers. Throw them to the mat and they will bounce up again so quickly that there is no time to strike or kick when they are in a disadvantageous position.

245

In reality, however, much of this training in falling goes to waste when the fighter using Oriental methods faces an opponent on a hard sidewalk or a bare wooden floor. Even if you are quite skilled, it's difficult to fall on concrete or bare wood without some damage. Therefore, the methods of falling taught in modern courses are used mostly for sport judo when opponents meet in a well-appointed gym with good floor mats. As any experienced street fighter knows, it's best not to lose your footing. Once down, you'll probably never get up again. And yet, the Oriental methods of falling can be life-savers if they are properly applied. It takes a great deal of skill to fall on a hard surface without damage. Yet, if worst comes to worst, the Oriental methods may prevent severe harm. Using them will often prevent the head from hitting the sidewalk or floor with great force.

In the Orient, great attention is paid to conditioning the mind for combat through contemplation. The teacher instructs his student in developing an attitude toward combat that stands him in good stead. The good Oriental fighter is calm, and yet he is exceedingly aggressive at the same time. The best attitude cuts off all awareness of pain or possible permanent damage and concentrates the attention solely on effective fighting. In American courses, this aspect of the instruction is almost always omitted. Veterans of serious combat will tell you, however, that a hotheaded, wild-eyed aggressiveness almost always leads to recklessness and loss of the fight. On the other hand, timid concentration on defense gives to the opponent all the opportunities for initiative and almost always results in defeat. In a dangerous situation, if you can remain calm and be aggressive at the same time, you have a tremendous advantage.

There you have it—a complex system of fighting which takes years to learn. A thorough study would involve long periods of contemplation and philosophical instruction. In many of the courses offered in the United States today, the chief aim is to convince the student that he or she is getting his or her money's worth. The easiest way to do this is to present the student with a certain number of set defenses against standardized attacks so that confidence and limited skills are built up rapidly. The instructor always approaches the student in the same, set way until the student learns the exact defense for that attack and uses it quickly and effectively. Then the instructor moves on to another set form of attack, and so on, until the course is complete. The student, glowingly confident, may then encounter an experienced thug who attacks in a way the instructor never mentioned. The result is a shattering experience for the student.

It's much better to build up an attitude of respectful fear of any form of violence. Avoid it as the plague, but if it comes, use every possible means to defend yourself including bites if they fit into the particular situation. Sometimes the only way to make a thug let go of you is to bite his nose, and yet I have never seen this particular defense mentioned in any book on unarmed combat. An aggressive street fighter will use this defense instinctively.

Many sport judo courses offered in the United States omit all mention of kicks and blows with the edge of the hand. These are thought to be too dangerous and very unsporting. In defending yourself against a dangerous attack, don't worry about sportsmanship.

It's true that many of the defenses shown in the following photographs are intended to be used against certain specified forms of attack. Whenever possible, however, the author has added a caption that points out unexpected variations which may be used by the criminal and effective variations for the defender. Try always to learn the *general* principle behind each defense so that you can improvise variations to suit the circumstances. There's no rule that you should refrain from slamming a door on a criminal's hand, for instance, rather than use a complex Oriental wrist grip.

The defenses presented in this chapter can be divided into two large classes—those intended to be used against drunks and other people who are merely annoying, and defenses that should be used only against a criminal who is making a dangerous attack. The latter class of defenses includes a few to be used against armed attack.

The defenses against mild attacks hardly require practice. Studying the pictures will often be enough since these defenses are very simple and are only intended to give you a way of breaking a hold on your body or clothing. These simple releases, however, are very

247

useful because they prevent the aggressor from thinking that you are an easy mark. If an intoxicated person, for instance, grasps you around the neck, and you break the hold instantaneously, he is informed that it's best to keep away from you. If you were unable to defend yourself at all, he would be assured of an easy victim, and robbery or rape might follow.

If you break a weak aggressor's grip, he will usually depart rapidly. In some cases, however, a more forceful attack may be made. If it is, you must be ready to squelch it with a very powerful blow or kick, or with a throw. In some cases, these follow-ups should be delivered very quickly— —as soon as the aggressor shows the first sign that he is about to renew his attack. With more dangerous aggressive people, the follow-up should be delivered as quickly as possible in an effort to disable the attacker before he can do any damage. You yourself must know what you should do— merely break the hold and then "laugh off" the incident, or immediately disable the aggressor. If you disable or even kill under circumstances that do not warrant it, you may find yourself charged as the aggressor by the law. And yet, you should not give up the advantage of a quick response if the attack is really dangerous. As with all means of self-defense, you are the only judge of the circumstances and you must be willing to stand on your decision.

PRACTICE

Mere study of the photographs in this chapter will give you a useful knowledge of the best ways to break clumsy grips by an unskilled aggressor. The methods presented for defense against more serious attacks should be practiced if they are to be of any use. Even the more simple defenses, however, should be practiced if you are completely inexperienced in unarmed defense. The essence of practice is duplicating the circumstances under which the attack may occur in reality. Run through the defenses with a partner several times, alternating the roles of defender and attacker until you really understand them. Then try to duplicate real attacks. The defender should not know which grip or other attack is going to be used. Place yourself in the center of the floor in a relaxed position and tell your partner to use any attack he or she pleases.

Of course, the attacker should not use violent or disabling blows or kicks in these sessions, but it's very easy to pretend to be doing so as long as the kick or blow is stopped short just before it lands.

Let the pretended aggressor circle you and even make simulated attacks from the rear without telling you what he or she intends to do. You'll soon find that it becomes quite an interesting contest, but it should not become too realistic. The defender's chief object is to meet that first attack as quickly and effectively as possible. If the initial grip is broken or the blow is warded off, and the follow-up can be delivered, the practice is real enough. It's important to remember that the attacker should not become too sophisticated. By studying this chapter, and practicing the defenses, you cannot build up defenses against a trained aggressor. Therefore, the aggressive tactics used in practice sessions should not be complicated. The pretended attacker should *not* allow in advance for the reaction of the defender. Instead, he or she should attempt to simulate the actions of the ordinary, untrained, rather clumsy thug. For practice in more sophisticated defenses, you should take a course at a good school of defense.

To practice, you really need gym mats to preclude the possibility of a punishing fall. At the very least, you should practice on a soft lawn. A child's toy pistol, a length of soft rubber hose to simulate a club, and a rubber toy knife are useful props. Remember that some of the blows and holds described in this chapter can inflict severe and permanent injuries or even death. Your partner must be a calm, controlled person who understands exactly what the object of these practice sessions is—to familiarize both of you with methods of defense, not to use them in any sort of competition with one another.

THE LAST RESORT

If you are overwhelmed by a sudden attack and cannot use any of the releases, much less follow-up tactics, you can at least try to limit the damage that the criminal is trying to inflict. This particular defense needs no practice. In fact, if you ever find yourself in this unfortunate situation, you'll use it as an instinctive defense. Try to fall to the floor in a corner of the room or elevator, or if you are outdoors, against the front of a building or some other solid object. Draw your arms up over your head and throat to protect them and pull your knees up as close to your chin as possible to protect your stomach and crotch. Your back should be against the wall. Sometimes it helps to roll over halfway onto your back if the criminal tries to kick the side of your body with a downward motion or "stomp." The floor and the walls protect most of you, and you present the attacker with arms and legs so that he cannot reach a vital part. In this position, the attacker may inflict considerable pain, but it's difficult for him to reach a vital part or to knock you unconscious. Of course, you should shout your lungs out if that seems the best course. On the other hand, it may be best to pretend to lose consciousness. If you have a weapon, this position will sometimes permit you to get it out, though it is necessary to remove an arm, and a kick in the head is usually the immediate result.

Successful unarmed resistance to criminal attacks often involves much more than a few graceful sport-judo exchanges. In using any form of physical defense, always make sure that you are acting within the law.

CHAPTER VIII

Selecting and Training a Defense Dog

O^N a fairly calm day, a dog with a good nose can detect an animal as much as a quarter of a mile away if the wind is blowing from the animal to the dog. Even when the air is still, a good dog can sense an intruder when he is some distance away. The dog's hearing is so acute that it is capable of detecting sounds that would escape its master. In addition, the animal hears sounds so high in pitch that they cannot be detected by the human ear. Acuteness of hearing and perception of high-pitched sounds make it possible for a dog to detect the sound of breathing or rustling, scuffing noises that no human being could ever detect.

CANINE SENSES AND BEHAVIOR

A dog is particularly effective as a guardian during the night when there are few distracting noises and the smells of cooking, smoking, and so forth are absent.

At night, a good dog's perception may seem to border on the supernatural. Many a dog can easily detect the presence of its master at a gate 50 or 60 feet from the house, and will go to the door to welcome him even though the man arrives at irregular times after dark.

I knew one wise old farm dog that could detect the opening of a door or window at night anywhere among a group of farm buildings. Whether this mongrel hound heard the movement or smelled the person is difficult to say, but he would pad quietly onto the scene any time a door or window was moved, and it would not have gone well for a criminal.

Good watchdogs are on the alert to some extent even when they are asleep. Slight noises and odors will wake them instantly if there is any danger. Dogs are also remarkable for their ability to track down intruders. A good German shepherd can follow a person through thick brush and across many distracting trails and will finally locate the quarry even though the person is hidden. The animal does this by picking up scent on objects a person brushes against and the odor left on the ground by the feet, or perhaps, on a garment left behind. The nose of a well-trained bloodhound is so accurate that the "testimony" of bloodhounds has sometimes been accepted in court when the dog picked out a suspect from among several people.

The dog is an intelligent animal, but its intelligence is much lower than a human being's. The proof of this is that the chief method of teaching a dog is repetition. The trainer carefully repeats the command and indicates the response the dog ought to make over and over again until the animal finally grasps what is wanted. Training a dog is much like instructing a willing but rather dull child, and the trainer must have considerable patience and affection for the animal in order to do it properly.

It should be remembered that the dog's sense of smell depends largely on the wind. If the wind is blowing from the intruder to the dog, the dog will catch it very easily. If the wind is blowing fairly strongly from the dog to the intruder, the animal will not easily detect a person. Hunters and those who use military sentry dogs know this very well. When no wind is blowing, however, the dog's "covering" ability is more limited. Nevertheless, a good sentry dog can usually detect the presence of an intruder at least 10 or 15 yards away when there is absolutely no wind. Of course, the dog's sensitive hearing helps. The dog may hear the intruder's breathing long before it detects the intruder's scent. This ability varies considerably from dog to dog, even if they are of the same breed. One German shepherd may be an absolute genius at detecting an intruder under adverse, still-air conditions, and another may be quite poor at it. It's only by working with the dog that one gets an idea of its ability.

A dog does not see color. Everything looks like a black-and-white photograph to a dog, and there's considerable evidence that this canine black-and-white is out of focus and very blurred. If a dog does not smell or hear an intruder, it's very unlikely that the animal will detect him unless he moves. The animal sees motion very well, perhaps because everything *else* it sees is an unmoving blur. This is why experienced trainers stand still if a dog shows any signs of aggressiveness. If a dog is nervous and may bite, it's best not to make any sudden movements. If the dog looks vicious, don't run unless you are absolutely sure that you can get away, perhaps by slamming a door behind you. Don't suddenly raise your hand because the dog will almost certainly leap for the moving hand with snapping jaws. If possible, ease slowly away while saying soothing things to the dog.

This sensitivity to movement is of great use in guard dogs. If the animal is told to stay and guard an intruder, the animal has a natural instinct to leap at movement and attack. As long as the intruder remains still, a well-trained dog will simply stay on guard. If, however, the intruder makes a sudden movement, perhaps to reach for a weapon, the well-trained guard dog will instantly charge and bite at the moving hand. German shepherds and Doberman pinschers seem to have a very highly developed instinct along these lines. If the animal is on the alert, and the intruder raises a club or knife, the dog will be chewing the man's wrist in a split second. In training, therefore, you should be very careful to avoid sudden motions.

There's a theory about animal behavior that one often hears from dog trainers as well as those who work with lions, tigers, trained bears, and other large, dangerous, circus or zoo animals. Whether the theory is correct or not is anyone's guess, but it does explain a great deal about animal behavior, and many trainers act on it. If the trainer or other person is in a calm, confident frame of mind, the theory goes, the smell the dog gets is pleasant and reassuring. If, on the other hand, the individual is uneasy or fright-

253

ened, the sweat glands exude a smell that is very unpleasant to the animal. If the animal is aggressive, it will attack as soon as the smell reaches it.

This theory may explain why dogs can detect untrustworthy persons. Put yourself in the place of a criminal who enters a home or place of business. Since the activity is dangerous, and the criminal may be apprehended or injured, he is uneasy or fearful, though he may show no outward sign of it. The dog, however, gets one whiff of the criminal, and will sense that there is trouble brewing.

People who know and love dogs often defer to this judgment by nose. If a dog reacts unfavorably to a given person, the dog's owner often regards that person with distrust. The dog is probably correct. An untrustworthy person may not show that he has bad motives, but he himself knows that he is guilty of some dishonesty and is at least fearful of being detected. The dog literally smells out the criminal. Pay attention when your dog consistently growls at one particular delivery man or one individual in your circle of acquaintances. Of course, there is one exception. If a person has a fear of animals caused by a bad experience in childhood—perhaps an attack by a dog—he or she will exude the odor that annoys dogs whether or not bad motives are involved.

If you fear dogs yourself, it's impossible for you to conceal it from an alert animal. It is unfair to expect the dog to overcome its natural dislike merely because you have paid out a few dollars to buy the animal. Even though a dog is a very useful, almost unique security device, it's not worth buying one if you cannot train it and use it properly. It may be very dangerous. If someone else in your family is afraid of animals, don't buy a watchdog. The dog would be a source of danger to that person.

How and Where the Dog Is Used

In a disturbed neighborhood where many crimes occur, a house where a large, powerful dog is present is usually not entered. With women spending a great deal of time alone at home, sexual criminals sometimes invade homes, but they do not usually do so, if they know that a good watchdog is inside. If a German shepherd or other large dog is seen around the home or when being walked, it's often enough to preclude any criminal attack. Even if the criminal does not know of the dog's presence, its barking will often warn him off when he first approaches the house or apartment. "Beware of the Dog" signs help.

In addition to this guard duty, dogs are also sometimes used to locate criminals already known to be on the property, and they may also be used to attack, though these two jobs are rarely done by civilian dogs. You are responsible for the actions of your dog just as you are responsible for your actions with a dangerous weapon. If your dog injures an innocent person, you are subject to two kinds of consequences—civil suit for damages by the injured person or his relatives, and criminal prosecution for breaking the laws controlling dogs in your local community, provided of course that you actually did violate these laws. It is best to regard the dog as a dangerous weapon. If you do this, you'll immediately see that you must follow the law of the self-defense as explained in Chapter IV. Do not release the dog for attack or urge the animal on unless your life or the life of a near relative is in danger. In Chapter IV, it was stated that the only form of danger to property which justifies the use of weapons in defense is an attempt to burn a home or to destroy it with explosives. In such situations, the homeowner and his family may use weapons in defense, and in cases of attempted arson and bombing, he or they have the right to use a dog as a weapon. If you have any doubts about these points, it's best to reread the material in Chapter IV on self-defense.

Usually, town or city laws and ordinances have provisions intended to prevent accidental attacks by dogs. Commonly, the law provides that the dog shall always be on a leash when outside *or* that the animal must be muzzled. That is, you can usually release your dog from the leash provided it is wearing a muzzle, though there are some towns that do not even allow this. You should carefully check your community's regulations, and you should abide by them. If you do not, you are courting a lawsuit or a criminal charge. And don't make the mistake of thinking that if you comply with these regulations you are completely absolved of any damage that your dog may do. For instance, if you live in a town where the dog may be released as long as it is wearing a muzzle, you may still be liable for damages if your dog digs up a flower bed or knocks down a child. In such a case, the owner of the dog will probably not be charged with a violation of the law, but he certainly may be sued for damages.

If you live in an apartment, there's obviously no question about the fact that your dog will be an inside watchdog. You couldn't leave it outside in the hall if you wanted to do so. In rural areas where there are no restrictions against allowing a dog to run loose, many farmers keep their watchdogs outside and do not chain them. Many rural people simply provide a doghouse and let the dog shift for itself except for one feeding a day. Sometimes the dog develops into a superb guard dog because it is allowed a great deal of freedom. Many of these animals have an almost uncanny ability to be anywhere on the farm where needed, night or day. Yet, these farm dogs sometimes get into trouble by attacking game, domestic stock, and even innocent people. If the dog gets into trouble, it may be shot by a conservation officer or its owner may be sued. More often, the dog simply vanishes one night in a trap or after a blast from a neighboring farmer's shotgun. Remember that deadly weapons may not be used against ordinary trespassers, and that a dog's attack is equivalent to the use of weapons.

I'd therefore advise you to keep your dog inside your home, except when the animal is firmly controlled by a leash or muzzle. This is the only possible course in the suburbs unless you have a yard with an extremely high, dog-proof fence—something that few homeowners have. With the watchdog inside the home, the animal is a safeguard against entrance by a criminal. If the dog is outside, the criminal may find it possible to silence the dog before approaching the house.

Here again, good security hardware and a security room help. In some homes, the dog is given the run of the lower floor and cellar but not the upstairs bedrooms. It's the dog's job to give the alarm and delay the criminal if possible while you retire to the security room, call the police, and get a weapon ready. Don't go to the dog's assistance, and don't leave the security room unless it's absolutely necessary. Even though you love the animal, the risk is not justifiable. If your dog is intelligent, the tone of its barking and snarling will tell you whether or not the emergency is serious enough for a call to the police.

CHOOSING THE RIGHT BREED

There is one exception to the general rule that dogs learn by repetition. Certain breeds have *inherited* abilities and instincts. For instance, it's usually quite difficult or impossible to get a German shepherd to look for game birds and point at them with its nose for the benefit of the hunter, but a good pointer or English setter usually does this at an early age without much urging from its master. Inherited instincts, sharpened by selective breeding, make it easier for dogs to learn certain things. Each breed has a specialization, and if you want a good watchdog, it's best to employ one of the breeds that specializes in this work. Otherwise, training is difficult, and you'll probably wind up with a poor watchdog.

If you live in an apartment or other confined quarters, it's foolish to keep a large dog. German shepherds, Doberman pinschers, and other large breeds rarely adjust to close confinement and often become surly or vicious. For an apartment, select an alert small dog with a loud bark, of a breed that has watchdog instincts. The bites of these dogs are very seldom harmful, but even a small dog can give warning of an intruder and may frighten him away by barking.

For confined quarters, the dachshund, the fox terrier, and almost any of the medium-sized terrier breeds are usually quite satisfactory. Terriers have been used as watchdogs on European farms for centuries. The dachshund is very good for this kind of service. This dog is small, but it is usually deep-chested and therefore has a loud bark. The dachshund is small only because it has short legs. If you examine its mouth, you'll find that the teeth are large and seem to be intended for a much taller dog. Most dachshunds are alert and quite courageous, though sometimes you'll run across a lazy one. Bulldogs may also be a good choice for an apartment, but some small bulldogs have high-pitched, weak barks. The fox terrier is a good choice since it is usually very brave and alert.

257

Where large quarters are available and the dog will have much outdoor exercise, the best choice is a German shepherd. The German shepherd is the *only* breed used by the United States Air Force, the largest user of sentry dogs, and this dog has a remarkable record of service in both World Wars. This animal is remarkably intelligent and has an excellent nose. If the animal has not been mistreated, it is usually not *too* aggressive, something that cannot be said of some other breeds. The ordinary civilian does not want a dog that will automatically attack all strangers.

Several other breeds work well as guard dogs provided they are not confined too closely. The Airedale and his German relative, the giant or standard schnauzer are excellent, and any of the larger terriers will work well provided they have adequate training and a good relationship with the owner and his family.

Avoid the bird-hunting breeds. Pointers, setters, and most spaniels have been bred for obedience when hunting, and it seems that this has deadened almost all their aggressive qualities. The same is not true of the hunting hounds used for furred game such as the dachshund, the English foxhound, and terriers. Of course, there are exceptions. There *are* such things as vicious bird dogs and cowardly German shepherds, but they are comparatively rare.

A few breeds are too aggressive for guard service with the average family, and I'd number the Doberman pinscher, the Russian wolfhound, and the chow among them. These dogs are remarkably intelligent and can be formidable adversaries to the criminal. These breeds, however, are often individualists, and they are difficult to train unless the trainer has considerable experience and a natural understanding of their temperaments. The Doberman, for instance, is the official war dog of the U.S. Marine Corps, precisely because it is so aggressive. The Air Force, on the other hand, uses the German shepherd because that service is interested more in a good sentry or scout dog than an aggressive fighter or man-killer. Some of these dogs are remarkably "one-man" minded. They will often select a single individual in a family as master, and will only obey commands given by that person. If the dog happens to select the man of the family who is often away from home, the dog may be very hard to handle.

258

The medium-sized mongrel with some shepherd or terrier blood often makes a superb guard dog. A fairly large mongrel with a deep bark, a good nose, and brains often outshines the fancier breeds in protecting a family. If you have such a dog, don't sell it or get rid of it because you think a German shepherd or an Airedale might do better. Your mongrel may be the best possible choice. Few people, however, will buy a mongrel for guard-dog service or acquire one from the city pound. The buyer does not know what to expect from a cross-blooded dog. The cross may be an excellent all-round guard dog, but it may be a coward or too vicious to be trained. With the established breeds, you at least know what to expect.

If you do purchase a standard breed and subsequently discover that the animal is deficient in intelligence, hearing, nose or eyesight, get rid of the dog at once. There's always some friend who merely wants a pet. Don't rely on a defective dog for guard service —it's like using a defective weapon.

If you do not know enough about dogs to select a breed that will make a good guard dog, you cannot go too far wrong if you choose a German shepherd or an Airedale for roomy living quarters or a dachshund or fox terrier for alarm duty in a small apartment.

AGE AND SEX

The Air Force accepts dogs that are between 12 and 36 months of age. Dogs younger than that are too much trouble to handle in a military installation. Dogs older than 36 months may be so set in their ways that it would be difficult to train them for guard service. The military services accept males or females, except that female dogs must be spayed. The reason is obvious. A female dog in the excitement of heat is undependable for guard service, and spells of heat come on every five or six months and may last from fifteen days to six or seven weeks.

Once you've decided on the right breed for your situation, look around for a kennel that handles the breed. Various dog magazines carry frequent advertisements from kennels, or write to the American Kennel Club, 51 Madison Avenue, New York, N.Y., for the address of the breed association for your breed. The breed association, a private club of owners and breeders, will put you in touch with a reputable kennel. Some people who sell dogs don't mind in the least if they can pass off a sick or defective animal. If possible, take a person who's familiar with dogs along on your buying expedition, so that he can advise you if a given dog is sick, stupid, deaf, or vicious. There are some advantages in buying a mature dog (they're usually over the puppy sicknesses), but I'd advise you to buy a very young animal. Buy a male unless you are willing to pay the additional cost of spaying.

Kennels usually offer pups as soon as they are weaned, which is about six to eight weeks after birth. If you buy an animal at this age, your first training tasks will be to housebreak the dog and to prevent it from chewing up the furniture, shoes, and everything else it can get hold of. This early training will get you acquainted with the dog, and the animal will begin to know and trust you and your family. This trusting relationship is the most important requirement in training a family watchdog, and it's easier to establish it with a puppy. Your local library will provide you with a good book on housebreaking and puppy training.

Play with the pup frequently and talk to it as much as you can. Encourage your children to be kind to the dog, but don't let them play with it too roughly. Children can be very cruel to small animals, and puppy teeth are very sharp. If the puppy nips a child, the puncture should be thoroughly disinfected. If the slightest sign of infection does show up, take the child to a doctor immediately.

You'll run into the puppy's desire to chew anything and everything it can get hold of except the rubber bone or other chewing toy you've bought for it at the pet shop. The same technique you used for housebreaking should be used to correct this trouble. A calm but forceful "No!" and showing the pup the device that it should chew on is enough. By the time the dog has its permanent teeth, you should be feeding it on solid food rather than puppy mush and you should be able to give it a bone once in a while (never bird bones and other bones that shatter easily or the dog's intestines may be punctured). Then the chewing problem should be over. Use the command "No!" and much scolding whenever the pup makes a mistake, just as you do in housebreaking.

In doing all this, you will teach the animal to obey the command, "No!" instantly. On hearing the command, the dog should immediately stop *whatever* it is doing even if it is in a highly excited state. Obedience to this command is very important in any watchdog.

If you buy a mature dog one or two years old as the Air Force does, you will encounter some difficulties. The animal has obviously become accustomed to other people while growing up, and it will take some time before it gets used to you and your family. You also lose all the advantages of housebreaking and other puppy training. Puppy training trains the dog but it also trains the dog's family since harsh discipline and rough handling just don't work with a puppy. You're forced to use the right methods. If you find you haven't the patience, start looking for another home for the dog.

If you buy from a dependable kennel, the owner or handler will be glad to spend a few minutes with you to tell how the dog has been fed and to give you advice about care. Many kennels have printed brochures on dog care which are carefully prepared with the kennel's breed in mind. Ask the kennel for the name of a good veterinarian who will administer the right course of injections to prevent distemper and rabies and other diseases at the right age for your dog and who will also spay females.

With a careful, understanding new owner, even a mature dog has little difficulty in adjusting to new circumstances, provided the dog has been treated decently in the past. You don't want a canine neurotic in your home.

Make an effort to determine the right food for a dog of the age and breed you have selected, and make a special effort to inform yourself about grooming and hygiene. For instance, if you choose a dog with a thick, curly coat, you're going to have to devote considerable time to combing, brushing, and clipping unless you're willing to hire a professional. If you expect an animal to act as a guardian, you owe it the best of care. Ordinary dog care, including hygiene, feeding, and grooming are not within the scope of this book.

MILITARY DOGS

The United States Army, the Marine Corps, and the Air Force use dogs for sentry, scout, and combat duty, and their training methods are quite similar in many respects. The Air Force, however, uses its dogs as guards at missile-launching sites, warehouses, airstrips, and other places where security is a problem, primarily at night. The civilian can learn a bit about training a watchdog from a brief outline of how the Air Force handles sentry-dog training.

As soon as possible, each young German shepherd is turned over to an enlisted dog handler who manages that dog and that dog alone for the entire term of its service life. The animal very seldom comes into close contact with any other person. The first step is obedience training. The handler works with the animal to teach it to walk sedately by his side without lunging at the leash, to come when called, to stop when the command "No!" is given, and to learn all the other ordinary obedience responses. In this basic obedience training, the handler and his dog work through the course under the direction of an experienced trainer who teaches the dog handlers, who in turn train the animals. In this training, the supervising trainer is careful to avoid giving commands directly to the dog. In a quiet voice, he gives orders to a group of handlers who relay the commands to their animals. The handlers remain in exclusive control of their animals. In order to instill quick obedience and precision, both the handlers and the dogs spend long hours at close-order military drill, including responses to such commands as parade rest, about face, to the rear march.

After obedience training, the handler takes his dog into intermediate training in which the animal learns to jump obstacles on command, to crawl through tunnels, and to respond to commands when off the leash. Only after all this is learned does the dog undergo field training for military guard duty.

In field training, the Air Force sentry dog undergoes agitation. An enlisted man is dressed in a heavily padded "attack suit." The suit completely protects the body and prevents the dog from reaching any part of it with its teeth. At frequent intervals, the dog is

262

"agitated" by a complete stranger in this protective clothing. At times, the animal is chained to a stake and the stranger approaches and teases the dog from a short distance with a leafy switch or with the heavily padded gloves of his attack suit. In more advanced training, the stranger hides in a field and the handler uses the dog to seek out the agitator either by following a carefully laid scent trail or by scenting the intruder at a distance. When discovered, the agitator sneaks away quietly and the dog is allowed to follow for a short distance, snarling and barking, and occasionally sinking its teeth in the attack suit. In all these encounters, the dog wins by driving the intruder away. In the final stage of sentry training, the dog is taught to stay on guard when the handler apprehends the intruder and disarms him. If the agitator pushes the handler away, strikes at him, or breaks away, the dog automatically reattacks the agitator without command. The dog is tested to be sure that the handler can halt aggressive action by giving the command "Out!" which causes the dog to stop its attack and move away.

The Air Force relies heavily on the natural but not excessive aggressiveness of the German shepherd but an unusually passive animal receives more agitation training than the others. Some shepherds, on the other hand, are so aggressive that little agitation is needed. In other words, individual modifications are made to suit the individual nature of the dog.

In the entire training course, the dog's handler is the only person who issues commands to the dog, and he is the only person to come into close contact with the animal. Because of the frequent agitation sessions with complete strangers, the dog develops a distrustful, vicious attitude toward them. It is such an automatic response, that the dog can normally be expected to attack every stranger who comes within reach unless restrained by the handler.

This military method of training develops a remarkably effective guard dog, but the animal is very vicious. Few civilians want this kind of animal because it would be extremely dangerous even to members of his own family. The military method of training would be impossible for many civilians. In the military system, the dog has only one master who is seldom out of contact with the animal. In civilian life, any family dog must have several masters

263

and it must learn to obey all of them. For instance, if the dog is trained by the man of the family, it must also learn to obey the commands of the wife and the elder children. The military system of agitation is also quite difficult because it's often impossible to find complete strangers who would be willing to act as agitators, and it would also be quite risky since the dog might possibly injure an agitator no matter what kind of attack suit was rigged up. In the Air Force, the agitator is an enlisted man who volunteers for the duty and there are no lawsuits.

CIVILIAN DOG-TRAINING

The civilian needs a form of training that will develop a good watchdog, but it should not make the dog too aggressive. Much of the remainder of this chapter details methods used for years by people who understand animals and who know what they want in performance by their dogs. There is little in print on this form of training.

The system presented here omits many commands ordinarily taught to show dogs. It's not necessary, for instance, to teach an ordinary watchdog to sit or lie down on command.

If you are only interested in a small "alarm dog," you should still give it some training in order to maintain control. Even a small dog's bite may lead to a costly lawsuit. If you are training a large dog such as a shepherd or a big terrier for more active work, you may not wish to include all the steps in this program such as training to assure confidence in spite of gunfire. Leave out those forms of training which are not suited to your own situation.

Before you purchase an animal, you should examine your home situation carefully. Dogs sometimes do injure children or adults even though they have been carefully trained. To maintain a watchdog, you must be prepared to undergo this risk, though a good dog and careful training makes it small indeed. Safety to yourself and the members of your family will depend mostly on everyone's ability to understand the animal and build up a confident, trusting relationship. Almost all dogs respond to this form of training with a love and respect that is more dependable than the friendship of most human beings, but if you are not able to build up such a relationship, it's best not to have anything to do with dogs. They're much too intelligent to allow themselves to be deceived by people who do not have the right attitude.

FAMILY TRAINING

To train a small alarm dog, you'll probably only need a short leather leash, a leather collar or harness, and a muzzle. Buy them at a reputable store and make sure that they are strong enough for your dog. In towns where it's required, the license tag or plate should be attached to the dog's collar and the collar should be worn whenever the dog is outside.

You do not need a stick, switch, or whip of any kind to train a watchdog. If the animal requires discipline, a jerk on the leash and a few forcefully-delivered repetitions of "No!" should be enough. If you begin beating your dog, it's a sign that either the dog or yourself (probably yourself) is unsuited for training. Excessive physical punishment is definitely not part of a good trainer's bag of tricks. If you've built up a decent relationship with your dog in early housebreaking and other puppy training, the animal will want and need your approval, and the tone of your voice will be enough to insure control. Yet, it cannot be denied that sometimes a pup will only respond to some form of physical punishment. A slap or a light blow with a rolled-up newspaper should be enough. It hurts the dog's feelings, and that's all you should need.

Don't reward the dog with food when it obeys your commands or does something special. Profuse approval expressed in your tone of voice and petting the dog is enough. No other special rewards should be given to the dog for doing what is expected of it, and one meal a day is enough for any mature, healthy dog provided it is given promptly at the same time every day.

Never allow visitors, friends, or strangers to give your dog candy or food. Besides ruining the animal's food discipline, this practice endangers the dog. Criminals have often fed dogs poison, and there are people who hate dogs and are very happy to feed them corrosive substances disguised with a tidbit in order to watch their suffering, or in order to rid the neighborhood of what they describe as "a pest." Yes, that's no exaggeration—many dogs are poisoned for

265

no better reason. It's best if only members of the family put out food and water for the dog, and it's best if the same dishes are always put down for it in the same place. If you discourage the dog from feeding on things given to it by strangers for a long enough period, the animal will usually get the idea that it should not accept anything unless a member of the family offers it.

If the different members of the family use different commands for the same action, the dog will become unbearably confused. For instance, if the man of the house uses the command "No!" when he wishes the dog to stop doing something, but his wife says, "Stop it," the dog may never learn to obey. All members of the family should use the same words in giving commands to the dog, and they should also use the same tone of voice for each command.

Even more important than standardized commands are the attitudes of the various members of the family. In child psychology, it's known that both parents should have similar attitudes on important matters so that they will not simultaneously teach the child conflicting behavior. A good dog has much the same attitude as a child, and an effort should be made to avoid confusing it. Take such a simple thing as a dog's desire to lie on a sofa or in a chair. If the woman of the family constantly orders the dog off the furniture while the man of the family often invites the dog to sit on the sofa beside him, the dog may become confused, or still worse, the animal may build up considerable resentment against the woman. If the dog's mistress is always willing to feed the dog whenever the animal wants to eat, she'll help to make the dog antagonistic toward those members of the family who refuse to feed the animal except at the regular hour. All members of the family should insist on the same behavior from the dog in important matters. That is not to say that children shouldn't play with the dog if the parents don't do so or that the man of the family can't be a little more stern than others, but on important matters, all should use the same commands and insist on the same responses.

After housebreaking and chewing are under control, you'll begin walking your dog regularly, and it will become accustomed to collar and leash. You should also make every effort to accustom the animal to a muzzle while it is quite young since the muzzle is important in training a watchdog. Even if the animal is on the leash, occasionally muzzle it simply to accustom the animal to the device.

Walk your dog at least twice a day to make sure that it gets all the opportunity needed to relieve itself and so that it gets sufficient exercise. If you can trust the dog off the leash, perhaps with its muzzle on, give it every opportunity for a carefree romp.

If you do all the things mentioned so far, your dog will probably develop love for you and your family, and anyone who's at all familiar with dogs knows that love is *not* too strong a word. Such a dog obeys naturally and will do everything in its power to protect and help its master and the family.

Let us assume that a family lives in an apartment or a small suburban home and that the dog is a naturally spirited, intelligent, but small animal such as a dachshund, a fox terrier, or perhaps one of the other terriers. If the family follows the ideas presented so far, *very little if any additional training will be needed.* The dog will be a reliable watchdog, provided the animal responds quickly to the single command: "No!" The dog's natural instincts will take over. A good dog is interested in all that goes on. When someone leaves or enters the house, the dog notices it. If someone rings the bell or knocks, the dog will be right there barking as loud as it can. If the dog is as alert as it should be, it will wake up out of a sound sleep anytime an outside door or window is opened or a lock is turned. It will announce the fact with loud barking. If it ever happens that an untrustworthy person visits your home, you'll probably find that the dog will bark, snarl, and show every intention of biting. A good dog does all these things naturally.

The final test occurs if the dog encounters an intruder. With a friendly family dog, it's sometimes quite difficult to know what the animal would actually do if a criminal tried to enter the home. Try to get the cooperation of a friend whom the dog does not know. Perhaps on his first visit to your home, give the friend the key to your house or apartment and ask him to enter it unannounced and with only a little noise, at a time set in advance. It's best to conduct this test when the house is quiet. Half an hour before the test, muzzle the dog so that it gets used to having the muzzle on. Fasten

267

the muzzle securely. Your unannounced visitor should be wearing old clothes. The dog's behavior when the door opens will tell you whether you have an alert guard dog or a lazy animal that should be sold as soon as possible. A good dog will ignore the muzzle and try to tear the visitor to pieces, and it will make a lot of noise as it does so. Certainly, any animal used as a watchdog should run to investigate and should make a lot of noise.

Don't try this test with the more powerful dogs such as an Airedale or German shepherd. Actually, you should train all large dogs a lot more carefully than called for by the "natural" system. If, however, you do wish to test a large dog, perhaps because you are considering buying it, ask the unannounced visitor to rattle the doorknob and make a bit of noise without opening the door. If the large dog's reaction is satisfactory, you can be fairly sure the animal is reliable. Even in strange quarters, a good watchdog is aware of noises at doors and windows.

If your dog is a good natural watchdog, it's important to make sure that he stays alert. The author has witnessed the ruin of several good, natural watchdogs. Almost always, the dog was overfed. The family just couldn't resist giving good old Towser table scraps and candy any old time, day or night. As a result, the dog swelled up like a bladder in a sausage machine and slept most of the time. In spite of their "kindness" with food, the family never took the dog for long walks, and so it got lazier and lost interest in people. The animal was treated with much mistaken kindness and was never allowed to believe for an instant that any human being could possibly be dangerous. Every time it barked or showed aggressiveness, it was scolded. One member of the family—usually the wife— could not stand "all that terrible barking" the dog set up when a visitor came to the house. If the dog barked too much, unfair discipline was imposed. In one case, the dog was severely whipped for barking at visitors a bit too long. After a while, the dog simply gave up barking at callers and would have greeted a thief without a sound. It's difficult to ruin a good dog, but these steps will do it.

Sometimes, however, a watchdog is actually too aggressive and does make life really uncomfortable for legitimate visitors. If you are sure that the visitor is trustworthy, and that the dog is making a mistake, don't beat the animal or show very marked disapproval. Merely tell the dog "No!" several times in a calm, controlled tone until it stops barking or snarling. More important, shake the visitor's hand or touch the person in some other way, demonstrating friendliness and trust. If the dog continues to show extreme aggressive behavior, it may be necessary to muzzle it and fasten it to a radiator or some other solid object with its leash, and if the dog tries to lunge at the visitor, use a choke chain. Be patient, keep the dog in the same room with the visitor, and try to show it that the visitor means no harm. Sooner or later, the message will come through, and the dog will learn to cease barking as soon as it has notified you in no uncertain terms that a visitor has arrived and you have notified the dog that the visitor is "O.K." Quite literally, talk to the dog and tell it that your father-in-law is a nice man who has come to dinner, and thank the dog for telling you that he was at the door. Dogs may not understand each word we say, but most of them understand what is meant very, very well.

Occasionally, an owner acquires a dog that barks very little at visitors. Instead, the dog—often a Doberman or a Russian wolfhound—waits patiently by the door until it can get at the visitor. Then it will make a silent rush and plant its teeth in the visitor's leg if not his throat. This type of animal might well make an excellent war dog in the Marine Corps, but it's scarcely a good civilian watchdog. There's too much chance that such an animal may get hold of the postman, the milkman, or a child. If you have such an animal, you'll find that it's necessary to keep it muzzled most of the time and that shouldn't be necessary. Get rid of the animal, buy a new one, and start all over again.

The training methods outlined so far will work with a good small dog. In most cases, however, a careful owner will want to train a large dog more carefully. If a big, aggressive dog is not carefully trained, it may severely injure or possibly kill some innocent person. With these larger, more powerful dogs, you must make every effort to assure yourself that the dog responds immediately to your commands and will not be dangerous to innocent people. You'll also find that a large, powerful dog can wear its owner out if it is not obedient. Even with a choke collar, a disobedient shepherd or Airedale can practically pull your arm out of its socket during a walk if it has not learned to walk properly by your side without lunging against the leash. If your training efforts have been inadequate and the dog is really aggressive, it may injure you. The first object in training a large dog should be to establish the fact that the animal is the servant of the members of the family and that it should behave properly at all times with, of course, a decent and kindly allowance for a few mistakes.

Owners of small dogs may also wish to give them ordinary obedience training since it makes for a much more pleasant relationship between the family and the animal. Though the "natural" system of dog training will ultimately result in a well-behaved small dog, obedience training can achieve the same results much more quickly.

Of course, you can send the dog to a training school where it will be taught all the standard commands and the correct responses. The kennel owner from whom you bought the dog may be able to recommend such a course. Some of these schools train both the owner and the dog together; others train only the dog. In the latter case it's important for the owner to obtain a detailed statement of all the things the dog has been taught and the exact commands that were used so that the owner can run through the dog's responses from time to time after the dog comes home in order to keep up the training. These courses, however, are rather expensive and they do have one disadvantage. In the instruction, the dog learns the standard responses to obedience commands. When the obedience-trained animal returns home, it will probably obey all the standard commands quite readily, but *someone else* has taught them, and the owner may find it difficult to teach the dog additional commands.

EQUIPMENT

To train a large watchdog, you'll need the following equipment:

- A leather collar with a heavy buckle and a D-ring for the leash snap. In areas where licenses are required, the tag or plate should be attached to this collar.

- A well-made leather leash five feet long with a strong loop in one end and a snap swivel in the other.

270

- A strong 30-foot woven-fabric leash with loop and snap swivel. If the woven-fabric leash is difficult to obtain, a 30-foot length of $\frac{1}{4}$-inch nylon rope can be used instead, if the snap swivel is securely spliced or tied into one end, and a good loop for a handle is spliced or tied into the other.

- A heavy leather muzzle that fits the dog well and completely precludes all possibility of a bite.

- A choke chain.

The leather collar is used when the dog is in a calm situation and does not need restraint. This collar should be tightened so that only two fingers of the hand can be inserted under it. This allows you to grab the collar to control the dog, but makes it tight enough so that the dog cannot work it off, and tight enough so that it will not catch on twigs and other objects.

The choke chain is used in training situations when the dog may become excited. Be careful to select the right length for your dog. It should encircle the animal's neck with three or four inches of chain left over. In putting the chain around the dog's neck, first form a loop by letting the chain fall back into one of the rings attached to each end of the length of chain. The rings at both ends of the chain are the same size and you cannot put one through the other to form a loop. Put the loop around the animal's neck and attach the snap of the leash to the ring at the free end. The ring used to form the loop is never placed right at the nape of the dog's neck. It's placed on the side of the neck. This arrangement takes up slack in the loop quickly if the dog lunges and cuts off the dog's air by closing its throat. If you have a firm grip on the leash and the dog surges forward suddenly, the chain automatically closes, and the dog is brought to a positive stop. The choke acts as an automatic disciplinary device and will stop even the most active dog. With large animals such as the German shepherd and the Airedale, this choke chain is often needed. It does no real harm to the animal if it is used intelligently. Of course, you should not allow a dog to keep lunging against the choke chain. If you do, permanent harm may result. With smaller, more delicate dogs, the choke chain should not be necessary. One seldom needs the choking device with dogs that weigh only 10 or 12 pounds.

The choke chain should only be used in training sessions in which the dog will undergo an experience that might excite it beyond the control possible with the ordinary leather collar and leash. After the dog has been sufficiently trained so that you can rely on its obedience, the choke chain should not be used except in very exceptional circumstances when the animal shows a great deal of agitation. If you use the leather collar under ordinary circumstances and reserve the choke chain for more important occasions, the dog will soon learn to associate the choke chain with discipline and you'll find that it will usually stop skylarking or misbehaving as soon as you rattle the chain. Some trainers use rattling of the chain as a disciplinary device.

On occasion, the dog will be wearing its leather collar, and you will wish to substitute the choke chain because there's a need for increased discipline. Always leave the leather collar on until you have put the choke chain in place. Grasp the leather collar with one hand and attach the choke chain with the other. Before letting go of the leather collar, make sure that the leash's snap swivel is attached to the ring in the choke chain. The same should be done when changing from the choke chain to the leather collar unless you are indoors or inside an enclosure so that the dog cannot get away from you. If necessary, fasten the leash to a stake or tree while changing collars or putting on or taking off the dog's muzzle.

All these items should be strong enough to handle your dog safely. The advice of a kennel owner or a reliable storekeeper specializing in dog equipment is very useful when selecting this equipment.

OBEDIENCE TRAINING

Military and police dogs are trained by people who emphasize every order with a gesture. Gradually, the dog learns to respond to either the voice command or the gesture. Since using gestures allows completely silent scouting, they are very useful to those who may encounter armed opponents. The gesture helps the animal to learn what is wanted. Most dogs are quite responsive to petting, fondling, and good-natured rough play. They also respond well to properly executed gestures, and some dogs may learn more from gestures than they will from voice commands. Because dogs learn by repetition, voice commands should always be given in exactly the same words and tones, and the gestures should always be made in exactly the same manner in order not to confuse the animal. At first then, always reinforce every voice command with the appropriate gesture. Later, you may be able to use the gesture or the command alone.

At the very least, your dog should learn to respond to the following commands without the slightest hesitation: heel, stay, come.

To walk at heel is the mark of a well-trained dog. When a dog walks in this position, the animal moves at the same pace as the person holding its leash. The dog does not lag behind and does not lunge ahead. Instead, the dog's shoulder remains in line with the leash-holder's body, and the dog never strains on the leash. The dog should also learn to stand naturally in this position or to sit and lie down in it when the handler halts. A healthy dog is always anxious to be on the move, however, so it's easier to teach the dog to heel while walking than to sit or stand in the at-heel position.

If you are right-handed, a guard dog should walk and heel on your left. A right-handed person holds the loop of the leash in his right hand and grasps the leash a few feet from the collar with his left hand. Immediate control is exercised by the left hand and the right hand is used as an "anchor." After the dog has received considerable training, you'll find that only the left hand is needed for controlling the dog with the leash, and this leaves the right hand free for a weapon or a flashlight. Police often fasten the leash to their belts so as to leave both hands free.

Start your regular walk at a brisk pace and encourage the dog to keep its shoulder in line with your body. With both hands on the leash, the handler can exercise strong control over the dog if it should attempt to break away. If the animal suddenly stops, hold the leash firmly near the animal and let the hand fall back to your thigh as you continue to walk. The sudden tug will put the dog into motion again. At the same time, give the one command that the dog already knows—"No!" and repeat it as often as needed to

273

keep the dog moving. If the dog surges ahead, clamp the hand to the thigh in precisely the same way and keep walking at the same pace. The pull on collar or choke chain should tell the animal (with several repetitions of "No!") that it is not to surge ahead. If your dog is really a lunger and the hand near the collar can't hold him back, loop the leash *behind* your back and continue to hold the leash firmly with both hands, one on each side of your body. Even a Saint Bernard will find it difficult to pull against the entire weight of the body and two restraining hands. Don't attempt to do this, however, if you haven't sufficient weight and strength to do it safely. Above all, keep walking and control the dog with the leash.

If the animal should ever put all its strength into an attempt to pull away, you'll find it necessary to haul it back into the position with the full strength of both arms, meanwhile delivering a stern lecture on the need for obedience in a loud, disapproving tone. After a while, the dog will begin to understand that it is to keep pace with you. One of the most important principles of animal training is to anticipate the wrong action before it occurs and forestall it. If you sense that the dog is about to surge ahead or lag behind, control it with the leash, but quite gently since the animal is not *yet* really pulling, and repeat the command, "Heel!" as often as needed. The very fact that you are repeating this command and using the leash even to a slight degree should be enough.

Repeat this training exercise as often as possible. In fact, you'll scarcely be able to avoid it if your dog is large and you walk it frequently. You don't want to sprain your arm or shoulder controlling the animal, and the only way to avoid it is to insist that the dog walk in the heel position, so you'll be wise to use the commands "No!" and "Heel!" often during your walks until your dog learns to obey them without question while in motion.

With the command "Heel!" the gesture is, of course, control with the leash. A good animal should respond to a very slight tug on the leash in the same manner as a good saddle horse neck-reins. After the necessary number of walks (and it depends on the animal and your own behavior how many this will be), the dog will heel and stay in that position while you walk after only one "Heel."

After a while, even that will be unnecessary. A really obedient dog will not break from the heel position even if you encounter another dog, a cat, or other distractions. Halt from time to time in convenient locations so that the dog can relieve itself. As the dog's master, *you* should choose the spots where you will stop, not the dog, and this is doubly important in crowded areas where the dog must be curbed when voiding wastes.

At first, the animal will be impatient and will only stay in the heel position for a short time. You must learn to gauge how long that period is and you must gradually increase it. Try to gauge the dog's reactions so that you're never really forced to discipline the animal. As long as it continues to show improvement, insist on only a few more minutes in the heel position each day. Then give the dog your approval by petting it, praising it and allowing it to play for a few minutes. If possible, release the animal from the leash as a reward, and let it romp for a while. Do this *before* the dog begins to show extreme impatience. Use this praise-and-reward system for all training exercises.

All through training, another basic principle will apply. Always start the animal off on its training session by having it do something that it already knows and does not resist. Then move smoothly into the next command without a break. For instance, if your dog now knows how to heel, walk in this manner for a while and then stop, giving the command "Heel." At first, of course, the dog will simply continue walking, but the choke chain or collar will halt it quickly enough. If the dog is a pace or two ahead of you when it is stopped, ease up beside the animal and repeat "Heel," a few times while petting and praising the dog. Then continue your walk for a few yards and repeat the exercise. After enough repetitions, the dog will learn to come to a halt in the heel position as soon as it hears the command. After a little more time, the dog will halt in the heel position as the result of a slight tug on the leash. Finally the dog will stop at heel whenever you halt.

Now that the dog has learned to walk and halt in the heel position, you should begin to teach it to stay in one place. A healthy dog almost always prefers to be in motion, and you will probably

275

encounter some difficulty with this command. To teach the dog to obey the command "Stay," you'll probably need the 30-foot woven-fabric leash or the $\frac{1}{4}$-inch nylon rope mentioned earlier.

Walk the dog in the heel position and halt with the dog at heel several times to make sure that the animal has its mind on its business. Then stop by a tree or a post. Attach the long leash to the collar and afterward detach the short leash so that you maintain control of the dog. Put the short leash in your pocket or loop it several times through your belt so that it will be out of the way. Now loop the long leash once around the tree or post and hold the coiled leash firmly in your left hand. Kneel beside the dog and pet and praise it for a few seconds, and then start to ease away from it, walking backward, and playing out the long leash as you go. Repeat the command "Stay," as though you really meant it—long drawn-out, and in a soothing but firm tone. Accompany the command by the gesture. Hold one hand up like a traffic policeman signalling a motorist to stop, and push the open palm toward the dog. While doing this, you should always maintain firm control with the leash as you should in every early training exercise.

You'll be lucky if the dog stays where it has been stationed. Usually, the animal will try to follow you. If it does, simply hold the leash firmly and the dog will be brought to a halt by the leash looped once around the tree or post. If the dog lunges toward you, it may be necessary to use both hands on the leash to pull the dog back into its original position.

You may encounter much resistance in this exercise because the dog's natural instinct is to follow you, but stick with it and repeat as often as necessary. After a while, you should be able to put the dog in a stay position without looping the leash around a tree or post. You should be able to move out of sight, perhaps around the corner of a building while the dog stays where it was stationed.

Some trainers make a great fetish out of teaching the dog to stay in a lying, sitting, or standing position. This is a required exercise in many dog shows, but it's unnecessary if you are training a watchdog.

Once the dog has learned to stay where stationed, you're ready to move on to the command "Come." This again involves using the long leash. The gesture is simply beckoning with the right arm just as though you were beckoning a person. Attach the long leash, give the command "Stay," and move away from the animal to the full extent of the leash. After you are sure the dog is fully obeying the command "Stay," give the command "Come," and beckon the animal with a wide sweep of the arm. Your sudden movement will alert the dog and usually it will look at you inquiringly. If at first the dog doesn't come to you, give the command "Come," and tug gently on the leash. The animal will usually rush to you. In fact, the dog's natural impulse is usually to follow its master, and it's actually very easy to teach a quick response to the command "Come." The great difficulty is to keep the dog in the stay position until you are ready for it to come. It's very rare indeed to be obliged to pull on the long leash when teaching a dog to come.

After several weeks of this obedience training, you'll undoubtedly find that your dog responds to one or two of the commands easily and naturally, but that one command puzzles or causes it trouble. Don't push the troublesome command too much. Introduce it in a training session only after the dog has done a few things that it really likes to do, and don't repeat too often if the dog finds it difficult. Always reward the dog by a good romp, off-leash if possible, and praise when it learns a new exercise. Never discipline harshly for simple failure to understand what is wanted. Reserve harsh scolding and strong tugs on the leash for situations in which you are very sure the dog knows what is wanted, but deliberately disobeys. In disciplining your dog, don't wait—scold the animal right after it misbehaves. Dogs can't form the connection between something they did an hour or two ago with the late punishment.

If your dog promptly obeys "Heel," "Stay," "Come," and "No!" it's a fairly well-behaved animal. One other command is really needed and that's "Give!" It's used when the dog has picked up some object in its mouth and is chewing or swallowing it—something that you should never allow it to do. This command isn't taught as a formal training exercise. Rather, it and the accompanying gesture are used only when necessary. In the usual course of things, however, you'll use it quite a few times until your dog learns that it's strictly forbidden to pick up food in the street or in any other place except the spot where it is regularly fed.

If your dog does pick up something, take it away as soon as possible. Hold the dog's leash or collar firmly with your left hand. Then place your right hand under the dog's jaw. Put your thumb in one corner of the mouth and the index finger in the corner on the other side and squeeze slowly but firmly. Try to keep your fingers as far back as possible so that the tips of thumb and fore-finger drive right into the corners of the mouth and compress the muscles. Experiment with your own jaw until you find the right position. The dog's mouth muscles are much the same as your own. As you press, the dog's mouth will open and you can usually shake or twist the dog's head so that the object will drop out. As you squeeze, say "Give!" loudly and firmly. If this happens often enough, the dog ought to learn to eject anything it has in its mouth on hearing the command. As soon as the object is ejected, examine it carefully. If there is any evidence of broken glass, poison, or dis-eased food, take the dog to the veterinarian immediately and ex-plain what has happened. In opening the dog's mouth, be cautious —this is a situation in which some dogs will bite at first.

Use the same technique if your dog sinks its teeth into another dog or even a person. You should keep your animal under control, but accidents do sometimes happen, and you should be able to make the dog let go. Never simply pull the animal away—it may result in a long, tearing wound. Another way to make a dog let go after it has fixed its jaws is to choke off the air supply with your right hand while holding collar or leash with your left. Grasp the upper throat firmly and squeeze in much the same way as the choke collar works. If the dog cannot breathe, it will let go. Then drag the animal away. If you must stop a dog fight, try to get some other experienced person to help by restraining the other dog. If you restrain your dog, the other may turn on you.

OFF-LEASH TRAINING

After your dog has learned to obey "No!" and to heel, to stay, and to come when called on the long leash, and you are sure you have good control over the animal, you're ready to begin off-leash training. If possible, work at first within an enclosure so that the dog cannot run off even if it wishes to do so. If this is not possible, it's wise to muzzle the dog at first even if this may not be legally required. When the dog is off leash, it should always be wearing its leather collar with its license tag.

Your first objective in off-leash training is to teach the animal to heel, stay, and come without using the long leash, though at first you may find that you'll have to use it from time to time.

Try the dog out at heeling in motion first. Without attaching the long leash, but carrying it for emergencies, take the dog for its usual walk and make sure it heels. If the dog surges ahead or lags behind, use the command "No!" and repeat "Heel," from time to time. You may just possibly get by with this, and the dog may never try to run off.

If the dog does run away, immediately use the command "No!" to halt it, and then try to use "Come," to make it return to you. Don't be impatient, and don't scold the dog for running off if it returns. Merely walk for a while with the leash on, and then start all over again. Try to be patient. If you don't alarm the dog, it won't go far even if it is off the leash. Of course, if you've been harsh with the animal and there is resentment on its part, the dog may go as far as Alaska. Off-leash training is a good test of previous training. If the training has been poor, you may never see the dog again.

If your dog really starts to run away, use the command "No!" If the animal responds, it will freeze. Then use the command "Stay," and keep repeating it until you can move up close enough to put on the leash again. Above all, talk to the dog as you approach and use all the soothing language you can. If the situation is not so tense, the dog may even respond to the command "Come." If it does, and comes to you instead of making you come to it, you're ahead of the game. If the dog does bolt and does not come back after you have waited a good long time, it's best to throw down your coat, sweater, or shirt at the spot where you last saw the dog. Very often, the animal will follow its own track back to the spot where it last saw you and it will find the garment. Usually, the dog will stay with the piece of clothing. Check back every hour or so,

279

and you'll probably eventually recover the dog. If all this doesn't work, there's a chance that the dog will be returned because of the tag on its collar either by officials or some good citizen. A lost dog without a muzzle should be recovered as soon as possible since it may bite someone and cause a lawsuit. Don't try off-leash training where the law does not permit it.

If, however, the dog does return from a run (and most dogs will), put the long leash on and keep walking for a while. If the dog breaks from the heel position, use the long leash to pull it back, at the same time saying "No!" and later, "Heel," as the dog comes into position. After a while, you'll be ready to try again without a leash and you will finally be successful.

Now go on to "Stay," and "Come," with which you should have little trouble, provided you hold the long leash in reserve for use when the dog is disobedient.

After a while, you should be able to station your dog, move off a considerable distance, call "Come," and get an instant response. This becomes something of a game with an intelligent animal and it's one of the best ways to give the dog exercise and training at the same time. If you can move several hundred yards away with the dog on station and then call "Come," the dog will enjoy the long run back to you.

After the dog readily comes when called, you should teach it the simple game of fetch in order to develop another method of giving it exercise without simply letting it run loose. Use the rubber bone or other object the dog habitually chews on or plays with. Using a bone that the dog has chewed a long time makes it especially easy for the dog to learn to fetch. With the dog in the halted heel position by your side, throw the bone down only a short distance in front of its nose and give the command "Fetch." Ten chances to one, the dog will reach down and pick up the bone or toy. Immediately put your hand in front of the dog's nose with an open palm and say "Give." If the object is not immediately forthcoming, tug gently on the bone or toy and repeat the command "Give." If the dog will not give up the object, use the procedure described previously to take objects away. If you repeat this exercise often enough, the dog will learn to give up the object easily enough. Now begin to throw the object farther and farther away. As soon as the dog seizes the object, give the command "Come," and take the object as soon as the dog brings it to you. Then increase the distance until you are throwing the object just as far as you can. Sooner or later, you'll be able to throw any object and have the dog retrieve it. It's a useful game since the dog will get its exercise while playing it, and you will not be obliged to walk all over the countryside if you do not happen to feel like it. By using this technique, you'll also be able to teach the dog to carry objects such as the evening newspaper or its own leash in its mouth and to yield them when you say "Give."

You can also use fetching to train a dog to jump obstacles. Throw the object to be fetched over low fences, walls, and hedges, and gradually increase the height of these obstacles. As the dog jumps, give the command "Hup," and sooner or later, you'll be able to get the dog to jump obstacles even though you haven't thrown anything. At this stage of training, it sometimes helps if you jump the obstacle yourself or walk around it so that the dog jumps over to join you. Teaching your dog to jump obstacles on command is sometimes useful with a watchdog since you may wish to get it over a barrier without going over yourself.

More Active Service

The whole system of training as described here is reduced to essentials and takes little time. You can do most of it during your regular walks with your dog. It can be carried out without special equipment such as hurdles and obstacle-course apparatus since you use trees, hedges, and fences. If you use this system intelligently, however, and suit it to the individual temperament of your dog, it will result in an obedient animal.

Some of the commands will also prove useful in active guard-dog service if you are ever forced to use your animal in that way. Earlier in this chapter, it was stated that you should call the police from your security room without aiding the dog if the animal gives an alarm by loud barking and snarling. This is good advice, but unfortunately, it's not always possible to follow it. For instance, there may be children in several different rooms in the house, and

281

you may not have the time to gather them all. In the riot situation where bombings and arson are possible, it doesn't help to retire to a secure place. More active defenses are needed in some situations, and then a good dog can be very useful.

Take, for instance, the command "Stay." If your dog has learned it properly, you'll be able to station the animal as a guard in any location you please. If the animal is intelligent and reasonably aggressive, it will attack any person who approaches even though it has been told to stay. Its nose will usually tell it what to do. At the very least, stationing a large dog as a guard may frighten off a criminal, and the dog will bark or snarl to inform you that something is wrong if you are attending to some other defense need within hearing. Avoid stationing your dog as a guard in any situation where it might possibly injure innocent people.

The command "Heel," enables you to use at least one hand for a weapon or some other security device, and the command "Come," is very useful if you are using the dog at some distance and wish to maintain control.

In an active defense situation, you may be using some sort of weapon, though if you are wise, you will be using any deadly weapon as a last-ditch defense device held in reserve for situations in which there is no choice except to use it in legal self-defense. Whether or not you should use a deadly weapon is a matter for your own best judgment, acting within the law of self-defense as discussed in Chapter IV. The dog merely adds to your capability. Using an animal instead of a weapon or with a weapon doesn't change the legal situation at all.

Normally, a good dog will attack or at least snarl and bark at an intruder. This may even prevent the criminal from entering, but if the criminal does succeed in getting inside the house or apartment, and you must actively defend your family, the dog will help. While the dog barks, snarls, and perhaps bites, you can remain at some distance and judge the situation. If the criminal merely tries to defend himself against the dog and does not try to use a weapon, you may not need to use your own defense device. In fact, you may be able to retire quietly and simply call the police while the dog keeps the intruder busy. You must judge the situation for yourself.

282

Always remember it's best not to use deadly weapons if you can avoid doing so. And don't allow your dog to continue its attack if the intruder seems completely defenseless.

Now let us consider the more common situation in which the dog's barking and snarling calls your attention to an intruder who is trying to get through a broken window or door. If you investigate, you may find that the intruder is making every effort to get away from your dog by retreating. If that is the case, I'd advise you to keep your distance. If the animal succeeds in driving the criminal back out through the opening, no one's life is in immediate danger, and there's no need to use weapons. Now, let's say that the dog jumps through the opening after the criminal. Should you follow? I'd advise you not to do so unless there is some overpowering reason that involves defense of life or defense against arson or bombing. If you go through that opening, you may be killed or injured by the criminal. Of course, you may want to help an animal that has given you such good service, but it's not worth risking your life. Remember that the criminal may have one or more friends waiting outside. It's not your duty to take on all of them. The best thing you can do at this point is keep your weapon ready, stay inside on the alert, and call the police.

Tell the police in no uncertain terms that your dog is pursuing a criminal in your neighborhood, and sit tight. It's not your job to pursue criminals. If the dog is killed or injured, it's unfortunate, but the dog is repaying you for all the care and feeding that you have given it.

If the dog follows the criminal, the owner has another worry. An excited, aggressive animal is following the intruder at some distance from the home. If it catches up with the criminal, it may severely injure or even kill him (though death is actually unlikely). Because of the noise that's likely at such times, the police will probably find it easy to locate and arrest the criminal, and in the process, the police will probably be obliged to restrain your dog. If so, they may request your assistance and you should cooperate fully. In the process, however, a policeman may be bitten by your excited dog and the criminal will probably be bitten quite a few times. The criminal will, of course, tell some sort of story to explain why he

283

was inside your home or breaking in. If the attempted entry took place during daylight hours, the criminal may say that he was trying to see you about a business deal or was delivering a package or trying to get a subscription to a magazine, and that he broke a window by mistake when knocking on it to attract your attention. Attempts to enter homes at night are not so easily explained, but sometimes the criminal can even be convincing about them. Remember that many criminals develop convincing "cover stories" in advance. The criminal may even convince the authorities that he was not the man who attempted to enter your house or apartment, that in fact, the dog mistook him for someone else. If all this happens, and the story is believed, you may be sued by the criminal and he may win the suit.

If at all possible, therefore, try to prevent the dog from following the criminal outside the building. This is especially true in a crowded urban area where an excited dog can get into trouble very easily. If you have trained the dog to respond instantaneously to "No!" and "Stay," it should not be difficult to stop the dog, but sometimes it may be necessary to hold the animal back physically. Do this only if there is no risk to yourself. The criminal may be standing outside the shattered door or window with a weapon.

In the active civilian defense situation, the dog may also be useful when it is on the leash. Even inside a building, the leashed dog can often lead you to an intruder when you yourself could never find him. In this situation, you may encounter an aggressive, armed criminal, and you may be forced to use a weapon in self-defense. At such times, it's almost always best simply to drop the dog's leash. Don't worry. An active German shepherd, Airedale, or schnauzer will know what to do. You usually don't have time to fumble with the leash snap or collar buckle, or let's say that it's dangerous to take the time. The criminal may be able to get hold of the leash and this may make it awkward for the dog, but the criminal's hands are occupied and that helps you. Don't be too anxious to use a weapon if the criminal cowers away and merely tries to defend himself against your dog, but if he tries to use a weapon, it may be wise to put him out of action on the spot. You must use your own judgment, acting within the law of self-defense.

284

In using a dog for active defense work, you should be sure that the animal is not gun-shy. The normal dog is "gun-green"—that is, it will shy away and cower when a gun goes off, not because it is afraid of the weapon or the noise, but simply because it is startled. A gun-green dog can be trained to tolerate the sound of gunfire, but it's best to start early—when the pup is about six months old. Use a child's cap pistol at first. Take it along with you on your walks with the dog and fire it from time to time. The dog may be startled at first, but it will soon grow used to the noise if you lean down and pet the animal and soothe it after letting off a cap. Don't try to surprise the dog. Show the animal the cap gun and talk to it as you fire. Take a good long time with this, and make sure that the animal is thoroughly used to it. Make sure the dog will not cower or run away even if you fire a cap unexpectedly. Then begin using a .22 blank pistol or a .22 rifle loaded with blanks if they are legally permissible in your town. Then work your way up to big-bore guns including a 12-gauge shotgun or a .38 pistol, fired quite close to the animal. This is a form of training that you can't force. If you hurry, you may cause the dog to become gun-shy because of the training. Sometimes it pays to chain the dog and back off a considerable distance. Then approach slowly, firing a shot now and then as you approach. A friend of the author's got his dog used to guns by gradually leading it closer to a trap and skeet field where heavy firing went on every day.

Some dogs are gun-shy because of previous experience with firearms and are so afraid of guns that they will flee whenever they see one. You should never use this kind of dog as a guardian. For instance, in the well-known Klutter case, described by Truman Capote in his book, *In Cold Blood,* Mr. Klutter had a large farm dog which was kept outside at night. The dog barked at unarmed intruders, but the animal was notoriously afraid of guns. When two criminals approached the farm one night carrying a shotgun, the dog fled without a sound. As a result, Mr. Klutter's throat was cut, and a few seconds later, he was shot in the head. The two criminals then killed Mr. Klutter's wife and his adolescent son and daughter. If Mr. Klutter's dog had not been afraid of guns, he and his family would probably still be alive today.

Those who are interested in very active field training for watch-dogs will want to conduct scouting and trailing exercises and they will also want to carry out practice attacks with their dogs to make sure that the animal will respond properly in any defense situation. As stated previously, the chief difficulty here is obtaining the coop-eration of strangers to act as decoys and intruders. If you can locate several other people who are interested in active training for watch-dogs, you may be able to exchange training sessions. You act as agitator, decoy, or intruder when someone else is training his dog, and the other person does the same for you. If you can find three or four people who will participate, this training makes an interest-ing hobby. At best, however, it's a difficult social situation, since anyone who acts as an intruder should never get to know the dog closely, and that's difficult, since the agitator-intruder should never visit your home. A compromise can sometimes be worked out, how-ever, by making sure that the dog is kept in the cellar or even in the garage when a member of your training group visits your home.

If you wish to undertake this form of training, remember that you should have a completely bite-proof attack suit, mask, and helmet, and that this active training may still be dangerous in spite of the protective equipment. If you train an active guard or sentry dog like those used by the Armed Forces, you must maintain strict control over the animal at all times. These dogs can be very danger-ous. If you're still interested after all these warnings, follow the training program described in, "USAF Sentry Dog Program," Air Force manual number 125-5 ($1.00), for sale by mail from the Superintendent of Documents, U.S. Government Printing Office, Washington, 25, D.C. This manual also contains excellent informa-tion on hygiene, grooming, and feeding. The basic training de-scribed in this chapter fits nicely into the Air Force system. If you train your dog according to the program suggested in this book, you may want to cap it with some of the exercises used by the Air Force.

CHAPTER IX

Protecting Your Children

AGAINST what or whom does a child need protection? In addition to the sex criminal, the drug pusher, and the kidnapper, children need protection against their own dangerous impulses and the careless or dangerous practices of parents.

Protection of a child requires a sense of proportion on the part of parents. Too much has been written by some child psychologists who favor permissiveness and "self-expression" to the exclusion of discipline. If an adolescent wants to take drugs or join a dangerous gang, should you permit him to do so in order to express himself? If your daughter takes a liking to an uncultured, irreligious, violent young criminal, should you permit her to date him? If you want your children to risk their futures and their lives, be permissive. You would not permit a two-year-old to crawl into a furnace. Why should you allow the adolescent to endanger himself or herself to an equal degree?

The problem is to maintain firm discipline while retaining the child's love and respect so that he or she will inform you of any dangerous situation that arises.

SEX

Some parents have an attitude toward trouble of any kind that soon communicates itself to the child without a word being spoken about it. The parent does not wish to be disturbed or troubled in any way, and it is evident to the child at a very early age. If the child gets into any sort of trouble or even suspects that there is danger, the parent's attitude prevents the youngster from speaking. This feeling on the part of parents is particularly evident in regard to sex. Many young children are attacked or molested by sex perverts in the United States. Many more are seduced by twisted people. Most sexual criminals prefer to establish a relationship with a child without resorting to violence. Actually, the violent criminal who attacks children is quite rare. How can the criminal be sure that the child will not tell its parents that the relationship exists? Most often, the criminal depends on the prevailing attitude of parents toward sex education. Eventually, the parents admit, the child will learn all there is to know about sex, but in the meanwhile, let's not talk about it. If any reference to the subject is made in the family, it is very vague, but the child almost always gets the idea that there is something deliciously attractive about this forbidden subject. Sooner or later, little Johnny or Nancy knows enough not to bring up the subject, and also that it is a poor idea to tell parents if any overt act takes place. At a very young age, children often innocently take part in what the psychologists call "sex play" and almost always they learn to conceal the fact from the family. A bit later, children learn to conceal acts that could not be considered play.

This secretive attitude on the part of children results from the moral attitudes of most American parents, and it can be dangerous. If an adult sex criminal makes an attempt to establish a relationship with a child or even uses mild force to compel the child, the victim will probably refrain from telling parents. The child has learned that, in the opinion of his parents, sex is a dirty, shameful, and forbidden subject. Because of the child's silence, a pervert may be able to establish a lasting relationship with a youngster based either on fear or pleasure. These relationships are extremely harmful because they lead the child into all sorts of perverse sexual habits and ultimately they may lead to violence. If the criminal runs into a situation where he knows exposure is possible, he may try to silence the child, and that may result in a murder. Most child mur-

288

ders by sex perverts are committed after a sex act or a series of them.

Therefore, it is best to see that your child learns the "facts of life" as soon as possible from yourself, from a priest or minister, in a school course, or from a carefully selected book. No one can tell you the precise age at which this should be done, but I suggest that it's a gradual process that goes on from about 9 years of age to 13 or 14. Certainly, no 15-year-old should be ignorant of sex. It's just too dangerous. The adolescent's knowledge should include an understanding of the dangers of sex perversion.

A loving parent can develop a trusting attitude in a child so that the youngster will be able to discuss sex and sexual problems at home. If this is not possible because of a weakness on the part of the parents, perhaps a priest or pastor can help either by counseling the child or by giving the parents worthwhile advice. Some religious institutions offer courses that are often labeled, "Preparation For Marriage." Ask your priest or pastor about them. Sometimes a child feels free to talk with a clergyman but cannot speak frankly with its parents.

If an open, trusting attitude can be developed, your child will come to you with problems, and among them you'll sometimes discover a sexual dilemma involving an older person who has made a sexual approach to the child. If this comes up, don't punish or discipline the child in any way if the youngster has been lured or forced into an illicit relationship. Your object is to get as much information as possible about what has happened and to retain the confidence of the child. If you lose your temper and resort to threats, violent language, or punishment, you may get no information at all.

What should you do if the child tells you about an overt sexual approach by a man or an older boy? (The female pervert interested in children is extremely rare.) There is no pat answer. Corrupting the morals of a minor is a serious charge in most states, and forced sexual acts and statutory rape may lead to a long prison sentence. Therefore, it's unwise to make public charges against any person involved in such crimes unless you have evidence that will stand up in court. If the charges cannot be proven, or if gossip starts, you

289

may be sued for slander. If you write down your charges, you may ultimately be charged with libel unless you can prove them. Some perverts can become dangerous if threatened or persecuted. The veracity of the child must also be weighed. Children have all sorts of fantasies and half-developed ideas that sometimes lead them to make mistakes. A child going through one of these fantasies may mistake an innocent action for a sexual approach, and lead the parent to make an accusation that is entirely unfounded and will have serious consequences.

Unless the sexual act or overture has been violent, or you have very good reason to believe that violence was intended, it's often best to remain silent but see to it that your child no longer comes in contact with the pervert or suspect. Keep your eyes and ears open, however, and if evidence that will stand up in court becomes available, it is your duty to go to the police. You must use your own judgment.

Discuss the whole incident completely and openly with your child, but avoid harsh discipline or punishment if you can do so. Once the air is cleared, drop the entire subject. Young minds are resilient and unless there has been violence, there should be no permanent harm. Though most perverts operate in secret and without violence, some of them can be extremely dangerous.

That violent crimes against children can happen for no understandable reason is evidenced by the case of Wendy Wolin, seven years old, who was stabbed in front of the fire department's signal headquarters in Elizabeth, New Jersey in 1966. She stumbled into the building and told firemen on duty that a man had punched her in the chest. The firemen tried to help her, but she fell dead a few minutes later. The child had not been molested before the stabbing. The descriptions of the criminal do not match anyone who could possibly have had any reason for harming the girl. The murderer is still walking the streets at this writing.

Violent crimes against children are extremely rare though they are so well publicized that many people believe they are quite common. A few simple rules, if followed, will prevent non-violent as well as violent crimes against your children.

The FBI Rules

The Federal Bureau of Investigation's guide to the prevention of kidnapping and abduction, prepared for educators and parents, is distributed by several publishing organizations. As a parent, you should follow these rules. Check to see that teachers and administrators in your child's school follow the rules that apply to them. If a security program must be set up at a local school to assure playground safety and the escorting of children to and from the school, it's best to work through the Parent-Teacher Association. If you can obtain advice from an experienced police officer, it helps very much.

The FBI statement follows:

The apprehending and convicting of kidnappers is a deterrent —but greater preventive action is necessary. Perhaps the realization of this fact is the motive which has caused many parents, teachers, youth leaders and local law enforcement agencies to analyze the protection they provide our youngsters.

Because schools are charged with the care of millions of children throughout a great part of the year, each education system should establish and enforce stringent protective measures. These measures doubtless will vary from community to community, but they should include at least the following basic rules:

1. Whenever possible before releasing a child to anyone except his parents during the regular school day, a teacher or administrative official should telephone one of the child's parents or guardians for approval.
2. When a parent telephones a request that a child be released early from school, the identity of the caller should be confirmed before the child is permitted to leave. If the parent is calling from his home, the school can verify his request by a return telephone call. In the event the telephone call is not being made from the child's residence, the caller should be asked intimate questions about the child. These questions might include the child's date of birth, the courses he is study-

291

ing, names of his teachers and classmates, and similar facts which should be known to his parents.

3. Faculties of schools should be alert to observe suspicious persons who loiter in school buildings and on the surrounding grounds. If such persons cannot readily provide a logical explanation for their presence, the police should be notified immediately. The identity and a description of all such suspicious persons should be obtained.

The responsibility of parents, however, greatly surpasses that of public and private institutions. As instructors in the world's greatest classroom, the parents have the obligation of teaching their children the fundamental rules of self-protection. Specifically, the children should be instructed to:

1. Travel in groups or pairs.
2. Walk along heavily traveled streets and avoid isolated areas where possible.
3. Refuse automobile rides from strangers and refuse to accompany strangers anywhere on foot.
4. Use city-approved play areas where recreational activities are supervised by responsible adults and where police protection is readily available.
5. Immediately report anyone who molests or annoys them to the nearest person of authority.
6. Never leave home without telling their parents where they will be and who will accompany them.
7. Loudly cry for help if a stranger attempts forcibly to detain them.

In addition to impressing their children with the necessity of following these rules, parents also must exercise a practical degree of supervision over their youngsters' activities. For example, grade-school children should not be permitted to travel the streets at night unless accompanied by a reliable adult. Other precautionary measures which parents should employ are:

1. Make certain that outside doors, windows and screens are securely locked before retiring at night.

2. Keep the door to the child's room open so that any unusual noises may be heard.

3. Be certain that the child's room is not readily accessible from the outside.

4. Never leave young children at home alone and unprotected and be certain that they are left in the care of a responsible, trustworthy person.

5. Instruct the children to keep the doors and windows locked and never to let in strangers.

6. Teach the children as early as possible how to call the police if strangers or prowlers hang around the house or attempt to get in.

7. Keep the house well lighted if it is necessary to leave the children at home.

8. Avoid obvious indications that you are not at home. Open garage doors and newspapers left outside the house obviously show that you are away from home and that your children may be inside unprotected.

9. Instruct servants not to let strangers into the house.

10. Do not advertise family finances or routines. Kidnappers frequently have their victims under surveillance for several days prior to the abduction, so that they may acquaint themselves with the family's habits.

If rules such as these are conscientiously followed, the criminal opportunity of kidnappers, sex offenders and others who prey upon children will be greatly reduced.

Whenever a kidnapping occurs, it is essential that the victim's family immediately initiate action to effect the safe delivery of the victim. This can best be accomplished when the family of the victim carries out the following suggestions:

1. Telephone the Federal Bureau of Investigation. The telephone number of the nearest FBI office is listed in the front of each telephone directory; the emergency number at FBI Headquarters in Washington is Executive 3-7100. The complainant should be prepared to furnish in an orderly fashion all facts relating to the disappearance of the victim.

2. Maintain absolute secrecy and do not permit any of the facts regarding the kidnapping or demands for ransom to be known to anyone outside the immediate family except the investigating officers.

3. Do not handle letters or communications demanding the payment of ransom. Turn these over to the trained investigators as soon as possible.

4. Neither touch nor disturb anything at the scene of the crime. Minute particles of evidence which are invisible to the naked eye can be destroyed.

5. Be calm and strive to maintain a normal routine around the home and office if possible.

6. Place full confidence in the law enforcement officers who are investigating the kidnapping. In addition to obtaining photographs and a complete description of the victim, it is essential that law enforcement officers have all facts relating to the personal habits, characteristics and peculiarities of the victim.

When kidnappings occur the first concern of the FBI and other law enforcement agencies is always the safe return of the victim.

In small towns, it's possible to maintain a fair degree of security if the parents know teachers, policemen, neighbors, and almost everyone who comes into contact with a child. Under these circumstances, you can allow a child a great deal of freedom of movement. In large cities, however, the problem is more difficult, especially when the child reaches an age when he or she must move about without the parents. Many quite young children must go to and from school and recreational activities alone because parents simply cannot accompany them.

If possible, it's always best to pair off your child with another who lives in your apartment house or immediate neighborhood going to the same school. A brother-sister team is excellent, but a neighbor's child can be of great help. If you can do so without unduly alarming the children, try to tell them about the danger of perverts and criminals. Quietly tell them that one of them should inform you, the police, a teacher, or any responsible adult if the other is molested in any way. This system works well if you can educate the children to do it without making them overly fearful. It resembles the "buddy system" used for children when swimming.

The telephone can be of great help in supervising children in exceptionally dangerous circumstances. Plan your child's ordinary school day and tell the youngster to telephone you at set intervals, even if the call must be made to your place of work. For instance, it may be wise to tell the child to call when he or she arrives outside the school, when leaving for home for lunch, when back outside the school after lunch, and when leaving school for home. If the child has regularly scheduled after-school recreation periods, make sure he or she calls when leaving for home. You can set up a daily schedule of telephone calls that even a very young child can follow. If one of the telephone calls does not come through on schedule, you must be willing to drop everything else and go looking for the child at the last-reported location, and if you can't find your youngster promptly, you should inform the police. Normally, the mother receives the calls, but if one fails to come through, the father should investigate if that is at all possible.

Many parents follow this system, and at first, they often run into the "I forgot" problem. The child simply does not remember to make one of the calls, and the parent perhaps leaves work to find out what happened. When the youngster is found playing ball in the neighborhood park, the usual reaction is anger, but try to suppress it. Talk to the child sensibly and quietly about the importance of making the calls promptly and regularly. After a few weeks, the calls become a matter of habit, and then you'll be sure something has gone wrong if Johnny doesn't call on time. Like so many other security measures, this one involves hard work until the habit is established. When your youngster leaves home in the morning, you should supply enough dimes to make all the calls including one extra dime for emergencies. Having an extra dime ready to make an emergency call can save your child's life or the life of his buddy.

THE GANG, SEX, AND CRIME

When a child reaches the teens, hazards multiply, but not dangerously if the child has understanding parents who provide a home that is a safe refuge, and an interesting, rewarding place. TV and the key to the family car are not adequate substitutes for love and discipline.

The chief hazards for the teen-ager are crime, sex, and drugs, and the chief agent for introducing them is the teen-age gang. The "gang instinct" is perfectly healthy and harmless as long as your son or daughter's friends are trustworthy and decent. Normal associations between children of similar ages leads to a sense of group solidarity, and this can do no harm as long as the group does not take on a criminal tinge. Because your son associates habitually with several classmates and spends most of his free time with them is no reason for supposing that trouble is brewing. If, however, you do not know his friends or their families, and allow your youngster an unlimited amount of free time, you're depending entirely on luck to keep him out of juvenile court or worse.

The way to deal with the gang instinct is to invite the gang into your home for parties, dances, card games, indoor sports, and just plain hanging around. If your child loves you, he or she will be ashamed of friends who disgrace your home by filthy language and uncivilized behavior. This is the way to eliminate bad company. Let them eliminate themselves by earning your child's contempt or hatred. There are quite a number of people who read books on child psychology and worry about the welfare of their offspring who would never think of participating in a party for the kids in which they could assess the attitudes of the gang. If you're in this class, I suggest that you interest yourself in your child's friends. Spend a little money for group activities and try to learn about the problems of your child's friends and their families. It's the best way to isolate one or two bad apples who may lead your child into dangerous escapades involving alcohol, sex, crime, and drugs.

Drugs are undoubtedly the most dangerous hazard to the American teen-ager. The illegal drug trade depends on pushers who make every effort to "hook" youngsters by introducing them to successively more dangerous drugs. Case histories of drug addicts demonstrate that lack of a decent family life and lack of a drive to achieve in sports and school commonly lead to a desire for drugs. The gang substitutes for a good home and normal energy outlets, and the gang usually consists of other youngsters in similarly deprived situations. The gang's interests under these circumstances are almost always anti-social. The outlets for their energy may be vandalism, sex, gambling, alcohol, or drugs. The competition is to see who can get into the most trouble and get away with it.

A youngster in such a situation is the natural prey of a drug pusher who knows how to offer the milder forms of narcotics in order to make the teen-ager dependent on him as a supplier. The gang may even start the pattern before the pusher appears on the scene. One variation is glue-sniffing in which the vapors from glue containing ether are inhaled until it causes a "cheap drunk" that many teen-agers find exciting. The next step is often alcohol or mild drugs such as Benzedrine. From there, the adolescent moves to marijuana—a mild narcotic, but one whose effects are unpredictable. Marijuana is usually a prelude to heroin or one of the other opium derivatives taken by injection or sniffing the powdered "snow" up the nostrils. Lately, the hallucinatory drug LSD has become very popular, especially among middle-class college students. Always, the urge of a weak personality is toward more powerful, habit-forming drugs. Once a habit is established, large amounts of money are needed to pay for the drugs, and crime is usually the only way in which enough money can be obtained.

It's a mistake to believe that only deprived children fall victim to the drug pusher. Many recent cases demonstrate that adolescents from middle-class homes often become drug addicts, and several affluent suburbs have been involved in widespread use of drugs by youngsters. One pusher who works at hooking adolescents can soon create a large group that is dependent on him to supply their habits. The drug pusher sometimes acts as a receiver of stolen goods who pays off in narcotics. In that way, the middleman is eliminated and the profit is greater.

The drug pusher most often finds it convenient to work through the neighborhood gang. One member of the gang is hooked, and

297

he is used to hook others. The pusher may supply narcotics free of charge at first to youngsters who are introduced to him by a gang member. It's like a "get-acquainted" offer from a store or a free sample. The first few times around the circuit, the drug is marijuana, but through group pressure and the "I dare you" attitude, the newcomer is induced to try heroin. If that first injection or sniff of heroin touches responsive nerves, the end of the road is probably imprisonment since the habit will grow and it will cost more day by day. Heroin sets up a chemical reaction in the human body that is extremely painful, physically and mentally, if the drug is withdrawn; this compels addicts to go on stealing and risking imprisonment to get more of the narcotic. The pusher who invests a few dollars in introductory doses of marijuana in cigarettes or a sniff or two of heroin is grooming a customer who may be worth $20,000 or $30,000 before he is finally put out of action by the police. This disastrous cycle is responsible for many deaths.

Even decent teen-agers are subject to this hazard because pushers are very skillful at getting a youngster started. You should be very alert to the attitudes of your children toward narcotics in order to detect the beginning of a drug habit. And don't think that a girl is immune. Girl gangs, drugs, illegitimate pregnancies, crime, and an early death go together. A male teen-ager usually steals to feed his habit; a girl most often becomes a prostitute.

Since drug addiction can crop up in the most unlikely places, it pays to know the signs. Here are some of the indications of drug addiction as reported by *The New York Times* from an official police source:

Has a youngster lost interest in education? Has he stopped being interested in the opposite sex? Has he lost a job because of some difficulty he cannot explain? Has he a new set of friends?

Does he get secretive telephone calls? Is he subject to sudden fits of excitement followed by depression? Has he become irritable, given to sudden bursts of anger? Does he remain alone in a bedroom or bathroom for long periods?

There are other symptoms as addiction progresses, such as an unhealthy look, fingers burned with cigarettes, disinterest in

298

appearance, tenseness and selfishness, blood spots, signs of emaciation, paleness, yawning, retching, glassy or dilated eyes, limb sores.

If you ever find a hypodermic needle or some unexplained white powder or very small pills, it's best to investigate thoroughly. The odor of a marijuana cigarette or "reefer" is very sweet, almost sickly, and it smells like no ordinary cigarette smoke.

What should you do if drug addiction strikes in your family? The best possible advice is to consult a reliable doctor and follow his directions to the letter. He's in a position to know the best way of arresting the addiction, and he can recommend a clinic if that should prove necessary.

Almost all youngsters have an adventurous instinct that can lead them into trouble. Try to channel this natural drive into sports. If you can interest your child in skiing, boxing, shooting, or even competitive team sports such as baseball or football, you'll be providing something that will give him enough competition and even danger to satisfy him. Furthermore, these sports help to provide skills that can be used in self-defense. These activities will give him enough opportunity for competitive achievement and the admiration of friends and yourself so that he will not work off excessive energy in vandalism or more serious crimes. Girls need similar if less active sports or hobbies.

If you become acquainted with your children's friends and provide enough satisfactory outlets for the normal drives, you'll be in a position to put your foot down if something does go wrong. If, for instance, you discover that your youngster's friends are interested only in hot-rodding, sex, drinking, and perhaps the beginnings of drug addiction, there's only one solution. You must resort to strong discipline to break the pattern of increasingly serious alienation and delinquency that can only lead to broken health and perhaps a violation of the criminal law. When you're sure that something must be done, do it. Tell your child that he or she must stop associating with anyone who is dangerous, and be in a position to specify their names. If you are forced to take decisive action, it may be best to send your child away for a week or two on some sort of vacation or to take a family vacation. Break the association sharply and cleanly and make sure that it is not renewed. All this takes time and effort, but it is your duty as a parent.

The best way to guard against the numerous hazards that beset adolescents is to provide them with a secure family life, with enough interests and real excitement to keep them out of trouble. If you love your children, and you can earn and retain their respect, your problem is almost solved before it arises.

Index

301

303

305

307